DISCOVERING MORE ABOUT HITCHIN

A wartime scene shows 'Jock' Thomson on the right standing proudly outside his garage in Queen Street with his sons Neil at the wheel of the family Hillman and Gordon firmly holding the door handle. (T N Thomson)

Lindsay Avenue and Oakfield Avenue under construction 1956. (NHM 10090-327-04)

Discovering More About Hitchin

EDITED BY
BRIDGET HOWLETT AND PAULINE HUMPHRIES

A Hitchin Historical
Society Publication

To Bob

Happy Birthday

All my love

Lucy
xxxxx

2019

About the Editors
Bridget Howlett – retired archivist and Hitchin Historical Society member since 1980.
Pauline Humphries – retired teacher and school librarian and Hitchin Historical Society member since 1977.
Mike Clarke, a retired psychiatrist and Society Publications Officer, has managed the realisation of the book working closely with freelance production consultant Debbie Wayment.

About the Contributors
This book is the work of fifteen main contributors but help, advice and material has been given by many more. Most of those involved are Hitchin Historical Society members and all are interested in the preservation and promotion of the town's unique history and identity.

A Hitchin Historical Society Publication 2018
Reprinted 2019
Copyright © Hitchin Historical Society 2018

ISBN 978-0-9926-162-4-3

Design, layout and photo-enhancing: Paul Barrett
Production services: Debbie Wayment, Wayment Print & Publishing Solutions Ltd., Hitchin
Printed in the UK by Cambrian Printers, Aberystwyth

A CIP catalogue record for this title is available from the British Library

About Hitchin Historical Society
The Society, founded in 1977, currently has about 400 members and arranges meetings and visits related to the history of Hitchin, Hertfordshire and adjacent counties and more general aspects of local history; it also looks after Hitchin's Physic Garden located near the Library. The Society is always keen to encourage the practical study of the town's past by its members and more widely. Further details are available on the Society website at **www.hitchinhistoricals.org.uk**

Front Cover: Hitchin Hill: houses mostly built in the 1820s on the north side of Stevenage Road (now demolished) *c*.1900. (NHM)

Back Cover: Novelty postcard. (Gerry Tidy)

Inside Front Cover: Colourful design by HUDC Surveyor Arthur T Blood for maisonettes initially for the Sunnyside Estate 1923 adapted for the Westmill Estate 1927. (HALS Off Acc 1104 Box 3)

Inside Back Cover: Design detail by HUDC Surveyor Arthur T Blood for end elevation for maisonettes on the Westmill Estate 1926. (HALS Off Acc 1104 Box 3)

FSC
www.fsc.org
MIX
From responsible sources
FSC® C005094

Title Page: Dragon finial on the gable end of 31 Whitehill Road. (Simon Walker 2018)

Contents

Dedication vii
Discovering Hitchin: Then and Now ix
Acknowledgements xi
List of abbreviations xiii

CHAPTER 1
The Fields Beneath 1
Bridget Howlett

CHAPTER 2
Gaping Hills Lane: a foot in town and country 11
Nafisa Sayany

CHAPTER 3
Hitchin Hill – A First "New Town" 24
David Howlett and Peter Ellis

CHAPTER 4
St John's Road and the surrounding area 34
Christopher Hubbard

CHAPTER 5
Hitchin's Victorian Photographers 43
Alan Fleck

CHAPTER 6
Oughtonhead, Oakfield and the Lucas Family 51
John Lucas

CHAPTER 7
The Oakfield Estate 65
Nigel Claydon

CHAPTER 8
Fruit, Veg. or a Privet Hedge. Home-Grown Wisdom in Hitchin 71
Derek Wheeler MBE

CHAPTER 9
Justice in Hitchin 80
Stephen Bradford-Best

CHAPTER 10
St Michael's Mount and the Poets Estate 87
David Howlett

CHAPTER 11
Walsworth 100
Janet Walker

CHAPTER 12
Highover and Farming in Walsworth 108
Bridget Howlett and Janet Walker

CHAPTER 13
Sir Francis Willes and Francis Lovell – from code breaker to landowner 115
Bridget Howlett

CHAPTER 14
"Fine Dry Plots for Better Class Houses": the Brampton Park Estate 129
Pauline Humphries

CHAPTER 15
"Fill her up!" Petrol supplies in Hitchin 138
Stephen Bradford-Best

CHAPTER 16
Origins of Hitchin's modern "Town Planning" 146
David Howlett

CHAPTER 17
Westmill Estate 151
Terry Knight

CHAPTER 18
Made in Hitchin: Backyard Industry and New Estates 160
David Howlett and Stephen Bradford-Best

CHAPTER 19
A look at some 1960s buildings in Hitchin 171
Chris Honey

Bibliography 187
Index 191

Dedication

To a True "Hitchin Worthy"
Priscilla Mary Douglas
1938–2015

Scilla Douglas at a Hitchin Historical Society book launch in 2004. (HHS)

Amere ten days after her birth, in Barnet, Priscilla Mary ('Scilla') travelled by aeroplane and boat to Bombay. Her father, Stephen ('Peter') Russell, was a member of the Indian Civil Service and so Scilla spent her early years – as one of the last children of Empire – in Bihar and New Delhi. After Indian Independence in 1947, the family moved to Calcutta and she boarded at a convent near Darjeeling. Returning home in 1951 Scilla attended St Philomena's Convent School in Surrey. The Russells settled in Hitchin in 1953 and Scilla's education concluded at the National Training College of Domestic Subjects in London.

A career in teaching beckoned! After cutting her teeth in Stevenage Scilla, together with husband Bob Douglas, moved to Hitchin. From 1964–73, whilst raising three children, she worked part-time at Hitchin College of Further Education. In 1973, with all her children by now of school age, Scilla moved to Hitchin Girls' Grammar School (HGGS) where she spent the rest of her career, as both teacher and Governor, retiring in 1993.

Scilla's aunt, Rosemary Cook (née Russell), had been a boarder at HGGS in the 1920s; from this Scilla developed a fascination with the story of the school about which she published two books commemorating its centenary in 1989. During the 1980s she also became closely involved with Hitchin Historical Society, eventually undertaking a number of Committee roles and then holding the positions of, successively, Chair then President.

To Scilla, Hitchin's local history was about much more than just 'the past'. It involved understanding the present in light of what had gone before and how this understanding contributed to Hitchin's strong sense of place and identity. In addition, to her, the study of local history should not be just a specialist or academic activity but involve as wide a cross section of the town's inhabitants as possible.

A key part of encouraging such involvement was through the Hitchin Historical Society's publication effort. Scilla took this to heart and, over about twenty years, was a catalyst and indefatigable worker in the production of more than twenty-five substantial books plus numerous leaflets, articles, a CD-Rom and two CDs of archive film putting Hitchin's unique and distinctive history firmly 'on the

Scilla Douglas and
Bridget Howlett
promoting Society
publications by the
Cabbies Hut in 2009.
Scilla motivated
its restoration and
resiting in Market
Place. (HHS)

record'. Above all, she nurtured this considerable output from a wide range of authors of very varied backgrounds and interests and did this with unwavering encouragement, enthusiasm, tact, (occasional!) correction and the tireless assistance of both Pauline Humphries in research and editorial tasks and David Jones in display production and many other practical roles.

One of Scilla's most important contributions in recording our local history came with the publication, in 1995, of *Discovering Hitchin: An exploration of aspects of Hitchin's history beyond the town centre.* Scilla was also involved with a variety of other local history projects such as the Hitchin Blue Plaque scheme; the celebration in innovative style of the 150th anniversary of the arrival of the town's first railway; the Society's contributions to the annual Hitchin Festival; the pioneering restoration of the Hitchin station Cabbies Hut; and looking after the town's built heritage more generally, as well as energetically supporting the work of the Hitchin British Schools Museum.

Following Scilla's untimely illness and death in 2015 the Society decided that *Discovering More About Hitchin* should be published as a fitting memorial to Scilla's unstinting contribution over many years to Hitchin's local history. So, read on, as here it is – we just hope that she would have approved.

Discovering Hitchin:
Then and Now

Discovering Hitchin, published in 1995, had its origins in a wish to produce a booklet calling attention to the interest and charm of areas away from the town centre, the streets where most people actually lived. Scilla had a passion for architectural detail, and many will remember the artefacts (chimney pots, hand-made bricks, locally produced ironwork) which she hosted in the garden in Wymondley Road. The book was based on reminiscences (some the result of 'cold calling') and contributions from friends, neighbours and Historical Society members. Scilla's charm and tact opened many doors, and an interested enquiry often led to cups of tea and access to treasured 'shoe-box' family photographs and memorabilia. We were backed up by resources and advice from the (then) Hitchin Museum; curatorial assistance helped uncover a wealth of material in its collections.

Discovering More About Hitchin also tours the town, avoiding the more documented areas, and concentrating on the origins and development of the places and themes that many of us associate with 'home'. The book comprises individual chapters, credited to their authors, some who have already had material published and others who appear in print for the first time. Again, a great deal of original research has taken place and, although our new Museum has been unavailable during the book's 'gestation', we have enjoyed staff cooperation in using its materials which we already had to hand. Researchers have also made frequent journeys to the County

Signing *Discovering Hitchin* at Burgess Books in Churchyard, November 1995. From left to right: Aud Eastham, Derek Wheeler, Scilla Douglas, Pauline Humphries and Laurie Hughes. (HHS)

Pauline Humphries and Scilla Douglas fronting the promotional window display in Burgess Books 1995. Note the drain cover and ridge tile from Scilla's collection of architectural ephemera. (HHS)

Archives in Hertford. This has been well-worth the effort; their ever helpful staff have aided discoveries that have widened both the scope and authority of this second book. However, there has still been a special place for the 'Hitchin-born-and-bred' contributions, the value of which cannot be over estimated. We have all tried our very best to get it 'right' but local history is always an ongoing project.

Discovering Hitchin was a 'paper-and-pencil' affair painstakingly transcribed from often almost illegible notes by the late Dorothy Hughes, wife of the (then) Society Treasurer. 'Cut and paste' really did mean just that. We now live with laptops on the kitchen table and easy access to search engines or packages such as Ancestry. This companion volume has been assembled, therefore, using the latest technology although pencil and paper (thank goodness!) have not entirely departed the scene.

So why did the Society embark on *Discovering More About Hitchin*? Almost as soon as the first book was published Scilla's fervent wish was to produce a sequel. We had unused material and ideas and, although some of this ended up in other publications over the succeeding twenty years, she always remained keen on a follow-up volume.

So, at last, Scilla, this is for you. The Editorial Team have at times (often!) felt your energising presence overlooking their efforts. We hope that we have not disappointed you.

Acknowledgements

Our thanks are due to many individuals, archives, libraries, museums and other institutions without whose generous assistance this book would not have been possible. We are especially grateful to Scilla Douglas' family for their support.

Hertfordshire Archives and Local Studies have been an invaluable resource, unstinting in their provision of advice, information, and illustrative material. Despite being unavailable for research, North Hertfordshire Museum has kindly allowed us to reproduce photographs, maps and documents from its collection. The availability of the Local Studies Collection and online resources at Hitchin Library has been essential. We are also indebted to Customer Services at North Hertfordshire District Council for access to planning applications.

Further afield, Dr Katharine Walker and the volunteers at the New Forest Centre, Lyndhurst, and Wiltshire and Swindon Archives have assisted research into the Lovell family. Thanks are due to both the British Museum and National Portrait Gallery for permission to use images. Closer to home, the Headmaster of Kingshott School kindly allowed us to photograph Oakfield House and images have been provided by the Estates Department of North Hertfordshire College, Hunting Gate, and Viking Johnson.

We have depended on the photographic expertise of Simon Walker who has enhanced images throughout the book, including some of a challenging nature! He has also assisted with research. We are greatly indebted to John Lucas whose photographic, computer skills, and patience are responsible for turning rough drafts of maps into a professional form. Alan Fleck has been of great help in the provision of photographs and information. Gerry Tidy and Terry Knight have allowed us to use postcards and other material from their personal collections. We have also greatly benefited from the archives of both the late Pat Gadd Thurstance and the late Scilla Douglas, now in the care of Hitchin Historical Society, as well as by the late Margaret Watson's research on the history of Walsworth.

Enormous thanks are due to our twelve authors who have not only laboured intensively on their own chapters, but have contributed information to their fellow scribes. Without them of course there would be no book! Especial thanks are due to Alan Fleck, Chris Honey, and Derek Wheeler MBE for additional proof reading.

The following have generously provided their time, information, memories and photographs which have greatly enriched this volume:

Doreen Barrett, Debbie Burstow, David Chivers, Kirsty Claydon, Anita Collis, Derrick Conder, Joanna Cooper, Alec Coutts, Adeline Darvill, Janet Dilley, Derek Dolling, Tim Dye and Charlotte Ransom, Alison Elliott, Andrew Fell-Gordon, Chris Finch, Patricia Foster (formerly Lawton), Mick Furr MBE, Nic Garner, Robert and Alison Germany, Steve Haygreen, Michael Hill, Pete, Emma and Elijah Howe, Mr and Mrs Hunnisett, Janice Hussey, Heidi Hutton, Andrew Hyde, Steve and Christine Johnson, John Joshua, Pat Lardner, June Leete, Vicki Lockyer, Terry and Sue McGinty, Iain Mansell, Kathleen Melot (née Pettengell), Pansy Mitchell, David Morgan, Cynthia Parker, John Pateman, Tracy Perry, George and Mary Prowse, Joyce Pullen, John Read, Richard Reeves, Andrew Rogers, Gillian Russell, Sarah Russell, Eileen Sanders, Stephen Sears, Derek Sheard, Mervyn Spokes, Andrew Staples, Janet Swan, Tony and Sue Thomas, Neil Thomson, Tracy Thomson, Irene and Robbie Todd, Jonathan Walters, Will Warburg, John Wheeler, Matthew Whiting and Sophie Rutschmann, Richard Whitmore, Robert and Frances Williams, Patricia Williams (formerly Wagg), Michele Wilson, Terry Wilson, Marion Woodbridge, and Brian Worbey.

Finally the onerous responsibility of seeing this book through to publication has fallen to Mike Clarke, Publications Officer of the Hitchin Historical Society, without whom it would have seemed an impossible task. We thank him for his good humour, patience, resourcefulness and technical competence which have made our work so much easier and more enjoyable. Phil Rowe, former Society Publications Officer, was instrumental in getting the project off the ground and has given us valuable support and encouragement throughout. The realisation of this book is due to the professional skills of freelance production consultant, Debbie Wayment, and to our designer, Paul Barrett.

Bridget Howlett
Pauline Humphries
Hitchin 2018

Computer free work station complete with files and boxes.
(Scilla Douglas 1995)

List of Abbreviations

BL   British Library
d   penny, and s shilling in pre-decimalisation currency*
GNR   Great Northern Railway
HALS   Hertfordshire Archives and Local Studies
HCC   Hertfordshire County Council
HHS   Hitchin Historical Society
HUDC   Hitchin Urban District Council
LMA   London Metropolitan Archives
LNER   London and North Eastern Railway
LTS   Lawson Thompson scrapbooks, North Hertfordshire
        Museum
NHDC   North Hertfordshire District Council
NHM   North Hertfordshire Museum, Hitchin
PH   public house
TNA   National Archives
UDC   Urban District Council
W & SA Wiltshire and Swindon Archives

*Note on currency

In February 1971 British currency was decimalised to create the present system of 100p equalling £1. In the pre-decimalisation currency 12 pennies (or 12d) equalled 1 shilling (or 1s) and 20 shillings equalled £1. There were 4 farthings to 1 penny.

Hitchin's Own Currency

In the 17th century, in common with many towns, Hitchin traders, in response to a national shortage, issued their own small change: mostly farthings and halfpennies. At least fifteen are known to exist, most dating from the 1660s. They went out of use in 1672 following the issue of 'official' farthings, and halfpennies a year later.

Here are two examples: Mary Tristram, a milliner, of 1666, and a John Rugley's halfpenny, issued a year later. Rugley is believed to have been a brewer. (Simon Walker)

One of the joys of research is finding previously unknown photographic gems. On looking through the collection held by the Thomson family, Stephen Bradford-Best discovered this 1920s photograph of a Triumph motorcycle sidecar supplied by 'Jock' Thomson to Squires Dairies of Bucklersbury as a milk float. On the back of the photograph are the words 'Rat Yard' and the stamp 'J. N. Thomson, Motor Engineer, 30, Station Road, Hitchin'. Jock Thomson started his business repairing motorcycles in buildings behind the Radcliffe Arms in Walsworth Road (formerly Station Road) later moving further along the road to Castle's Yard before he bought his garage in Queen Street from John Cain in 1935. With the owner's name being clearly visible, our research confirmed the type of motorcycle and probably the sidebox, the supplier and the location, but we still do not know the name of the milkman astride the Triumph. (T N Thomson)

The Fields Beneath

BRIDGET HOWLETT

M odern Hitchin still bears the imprint of the open fields which used to surround the town centre. Most extensive open fields like Hitchin's were swept away by enclosure in the 18th and 19th centuries and replaced by smaller rectangular individually owned fields which could in turn be easily developed for housing. This happened in much of Walsworth, but the slow and gradual process of consolidation of small strips of land in Hitchin's fields into larger blocks meant that when houses were built beyond the town centre in the 19th and early 20th centuries, they had to fit into the existing pattern of field boundaries, lanes and footpaths.

Frederic Seebohm, who lived at The Hermitage in Hitchin, published in 1883 a seminal book, *The English Village Community*, in which he argued for the continuity of field systems from Roman and pre Roman times in eastern England. He used the open fields of Hitchin as an example, describing them as they still existed when he was writing. Land within the fields was divided into long narrow strips each individually owned, separated from its neighbours by turf balks or baulks. Seebohm estimated that the standard strip was about 220 yards long and 22 yards wide making it an acre in area, which was ploughed into four ridges each 16½ feet wide.[1] A few such ridges can still be seen in Ransom's Recreation Ground and in the grass between Walsworth Road and the Dell. Here each strip is about 16 feet wide and runs down the slope to allow water to flow off the land along the furrows between the ridges. Strips running in the same direction were arranged in groups called furlongs or shots, for example Beggarly Shot, part of which is now included in the site of William Ransom School. The furlongs were divided from each other by footpaths or tracks or by wider balks usually overgrown with bushes.[2]

As strips and furlongs were separated only by turf balks or footpaths, all the land within a field had to be ploughed and harvested at the same time. Animals could not be allowed to graze on the stubble until all the corn in the field had been harvested. A document in the archives of Trinity College Cambridge outlines the working of Hitchin's open fields in the 1730s. The arable land around Hitchin was divided into nine open fields which were grouped into three seasons. In 1737 Moremead Field, Standhill Field and Bury

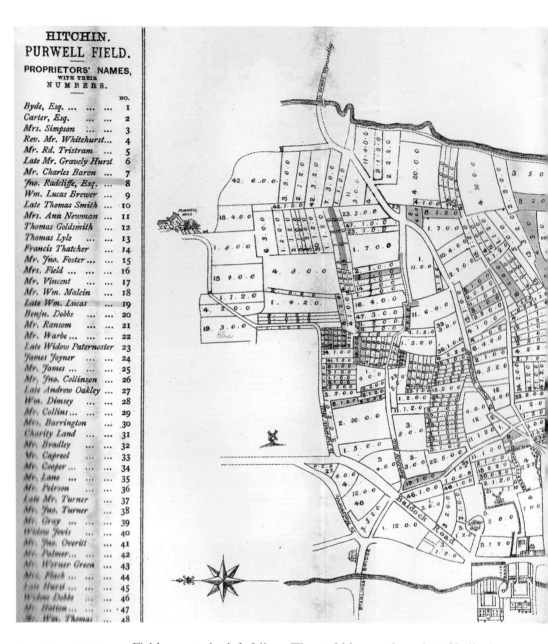

HITCHIN.
PURWELL FIELD.

PROPRIETORS' NAMES,
WITH THEIR
NUMBERS.

	NO.
Byde, Esq.	1
Carter, Esq.	2
Mrs. Simpson	3
Rev. Mr. Whitehurst	4
Mr. Rd. Tristram	5
Late Mr. Gravely Hurst	6
Mr. Charles Baron	7
Jno. Radcliffe, Esq.	8
Wm. Lucas Brewer	9
Late Thomas Smith	10
Mrs. Ann Newman	11
Thomas Goldsmith	12
Thomas Lyle	13
Francis Thatcher	14
Mr. Jno. Foster	15
Mrs. Field	16
Mr. Vincent	17
Mr. Wm. Malcin	18
Late Wm. Lucas	19
Benjn. Dobbs	20
Mr. Ransom	21
Mr. Warbe	22
Late Widow Paternoster	23
James Joyner	24
Mr. James	25
Mr. Jno. Collinson	26
Late Andrew Oakley	27
Wm. Dimsey	28
Mr. Collins	29
Mrs. Barrington	30
Charity Land	31
Mr. Bradley	32
Mr. Capreol	33
Mr. Cooper	34
Mr. Lane	35
Mr. Peirson	36
Late Mr. Turner	37
Mr. Jno. Turner	38
Mr. Gray	39
Widow Jevis	40
Mr. Jno. Overitt	41
Mr. Palmer	42
Mr. Warner Green	43
Mrs. Flack	44
Late Hurst	45
Widow Dobbs	46
Mr. Hutton	47
W. Wm. Thomas	48

Map of Purwell Field in Hitchin c.1770 divided into small strips of about an acre with a list of the 48 different owners. (Frederic Seebohm, *The English Village Community*, 1884 edition)

Field were to be left fallow. The stubble, weeds and turf balks in Bury Field would be grazed by cattle and in the other fields by sheep to restore their fertility. In the autumn these three fields would be ploughed and sown with wheat or other cereals. Once the crops had been harvested in 1738, the fields would again be grazed before being ploughed and sown with barley and other crops the following spring (1739). After harvest the fields would again be left fallow. Meanwhile Burford Field, Spital Field and Ridge Field would be

left fallow in 1738 before being sown with wheat to be harvested in 1739. In 1739 the final group of fields, Purwell Field, Great and Little Welshman's Croft, and Hillgrove Field would be left fallow.[3] Beside the River Purwell and River Hiz were individually owned meadows which after haymaking were thrown open for the communal grazing of cattle. Oughtonhead Common and Butts Close were permanent pasture where animals could be grazed.

Excluded from the open fields were Bearton and the area to the south, the Fish Pond Fields. In 1608 this was the most wooded part of Hitchin with over 2000 trees mostly elms.[4] On the earliest detailed map of Hitchin, dating from 1818, most of the area is coloured green indicating it was meadow or pasture rather than arable land. The ponds and the Capswell stream which rises from springs on Butts Close meant that this land was well watered, much better suited to grass than the chalk hills around Hitchin. It was divided into roughly rectangular fields as opposed to the narrow strips of land of the unenclosed large arable fields to the north, south and west. Bearton Green is now the name of a modern suburban road, but at one time it was a slight widening of the western end of Bearton Road, next to its junction with Bedford Road where there is still a small triangle of grass. Bearton Green and Butts Close may be the only remnants of an extensive area of common pasture, which stretched from what is now the junction of Old Hale Way and Strathmore Avenue as far as Bedford Road, Old Park Road, the rear of houses in Tilehouse Street, Bucklersbury and Bancroft, and Grove Road.

If this area was common pasture, what happened to it? Landscape historians, Anne Rowe and Tom Williamson, have suggested that both Ickleford and Great Wymondley originally had large commons, most of which were gradually enclosed or built on, leaving only

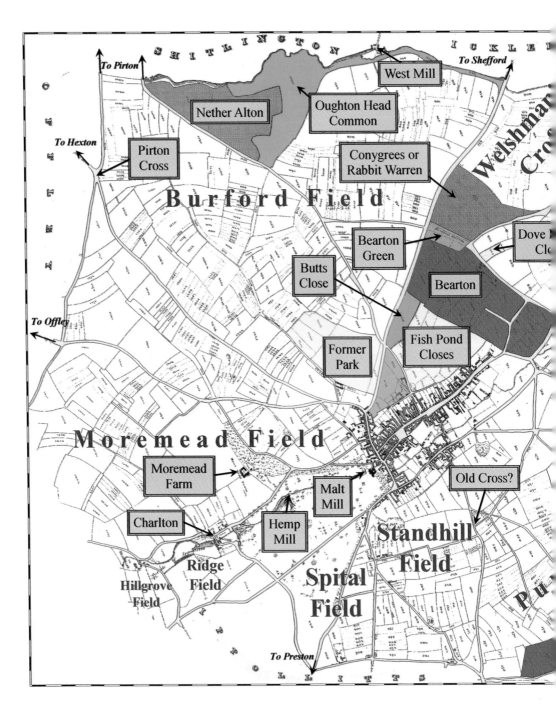

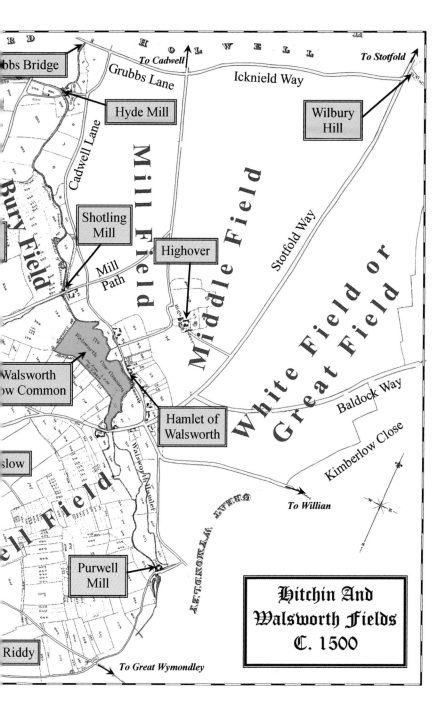

A conjectural map showing the open fields of Hitchin and Walsworth in *c.*1500 prepared by Bridget Howlett and John Lucas based on Henry Merrett's maps of Hitchin and Walsworth 1818. (NHM)

bbs Bridge

To Cadwell

Grubbs Lane

Icknield Way

To Stotfold

Hyde Mill

Wilbury Hill

Cadwell Lane

Mill Field

Middle Field

Stotfold Way

Bury Field

Shotling Mill

Highover

Mill Path

White Field or Great Field

Walsworth Cow Common

Walsworth ow Common

Baldock Way

Hamlet of Walsworth

Kimberlow Close

slow

ell Field

To Willian

Purwell Mill

Hitchin And Walsworth Fields C. 1500

Riddy

To Great Wymondley

small greens and other fragments of common land.[5] In the 12th and 13th centuries the population of England grew rapidly, increasing demand for food and for tenancies of land. Lords of the manor could substantially increase the value of their estates by converting pasture to arable fields, or, where the land was suitable, to meadows producing hay to feed livestock through the winter. If Bearton and the Fish Pond Fields were a large common pasture, the lord of the manor may have enclosed this, leaving just a few acres of common grazing for the inhabitants of Hitchin at Butts Close. Oughtonhead Common may also once have been considerably larger.

A grant of one third of two thirds of the Manor of Hitchin in 1381 details the demesne land which was directly under the control of the lord of the manor, growing crops for consumption by his household or for sale. This shows that much of Bearton and the Fish Pond Fields were part of the demesne. The 1381 grant includes "*a share of the pond with the fish and the trees about it, of a dovecot with the doves thereof*" and "*a park called Punfold*" providing fresh food for the lord's table.[6] In the 19th century the fish pond became the central feature of the extensive gardens of "Woodlands" described in sales particulars of 1880 as "*of large extent and through which runs a never failing supply of water called 'Capswell Stream', (with rustic stone bridge)*".[7] The garden became the site of Hitchin Boys' School and the pond was filled in. Dovehouse Close was on the north side of Bearton Road near the east side of Old Hale Way.[8] Field and street names suggest that there may have once been a small deer park between Old Park Road, Gaping Lane, Lucas Lane, Grays Lane, and its continuation towards West Alley, which was at one time called Park Lane.

Rabbits were another desirable commodity valued by manorial lords both for their fur and for fresh meat. The land immediately to the north of Bearton Road (formerly Bearton Green) and between Bedford Road and Old Hale Way, about 29 acres, was called Conygrees suggesting that it was a former rabbit warren. Accounts of the Manor of Hitchin from 1426 to 1538 include the farm or lease of the rabbit warren, though by 1496 it was worth nothing because there were no rabbits.[9]

Walsworth had its own three open fields, White or Great Field, Middle Field, and Mill Field, as well as the common beside the River Purwell. White Field was bounded by Willian Road, the parish boundary with Letchworth, and the original course of Stotfold Road. Mill Field lay between Woolgrove Road, Cadwell Lane, the Icknield Way and Middle Field. Middle Field was the remaining land between Mill Field, the original Stotfold Road and the Icknield Way, but excluding Highover Farm. Highover, an ancient settlement first recorded between 1287 and 1294, was surrounded by small enclosed

fields.[10] In 1766 an Enclosure Act replaced Walsworth's three open fields with smaller rectangular fields with ruler straight boundaries. Cambridge Road was widened and straightened and Stotfold Road was rerouted in a straight line starting further up the hill away from the houses of Walsworth. Footpaths running between the furlongs of the open fields disappeared.[11]

It was relatively easy to enclose Walsworth's open fields because 80% of the land was owned by just four men, Thomas Plumer Byde, the Reverend Thomas Whitehurst, Thomas Goostrey, and Thomas Blackhall. To obtain an Act of Parliament to enclose open fields it was necessary to have the consent of the owners of 75% of the land by value. Ownership of Hitchin's fields was far more divided. In

Walsworth Enclosure Map 1767 showing the open fields replaced by individually owned rectangular fields. (HALS 58882)

the 1770s 48 individuals owned 289 strips in Purwell Field with holdings varying from one to 38 strips.[12] In addition, not all the large landowners wanted enclosure. When in 1765 John Radcliffe of Hitchin Priory approached the Duke of Bedford, who held a lease of the tithes (the tenth of all produce originally due annually to the church), he was informed:

> "*The Duke of Bedford's Opinion in General I know is against inclosing because he thinks it has a Tendency to lessen the Inhabitants of the place and also the employment of the poor.*"[13]

In 1816 none of the 11 largest landowners in Hitchin owned more than 350 acres out of a total of about 2660 acres. Between them they owned about 66% of the land, well short of the 75% required for an enclosure act.[14]

Bury Field and Welshman's Croft beside the Rivers Hiz and Oughton were the only common fields suitable for grazing cattle rather than sheep when they were fallow. When in the 1580s or 1590s, a lawyer and royal official, John Bowyer, enclosed with hedges and ditches a parcel of meadow called Dolphins Slade in Welshman's Croft, the occupiers of neighbouring land could no longer turn their ploughs over it, nor could anyone pass through it.

> Some "*willfull desperate persons, arrayed & furnished in warlike manner – riotously did breake and enter the saide close and the hedges of the said complainant to the number of nynescore foote [180 feet] – did breake in peces pull up and cast downe*" and "*the ditches of the complainant there did fill up and make plaine*".[15]

By 1676 the manor court accepted payments from owners of strips in the common fields who wished to enclose them. In February 1819 the Quaker Joshua Ransom asked his cousin William Exton what legal authority he could claim for enclosing land in the common fields. William Exton's reply was basically to just do it. Later the same year the manor court stated that any owner of land in the common fields could enclose it provided that they gave up their rights to common grazing. The exception was land in Bury Field and Welshman's Croft which after harvest became cow commons. William Exton advised Joshua Ransom that if he wanted to enclose meadow land used for grazing cattle after haymaking, the best way to do this was to build a cottage on the spot.[16] In the 1820s or 1830s cottages were built along Russells Slip, a long narrow strip in Moremead Field.

During the 19th century, many of the wealthier owners of land in the common fields acquired adjoining strips and consolidated them into larger blocks of land which they then enclosed. Initially much of this was either for agricultural use or for building themselves substantial houses with large park like gardens. In the 1820s or 1830s William Bowyer built himself a large house in gothic style called Mount Pleasant (later renamed Rosenberg, then Tudor House, now the site of Tudor Court) between Pirton and Offley Roads. By the 1840s the Lucas family had acquired sufficient land near Oughtonhead to build a new farm out in the fields to replace their barns and yard in Grays Lane.[17] The first development of densely packed houses away from the town centre was at the top of Hitchin Hill which became known as Hitchin New Town as described in Chapter 3. By 1838 over 50 houses had been built on four small pieces of land owned by Thomas Field next to his brickworks.

From the 1850s larger blocks of land were sold for development and new streets laid out lined with a wide range of types of houses, but the remains of the open field system could still cause problems. In 1933 Messrs Wallace Brothers, Mr G P Roberts and other landowners complained that commonable rights had "*long impeded the free use and development of land on the north and east sides of the town*".[18] Here Bury Field and Welshman's Croft were cow commons where, unlike the other open fields, the manor court had not allowed the enclosure of land and its removal from common grazing after harvest. In 1934 an agreement was reached between all the owners and occupiers of land in Welshman's Croft and Bury Field for a mutual release of their common rights[19], which allowed

Mount Pleasant (later renamed Rosenberg, then Tudor House) built by William Bowyer. By 1883 it had become the home of Winchester Clowes, partner in the eminent London printing firm, William Clowes & Sons. (NHM sales particulars 1848)

The Baulk Path leading from Cambridge Road to Walsworth. Baulks or balks divided the furlongs in the open fields. The path shown in this postcard now runs through the houses of Meadowbank (still with a hedge on one side) then across Walsworth Common. (Gerry Tidy)

the rapid development of Strathmore Avenue and Heathfield Road in the late 1930s.

Although most of Hitchin's fields have now disappeared under bricks and mortar, the piecemeal enclosure of strips of land has preserved many of the old boundaries or baulks between furlongs or groups of strips. Hitchin is notable for the number of footpaths running between houses, gardens and schools which once ran along these boundaries and provided access to the fields, an enduring record of its agricultural past.

1   Frederic Seebohm, *The English Village Community* (Longman, 1884) pp 2–4
2   Seebohm, *The English Village Community*, p 4
3   Trinity College Archives 42 Hitchin 36
4   Survey of the King's timber and woods in Hertfordshire and Essex 1608 BL Add Mss 16237
5   Anne Rowe and Tom Williamson, *Hertfordshire a landscape history* (University of Hertfordshire, 2013) pp 40–42
6   TNA C54/220, Calendar of Close Rolls 1 Feb 1381
7   HALS D/EWS E/8
8   1818 copy of 1816 map of Hitchin plot 864 NHM
9   BL Egerton Rolls 8363–8365; TNA SC6/870/4–6, SC6/HENVII/258-HENVIII/265, SC6/HENVII/1567–1587
10 J E B Gover, A Mawer, and F M Stenton, *The Place Names of Hertfordshire* (1938) p 10
11 Walsworth Enclosure Map HALS 58882 and award HALS QS/E 67A
12 Seebohm, *The English Village Community*, pp 6–8
13 HALS D/ER C54
14 HALS DP/53/29/7
15 TNA STAC7/10/34: HALS 19185
16 Bridget Howlett ed, *Survey of the Royal Manor of Hitchin* (Hertfordshire Record Society, 2000) p xvii; HALS D/ESe C26/1; Seebohm, *The English Village Community* p 451
17 See Chapter 6
18 HUDC minutes 22 November 1933 HALS
19 HUDC minutes 29 November 1934 HALS

Gaping Hills Lane: a foot in town and country

2

NAFISA SAYANY

G aping Hills lie to the west of the town, a mere 15 minute gentle walk from Brand Street via Gaping Lane (Gaping Hills Lane as noted in old title deeds), an ancient field track that forks left at the foot of Oughtonhead Way at the corner of the former Sir John Barleycorn Public House (c.1852). The lane followed ancient field boundaries to where it crossed a north-south track (today known as Lucas Lane) from where a narrow bridleway extends over the ridge into the Ducklands fields and crosses the track leading to Ducklands Cottages. The earliest written references to Gaping Hill are in a title deed of 1565 and in the 1591 rental of the Manor of Hitchin.[1]

The ponds on Butts Close are fed by water from these hills, and the spring emerges at a position almost in line with the course of Gaping Lane. Today, the Gaping Hills define the western urban edge of Hitchin and the boundary of the town's green belt edge is just below the east side of the ridge. The top of Gaping Hills reaches 302 feet and climbs along the ridge to 325 feet on the Pirton Road, enjoying wide-reaching, panoramic views into the widening gap

Excerpt from map c.1770 showing the area between Bedford Road and Pirton Road. The arrow indicates the junction of Oughtonhead Way with Bedford Road and Old Park Road. (HALS DE/Ws/P/14)

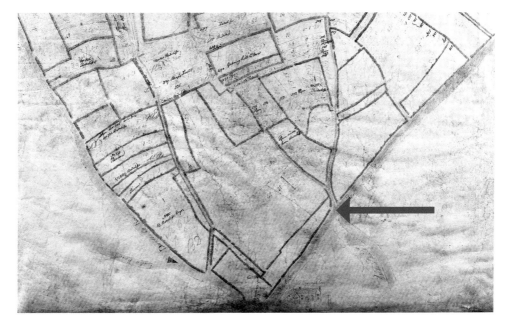

between the Chilterns to the North West and also eastwards across the town and the Hiz valley.

Fields and Gardens from Pound Lane to the Gaping Hills

Some of the land between Bedford Road and Gaping Hills was once part of a small medieval park called Punfold, from which Old Park Road most likely gets its name. The name Punfold, derives from the Anglo-Saxon term for a pound for keeping animals.[2]

The park extended from Grays Lane (formerly Park Lane) at the southern boundary to Chalk Dell at its northern edge where tenants of the manor were permitted to dig chalk for agriculture and building.[3]

The park had disappeared by the 16th century. The 1676 survey of the manor of Hitchin contains numerous references to Gaping Hill and Gaping Hill Field as well as references to pieces of land called Park Piece. Most likely these were remnants of the medieval park now apportioned as fields and closes and identifiable in the 1844 Tithe Survey namely: Park Piece Gardens (plot 1252) and Top of Park Piece (plot 1249). In addition Little Park Piece (plot 1246) and Top of Park Piece (plots 1247 & 1248) lay to the north of Gaping Lane. Most of this land was now owned by William Wilshere and the Reverend Wollaston Pym.[4]

The first built structure in the area was the Union Workhouse at Chalk Dell (1836) followed by the Cricketers Public House (est. 1844) which originally stood on the site of the Firs Hotel in Bedford Road. The 1834 Poor Law Amendment Act combined parishes into Poor Law Unions including the Hitchin Union. Older small

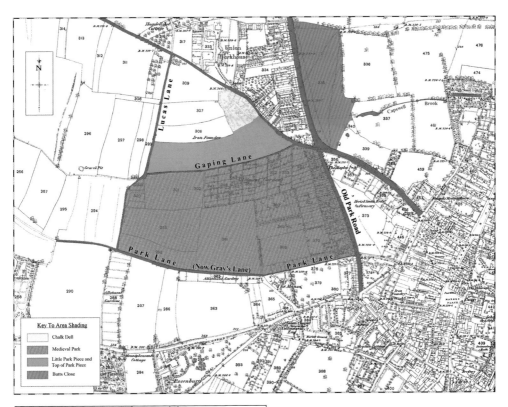

Above: Extent of Punfold Park superimposed on OS map 1881 25 inch to 1 mile XII.1. (Map prepared by Bridget Howlett and John Lucas)

Left: Excerpt from Hitchin Tithe Map 1844. Oughtonhead Way runs diagonally past the Chalk Dell towards the Union Workhouse. Park Piece Gardens lie to the south of Gaping Lane. (HALS DSA4/53/2)

parish workhouses such as the Hitchin Workhouse in Bancroft (now Bancroft House) were replaced by large union workhouses. Chalk Dell Path was soon to be renamed Union Road and then later Oughtonhead Way.[5]

Park Piece Gardens

Due to the rapid population increase in the first half of the 19th century mostly crammed into the town centre, some fields on the edge of the town had begun to be divided for use as detached gardens, cottage gardens and allotments. By 1851 the OS map illustrates how the detached gardens increased in number and began to replace farm land along roads such as today's Highbury Road, Grays Lane, Wratten Road, Old Park Road and Hitchin Hill. It is likely that the larger plots were formal, detached gardens for the wealthier classes and smaller plots for the "labouring" classes.[6]

In 1796 William Wilberforce, Shute Barrington, Bishop of Durham, Frances Elizabeth King and others established the influential Society for Bettering the Condition and Improving the Comforts of the Poor, which advocated the provision of allotment gardens. The Hitchin Society for Bettering the Condition of the Poor was founded in 1831 and minutes from the first annual general meeting held on 15 November 1832 show that besides the objectives of religious observance, education and cleanliness to mitigate the evils of sickness and poverty, the Society also provided for a number of gardens. William Wilshere MP, one of the trustees of the Society, rented no fewer than 13 pieces of his land to the Society as sites for gardens in Hitchin. The individual plots would have been allocated at affordable levels of rent for the "working poor".[7]

Park Piece Gardens shown in great detail in 1851. Excerpt from Hitchin Board of Health OS map 10 feet to 1 mile IV. (Bridget Howlett)

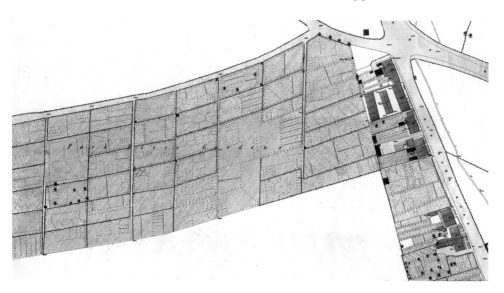

These included Park Piece Gardens on the south side of Gaping Lane. The varied size plots are separated by boundary hedges and narrow paths with main access via four pathways from Gaping Lane.

Garden Management

The Society for Bettering the Condition of the Poor 1835 meeting minutes record:

> *"The Garden Committee are requested to take occasional surveys of the Gardens, so as to notice the various states and modes of cultivation, and to give occasional Hints (if any occur to them) for their profitable management."*

> *"The Committee have recommended Eight Tenants for Prizes of 5s. each….and have great satisfaction in publishing….that a few men of questionable character, who have been two or three years in the possession of Gardens, have since exhibited a marked improvement in their general conduct."[8]*

The allotment movement in England was firmly established and Acts of Parliament were being passed, for example the Cottagers (Allotments) Bill in 1887. Documents from the Wilshere Estate confirm continued management of Park Piece Gardens under Charles Willes Wilshere, Esq., who inherited the estate from his brother William. By 1907 the gardens had passed to Miss Wilshere and remained in the ownership of the Wilshere family, unchanged in use until 1965, when the land was purchased by Hertfordshire County Council for educational purposes.

Park Piece Gardens were by 1879 referred to as Cottage Allotments and were let on conditions, as stated in a document *"Rules of the Cottage Allotments belonging to Charles Willes Wilshere Esq."*

Park Piece Allotment agreements with names and dates of tenants survive in the Wilshere Estate records held by Hertfordshire Archives. The gardens were mainly tenanted by people from the nearby growing neighbourhood on Gaping Lane, Bedford Street, Union Road (now Oughtonhead Way) and Old Park Road, adding to the village atmosphere and character of the neighbourhood. Records show Henry Tomlin in 1888 and William Tomlin in 1902 as allotment tenants.[9] After World War II Chris Hubbard lived with his grandmother at 17 Bedford Street and remembers "old man Tomlin" held pigs on an allotment near the Sir John Barleycorn. Occasional work, such as potato picking, was available on the nearby farms beyond Gaping Hills for the teenagers of the neighbourhood.[10]

Rules for Park Piece
Cottage Gardens
1879. (HALS DE/
Ws/E2)

RULES OF THE COTTAGE ALLOTMENTS
BELONGING TO

CHARLES WILLES WILSHERE, ESQ.

Every Occupier of an Allotment is to observe that it is held on the following Conditions:—

1. That he is to cultivate the land by manual labour alone, and with his best skill and diligence.

2. Not to plant potatoes, unless the ground be first properly manured.

3. No waggon, cart, or barrow to be allowed in the field in wet weather so as to cut or damage the roads, and no dung or rubbish to be permitted to lie in the roads.

4. No occupier is allowed to work on Sundays; or to take any fruit or vegetables out of the field on Sundays, after eight o'clock in the morning, under a penalty of one shilling for the first offence, and for a second offence he shall be deprived of his Allotment, and forfeit the crops.

5. In case the land be given up, the occupier to be paid for digging and planting according to custom, provided he leaves his Allotment in good condition, to the satisfaction of the Landlord or his Agent.

6. If an occupier be found or known to encroach or trespass upon, or in any way damage the crop of any Allotment except his own, or climb over or damage the gates or fences, or introduce any person into the field who shall so offend, he shall for the first offence pay, by way of fine, the amount of damage done (to be assessed by the Landlord or his Agent); for the second, twice as much; and for a third offence, be deprived of his Allotment and forfeit his crops.

7. The holders of these Allotments must agree to prevent depredations on each others' property, and assist in convicting persons who destroy or injure fences or crops of any description. And if any occupier be guilty of theft or drunkenness, or shall otherwise offend against the laws of his country, he will be subject to immediate ejectment and forfeit the crops.

The allotment rents remained pretty stable at 7s 6d / 10s and affordable for the local residents who held a variety of occupations; listed among the allotment tenants are: bakers, butchers, carpenters, grocers and a street lamp lighter.[11]

Even when I moved to Gaping Lane in 1997, neighbours were still exchanging greetings and stories on their way to and from their garden plots. Doug, retired postmaster living at 30 Bedford Street, always had a story about the neighbourhood for me. I remember one sunny afternoon, as he passed by with his wheelbarrow, he stopped and said, pointing his spade down the Gaping Lane, "*you do know there's a river under there?*" Was he referring to the water from Gaping Hills that feeds the ponds on Butt's Close?

The gardens once connected the residents providing for a sense of community. Today the local residents are hopeful that the remaining gardens can be protected as an historical feature and neighbourhood green space to be cultivated and enjoyed by the local community again. They have come together to form an association to register the remaining Gardens as an Asset of Community Value with the District Council. Kate Harwood from Hertfordshire Gardens Trust has produced a comprehensive historical record and statement of significance, which can be viewed online.[12]

Little Park Piece at Gaping Hills

Hitchin had expanded rapidly by the 1850s and residential housing development had begun to creep along Old Park Road by 1851. (See the map on page 14). This piecemeal development was characterised by its variety of architecture as a testimony to its gradual conversion from fields, enclosures and detached gardens into residential housing plots as land rental value became more profitable for housing over farm or garden use.

Little Park Piece (plot 1246 on the 1844 Tithe Survey map see page 13) was owned by the Rev. Wollaston Pym until his death in 1846. His heir was his nephew, Francis Pym of Hazells Hall, near Sandy Bedfordshire. William Lucas of Hitchin wrote in 1860:

> "A few years ago F[rancis] P[ym] was one of the most influential men in Bedfordshire, Chairman of the Quarterly Sessions, etc. with an estate of £14,000 a year, a religious, useful man also, but the last few years of his life were clouded with pecuniary difficulties."[13]

In 1852 he sold his lands in Hitchin. Little Park Piece was bought by William Braund, Secretary of the Hitchin Friendly Society. He laid out a new road *"intended to be called Bedford Street"* and 26 building plots were offered for sale by auction on 24 July 1852 at the Sun Inn, Hitchin. Plot 1 on the corner of Gaping Lane and what became Oughtonhead Way was bought by Samuel Taylor, a publican. Before his death in 1856 he had built two cottages which by 1860 had become the Sir John Barleycorn beer house. Long term local residents still remember a small butcher's and general stores adjoining.[14]

James Hack Tuke (partner in Sharples, Tuke, Lucas & Seebohm Bank, Hitchin) successfully bid for plots 2 & 3 and plots 4 & 5 paying £127. He subsequently built the five gothic style cottages (2–10 Gaping Lane) as well as Delta Cottages, 8–9 Oughtonhead Way, next to the Sir John Barleycorn.[15]

George Jeeves, a local brickmaker and builder who actively developed areas for housing on a speculative basis, bought plot 26 at the far end of Bedford Street fronting on to Gaping Lane, where he built Prospect Villas (46 & 48 Gaping Lane). He also bought plots 14 & 15 half way along Bedford Street where he built a large detached house which he sold in 1855 to the Reverend John Reynolds Wardale, Rector of Higham Gobion. The Reverend Wardale also purchased the plot opposite his house between Bedford Street and Gaping Lane which he used as a detached garden.[16]

More cottages were quickly built near the corner of Bedford Street and Oughtonhead Way, but many building plots further along Bedford Street and Gaping Lane took much longer to develop. However plots 23 & 24 near the western end of Bedford Street were bought in 1852 by John Gatward, the Hitchin ironmonger whose family home and business was in High Street near West Alley with

John Gatward Junior, ironmonger, photographed in 1865. (NHM LTS Vol 1A p95)

Bedford Street and
Gaping Lane in 1881.
Excerpt from OS
map 25 inch XI 1.1.
(HALS)

a small foundry behind. The house was destroyed by fire in 1853. John Gatward acquired the adjoining plot 22 in Bedford Street which was still undeveloped in 1857. On these three plots he built a much larger iron foundry. Bedford Street became known briefly as Foundry Road which did not find favour with the residents. One wonders what his brother-in-law George Jeeves thought about this! By 1884 John Gatward had bought The Swan Inn in Market Place adjacent to his shop, as well as the extensive yard behind The Swan and transferred his foundry here. The Bedford Street property was described in 1887 as *"2 cottages late Foundry"* and a building plot owned by William Allen & Barker, builders and carpenters, Numbers 30, 31 Victoria Cottage and 32 Vine Cottage now stand on the site of the former iron foundry.[17]

Little Park Piece itself is characterised by a diverse street scene of short terraces of three, five, six or seven houses punctuated here and there by a detached or semi-detached property. Several properties are set back from Bedford Street (that divides the close running east to west from Oughtonhead Way) and provide an enviable mix of tenure that no planner today could achieve by prescription. An interesting characteristic of the labourers' cottages built between the 1850s and 1900s is their generosity of size; spacious parlours, three bedrooms, a purpose built scullery, reception room and parlour – quite ahead of any prescribed building regulations which were not legislated for until the late 19th century.

The dating of many properties on Little Park Piece remains inaccurate, with formal construction detail unknown or only roughly described in conveyance documents indicating a best guess period of 1890s or 1900s. But we do know that owners of property on Bedford Street were frequently required to pay for its "making" between 1891 and 1896, when several more cottages were being built and required to meet the sanitary standards of the day.[18]

Logsdon and Jackson's Concrete Cottages

Research from older conveyance documents and information extracted from the Hitchin Local Board minutes has allowed for a more accurate dating of seven concrete cottages that stand on Gaping Lane numbered 6–12 (32–44 today).

Built on the steepest part of Little Park Piece with views over the Cottage Allotments and further south and east across Hiz valley, the town and Priory Park, these seven cottages represent a rare, but successful experiment of in situ unreinforced concrete building techniques. To date, it has not been possible to track down any planning/build application that could lead to uncovering the exact detail of the construction materials and methods. However we can learn more by probing into the two Hitchin characters responsible for their construction, Mr Edwin Logsdon and Mr Joseph Jackson. Much is written about Edwin Logsdon's role as Captain of the Hitchin Fire Brigade from 1895 until his death in 1912. He lived at the Sun Inn for 40 years, where his widowed mother was employed as manageress and he eventually succeeded William Hill as the landlord. The Sun Inn was, by coincidence, the venue where local land auctions were held and where Logsdon could have befriended Mr Joseph Jackson, auctioneer's clerk and later partner with Messrs Jackson (no relation), land agents and auctioneers of Hitchin. Joseph Jackson's obituary in 1909 notes *"his profession brought him into contact with a great number of people in the town and surrounding district….He had for many years been associated with Mr. Edwin Logsdon in business concerns…"*. Included in these concerns were the joint ownership of the *"Orten Head Road Gravel*

Below left: Concrete cottages viewed from West Hill.
(Nafisa Sayany 2018)

Below right: Prospect Villas and the concrete cottages viewed from upper Gaping Lane.
(Nafisa Sayany 2018)

Edwin Logsdon in his uniform as Captain of the Hitchin Fire Brigade. (NHM LTS Vol 3A p8)

Concrete materials: cement mix with pebbles surrounding flue inside chimney breast at 44 Gaping Lane. (Nafisa Sayany 2018)

Pit and Brickworks" (today the lower cricket pitch at Oughtonhead Way, belonging to Blueharts Hockey and Hitchin Cricket Club) and the purchase and development of building plots.[19]

The story of the seven concrete cottages begins in 1885, when these two gentlemen purchased a piece of land from James Hack Tuke (mentioned earlier as owning several portions of Little Park Piece) as recorded in an indenture dated 29 September 1885 *"made between James Hack Tuke ...of the one part and the said Edwin Logsdon and Joseph Jackson of the other part..."* which conveyed:

> *"unto the purchaser ALL that piece of land situate in the Parish of Hitchin in the County of Hertford being part of a Close formerly known as Little Park Piece and numbered 1246 on the Tithe Commutation Survey and plan of the same Parish and which piece or parcel of land is bounded on the South by a lane leading from Butts Close Corner towards Gaping Hills called Gaping Hill Lane on the West and North by a street called Bedford Street and on the East by other part of the said Close formerly belonging to William Williams but now to John Moore, and which said piece of land contains a frontage towards the said Gaping Hill Lane of one hundred and one feet or thereabouts and towards Bedford Street aforesaid of one hundred and seventy five feet or thereabouts…"*[20]

It is a mystery as to what would have inspired these two chaps to consider the use of concrete to build the cottages other than the fact that they had ready access to river gravel for the concrete mix.

However they must have been aware of a house constructed entirely of concrete in the early 1870s in Walsworth Road (now no 47, The Driver Hire Recruitment Centre).[21] They were ready to develop the land as, within less than two months, Hitchin Local Board Minutes record on 4 November 1885 *"plans passed on cottages proposed to be erected by Messrs. Logsdon & Jackson in Foundry Road, subject to Surveyors recommendations being carried out."*[22]

Logsdon and Jackson had a ready supply of river gravel and brick fragments from their gravel pit and brickworks close by in Oughtonhead Way. All they needed was a local supply of cement, which may have come from the Arlesey Lime and Portland Cement Company. Yellow gault bricks are present in the edging to the front entrance of the cottages, similar to the Arlesey Yellow Gault Brick, but were also made by George Jeeves in his brickworks at the corner of Bedford Road and Bearton Road.[23] During the build, Messrs Logsdon & Jackson were busy providing bids to supply gravel for road construction, but the cottages were most certainly completed by January 1887, as they were put on notice that month for failing to have given notice of completion of their buildings under the byelaws and that they were liable to proceedings!

The Local Board Letter Book of 29 January 1887 reads:

"Sirs,

I am instructed in addition to the verbal notice given to you yesterday in Foundry Road to hand you this written notice, that your two new cottages in Foundry Road must not be tenanted until you have received a certificate to confirm that this Board thinks these cottages are fit for habitation.

Your attention to the fact that the plans deposited with the Board show a brick wall on one side of the staircases which ought to have been carried out instead of the present lath and plaster stoothing."[24]

Stoothing is the wooden shuttering required for plaster or concrete construction.

Well, the lath and plaster were never replaced by brick walls. Maybe Mr Logsdon's role with the local fire brigade provided for excellent powers of persuasion?

Concrete, of course, is an ancient building material dating back at least to the Egyptians for the pyramids and famously much used by the Romans. By the 19th century, Portland cement had been invented by Joseph Aspin in England. A delightful book, *Concrete Cottages Small Garages and Farm Buildings,* published in 1918 and edited by Albert Lakeman (printed strangely enough nearby in Hertford by Stephen Austin & Sons Ltd for Concrete Publications Ltd. London), explains the different type of concrete used for buildings and recommends *"the fireplaces should be grouped to allow of the flues being combined into the minimum number of chimney stacks".*[25] The fireplaces in the cottages are grouped between the two front rooms on the party wall and angled in the corner. Each pair of houses in the terrace shares a single concrete chimney stack housing four flues for each house. The middle houses also share chimney stacks over the sculleries, though the end cottages would probably have had iron stove pipes instead.

The builders used concrete block for the frontages, but the majority of the structure, including the interior partition walls, match the construction description given for a pair of cottages that were built in the 1870s as part of the Gregynog Estate, Tregynon, Powys, Wales. These cottages were *"constructed from unreinforced concrete made from river gravel and brick fragments bonded with cement. It was laid in wet courses directly onto the wall using timber shuttering and finished with a skim coat of render".*[26] That's a

Bedroom fireplace
with concrete
surround and
mantelpiece at
44 Gaping Lane.
(Nafisa Sayany 2018)

perfect description for what can be found in the Logsdon and Jackson cottages, including the use of concrete for the chimneys, partition walls, sills and fireplaces.

The cottages remained in single ownership after Logsdon and Jackson sold *"the seven cottages or tenements erected upon the said piece or parcel of land here by conveyed"*, and now known as 6,7,8,9,10,11 and 12 in Gaping Lane, in September 1894 to Mrs Eliza Anne Moulden, of "Bandra" 7 Hitchin Road, Stevenage. Eliza was the widow of Joseph Moulden, a master butcher in Stevenage High Street who died in 1891.[27]

When Eliza died in 1915, her son Joseph E Moulden had predeceased her and her estate was left to trustees instructed with the sale of her estate. They sold the seven cottages to Joseph Williams of Bedford Road Hitchin, metal merchant, for the sum of £1,015. When he died in July 1930, he left them to Elisabeth Pratt of 2 Park Street Hitchin and Annie Tomlin of 5 West Hill. The house numbers were changed from 6–12 Gaping Lane to 32–44 Gaping Lane when a renumbering was carried out by Hitchin Urban District Council in 1935, probably in response to the development of the properties built further along Gaping Lane to where it meets Lucas Lane.

The cottages remained tenanted until the 1960s. Elisabeth Pratt died in 1955 and Annie Tomlin in 1969. The first cottage to be sold individually, possibly as tenancies ended, was in 1960 (Number 38). Numbers 42 and 44 were sold in 1967, number 40 in 1968 and number 34 in 1969 before Annie's death in December of the same year. Number 36 was not sold until 1972 and the sale of number 32 remains unknown.[28]

At the time of writing in 2018, the last fields of Gaping Hills are soon to disappear with development of the Cricket Club grounds already started on the former Gaping Hills Close. Further developments along the length of Lucas Lane are proposed in the District Local Plan, but hopefully Little Park Piece residents will still be able to enjoy having one foot in the town and one foot in the country.

1   HALS 87587; TNA SC12/31/12
2   TNA C54/220, Calendar of Close Rolls 1 Feb 1381; Bridget Howlett, *Hitchin Priory Park. The history of a landscape park and gardens* (HHS, 2004) pp1–3; Anne Rowe, *Medieval Parks of Hertfordshire* (University of Hertfordshire, 2009) pp128–129
3   Hitchin manorial accounts 1450–1453 BL Egerton Ch 8364–8365 and 1459–1538 TNA SC6/870/4–6, SC6/HENVII/258–265, SC6/HENVIII/1567–1587, SC6/HENVIII/6629–6632

4   Bridget Howlett ed, *Survey of the Royal Manor of Hitchin* (Hertfordshire Record Society, 2000) pp24–25; field names in 1818 copy of 1816 map and schedule of Hitchin NHM; Hitchin tithe apportionment 1841 and map 1844 HALS DSA4/53/1–2

5   Anthony M Foster and Lionel M Munby, *Market Town* (HHS, 1987) pp22–26

6   Rosemary Thornes and Terry Slater, "Detached gardens and the urban fringe of eighteenth-and-nineteenth-century English provincial towns", *Journal of Historical Geography* 53 July 2016 pp28–44

7   Foster and Munby, *Market Town*, p21; NHM LTS Vol 1B p155

8   NHM LTS Vol 1B p155

9   Kate Harwood, "Park Piece Detached Gardens (now Gaping Lane)" Hertfordshire Gardens Trust, 2017 http://hertsgardenstrust.org.uk/wp-content/uploads/2017/09/Gaping%20Lane%20Detached%20Gardens.pdf ; Park Piece Allotments rules and tenancy agreements 1879–1924 HALS DE/Ws/E2, DE/Ws/E9-E14

10   The author's thanks to Christopher Hubbard

11   HALS DE/Ws/E2, DE/Ws/E9–E14; See Hitchin 1913 Project www.hitchin1913. org.uk using Inland Revenue Valuation Office Field Books (TNA IR 58) and maps (HALS IR1) compared with 1911 census.

12   Harwood, "Park Piece Detached Gardens (now Gaping Lane)" Hertfordshire Gardens Trust, 2017 http://hertsgardenstrust.org.uk/wp-content/uploads/2017/09/Gaping%20Lane%20Detached%20Gardens.pdf

13   G E Bryant & G P Baker ed. *A Quaker Journal Vol II* (Hutchinson, 1933) p537; Hitchin manor court book 1842–1854 TNA CRES5/310 pp128–130

14   Foster and Munby, *Market Town* p169; Hitchin manor court books 1842–1862 TNA CRES5/310 pp296, 376, CRES5/311 p170; Pat Gadd, "Hitchin Inns", 1987 typescript pp116–117

15   Deeds to Delta Cottages, 9 Oughtonhead Way courtesy of Tony & Sue Thomas; Hitchin manor court book 1842–1854 TNA CRES5/310 p395

16   Tony Crosby, Priscilla Douglas, Steve Fletcher et al., *Jeeves Yard. A dynasty of Hitchin builders and brickmakers* (HHS, 2003) p57; Hitchin manor court books 1842–1862 TNA CRES5/310 pp351, CRES5/311 pp85–86; Hitchin valuation list March 1887 HALS Off Acc 1104 UN81/24

17   Hitchin manor court books 1842–1862 TNA CRES5/310 p352 CRES5/311 pp81, 162, 221 ; Hitchin Historical Society, *Hitchin Arcade Then and Now* (HHS, 2007) pp22–32; Hitchin rate book 1861 HALS Off Acc 1104 Box 5 UN81/4; Hitchin valuation list March 1887 HALS Off Acc 1104 UN81/24

18   Hitchin Local Board and HUDC minutes 16 December 1891, 30 December 1891, 5 October 1892, 22 March 1893, 26 July 1893, 9 August 1893, 13 November 1895, 27 November 1895, 11 December 1895, 23 December 1895, 22 January 1896 HALS Off Acc 1417

19   NHM LTS Vol 3A pp8–9,103; Hitchin valuation list 1887 HALS Off Acc 1104 Box 5UN81/4

20   Deeds to 36 Gaping Lane courtesy of Steve & Christine Johnson

21   Valerie Taplin and Audrey Stewart, *Two Minutes to the Station. The Tale of Hitchin's Victorian Triangle* (HHS, 2010) pp17–19

22   Hitchin Local Board minutes 4 November 1885 HALS Off Acc 1417

23   G P Page, Arlesey – The Pits www.onthebuttonarlesey.co.uk/Arlesey ThePits. pdf ; Arcangelo Lombari https://arcangelolombari.wordpress.com/2013/ 12/05/brickworks-at-arlesey-short-version/ ; Crosby at al, *Jeeves Yard* pp54- 55

24   Hitchin Local Board letter book 1886–1889 HALS Off Acc 1104

25   Albert Lakeman ed., *Concrete Cottages, Small Garages and Farm Buildings* (Concrete Publications, 1918) https://archive.org/stream/concretecottages00lakerich/concretecottages00lakerich_djvu.txt

26   www.coflein.gov.uk/en/site/29033/details/concrete-cottages

27   Deeds to 36 Gaping Lane courtesy of Steve & Christine Johnson

28   Deeds to 32–44 Gaping Lane courtesy of their owners

Hitchin Hill – A First "New Town" 3

DAVID HOWLETT AND PETER ELLIS

A Hidden Gem

Today the small housing enclave of "Hitchin Hill" often goes unnoticed lying, as it does, in an area dominated by the 20th century and focused on the large modern roundabout where Stevenage Road meets Park Way and the London and Gosmore roads. But Hitchin Hill has a surprising, varied and very distinct history which can still be traced through landscape features that survive today.

The name "Hitchin Hill" seems originally to have been applied, understandably, to the hill itself (today Park Street) which forms the route leading away from the town centre, south towards the Stevenage and London roads. Only later was the label "Hitchin Hill" used in the way that it is now for the area around the road junctions.

"New Towns" are not New

Hitchin historians often note how, as the town's large medieval open fields were never formally enclosed, it was difficult to build away from the central medieval centre. To do so usually required agreement between a varied number of separate owners and occupiers of the open field strips which had, in a sense, become fossilised. It was, therefore, into the 1700s before a start was made in overcoming these difficulties: then a small number of isolated cottages – such as those at Ninesprings and off Cambridge Road – were built. But these encroachments of the open fields remained the exception, not the rule, and a rising population was accommodated within the medieval town by cramming more inhabitants into the existing, and constrained, built up area.

Hitchin Hill is especially important because its development broke this established mould in a context of population pressures becoming particularly intense. In the early 1820s it emerged as the first major piece of building away from the historic town centre. This is why the area acquired the label of "New Town" in its earliest years. Hitchin Hill might have broken the mould but, in an important way, it did not break the landscape. The earliest detailed rate assessment plan of Hitchin of 1816 shows, at the junction of the Stevenage and London roads, a distinct triangular field pattern created from a bundle of strips carved from the ancient open field of Standhill and the new development was fitted within this framework.[1]

In 1816 we know much of this area was owned by Thomas Field (prosperous wheelwright, property owner and Baptist) and leased to Abraham Fells, a nurseryman who supplied plants to – amongst others – the Delmé-Radcliffes at the Priory. It is fascinating that this triangular plot (490 & 491 on the map below) can still be clearly traced as the core of the suburb; the three main paths (Butcher's Lane, Hitchin Hill Path and the unnamed lane to the south) can also be linked to early plot boundaries. Tantalisingly, the strip boundaries of Field's holding encompassed land on both sides of Stevenage Road (490, 491, 500 & 501 on the map) suggesting the field pattern was established before the road became a major route.[2] In the area of the large modern roundabout stood an obelisk. Evidence shows this dated from at least 1565 (then called High Cross) and it is also shown on maps of c1770 and 1851, but it had disappeared by 1881.[3]

In 1816 there was also a small house and barn nearby north of Stevenage Road, owned and occupied by Mary Foster (499 on the map) and a clay pit (502 on the map) which lay between Stevenage Road and St John's Road (then Bethel Lane). In addition, there were a few cottages on St John's Road and a few more much further east along Stevenage Road. By 1825 Thomas Field had developed a brickworks near the clay pit and Hitchin Hill's houses began to appear; by 1826 there were about ten new dwellings and the town rate collector introduced a new heading *"Moorhens and Hitchin Hill"* into his accounts.[4]

The varied sizes, shapes and materials of the surviving houses clearly show the area was developed piecemeal by the Field family

Below left: Hitchin Hill in 1816. Park Street leads south from the town centre between Priory Park and the Sand Pits to the junction of London and Stevenage Roads. (Excerpt from Henry Merrett's copy of map of Hitchin 1818 NHM)

Below right: The obelisk at the junction of London Road and Stevenage Road. (Excerpt from a map of Purwell Field c.1770 HALS DZ/72/P121605)

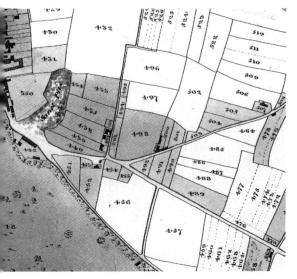

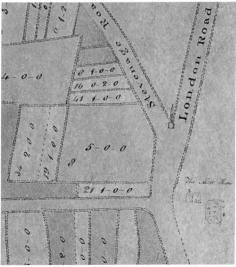

5 Hitchin Hill Path with carved date stone of 1834 and the name T. Field. (Scilla Douglas 2010)

T. Field date stone on 5 Hitchin Hill Path. (Peter Ellis 2018)

and others. These included carpenter James Russell, miller William Theobalds and banker, later also brewer, Joseph Margetts Pierson. Some evidence exists along Hitchin Hill Path of agreement on approximate common building lines to create attractive front gardens; it also seems the older brick boundary walls that survive may similarly date from a common approach to laying out the gardens. It is difficult to be sure which of the buildings was completed first. Nos 5–6 Hitchin Hill Path have a carved date-stone of 1834 and the name "T Field", although the architectural characteristics of the immediately adjacent house (Montserrat) could well mean that this is in fact one of the earliest houses dating from about 1830. No 7 appeared between 1825–30. Butcher's Lane and the unnamed south alleyway provided the wider accesses for horses and carts to the rear of the properties facing Hitchin Hill Path; a property on Butcher's Lane is still known as the Old Coach House, likely originally connected to No 7 and then converted to cottages after Nos 5–6 were built.[5]

A new settlement meant mouths to feed and thirsts to slake. Nearby the Moorhens had functioned as an inn since 1759. A public house, the Duke of Wellington, was built in 1828 on the south side of Stevenage Road just beyond Field's triangle of new houses. By 1841 two adjoining beerhouses were established opposite, on the north side, one of which was the William IV; when re-let in 1864, it had an established grocery business attached.[6]

By 1838 the rating list records that the "Hitchin New Town Development" was substantially complete and the tithe map of 1844 clearly shows most of the buildings that can still be found there today; one which remains prominent – St Elmo, near

Sales Particulars for The Wellington with stabling for six horses sold as part of Marshall and Pierson's Brewery Estate 1841. (NHM 2718/16)

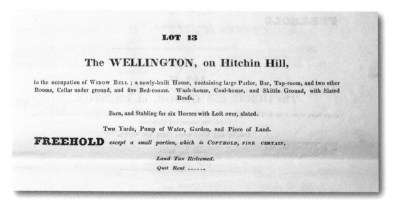

LOT 13

The WELLINGTON, on Hitchin Hill,

ia the occupation of WIDOW BELL ; a newly-built House, containing large Parlor, Bar, Tap-room, and two other Rooms, Cellar under ground, and five Bed-rooms. Wash-house, Coal-house, and Skittle Ground, with Slated Roofs.

Barn, and Stabling for six Horses with Loft over, slated.

Two Yards, Pump of Water, Garden, and Piece of Land.

FREEHOLD except a small portion, which is COPYHOLD, FINE CERTAIN.

Land Tax Redeemed.

Quit Rent ......

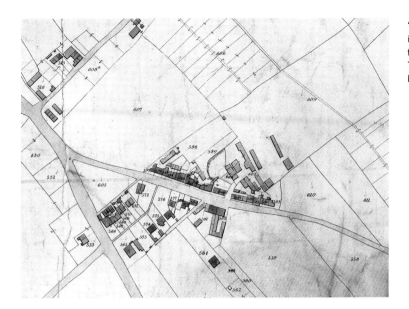

"Hitchin New Town" in 1844. (Excerpt from Hitchin Tithe Map HALS DSA4/53/2A)

Montserrat – was described in 1838 as *"New House"*. The line of generally smaller houses along the north side of Stevenage Road, now lost, is also shown. These stand in front of Thomas Field's brickworks (602 on tithe map above) and by 1838 one was home to his daughter. Somewhere here was also, after 1833, a schoolroom licensed for Nonconformist (presumably Baptist) worship connected to Thomas Field.[7]

Attractive residential enclave?

By 1841 Hitchin Hill was, therefore, firmly established as the town's largest out-settlement, effectively a separate hamlet with a distinct character. The Census of that year recorded 505 inhabitants there at a time when Hitchin overall totalled 6,125 people, an increase for the town of almost 94% since 1801. The variety and quality of the housing in the triangular portion of Thomas Field's land made it mainly a residential area. Perhaps its relatively high, dry and airy location made it more attractive than the increasingly overcrowded and insalubrious town centre below. William Ranger's public health report (of 1849) nevertheless identified problems at Hitchin Hill. It was an area where *"fever prevailed"* and where in parts there were open drains and dunghills. Overall, however, it seems conditions were not too bad compared to other areas of the town and the new buildings, such as Montserrat, could include ways of collecting rainfall to give a cleaner water supply.

The 1841 Census certainly reveals a segment of inhabitants who were of the 'better sort' such as Hitchin's Registrar James Coleman, the Parish Clerk Thomas Dimsey (son of the former master of

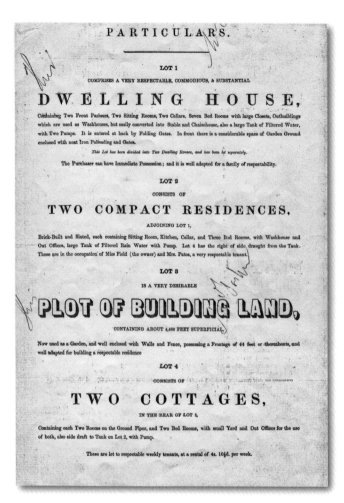

PARTICULARS.

LOT 1

COMPRISES A VERY RESPECTABLE, COMMODIOUS, & SUBSTANTIAL

DWELLING HOUSE,

Containing Two Front Parlours, Two Sitting Rooms, Two Cellars, Seven Bed Rooms with large Closets, Outbuildings which are used as Washhouses, but easily converted into Stable and Chaisehouse, also a large Tank of Filtered Water, with Two Pumps. It is entered at back by Folding Gates. In front there is a considerable space of Garden Ground enclosed with neat Iron Palisading and Gates.

This Lot has been divided into Two Dwelling Houses, and has been let separately.

The Purchaser can have Immediate Possession; and it is well adapted for a family of respectability.

LOT 2

CONSISTS OF

TWO COMPACT RESIDENCES,

ADJOINING LOT 1,

Brick-Built and Slated, each containing Sitting Room, Kitchen, Cellar, and Three Bed Rooms, with Washhouse and Out Offices, large Tank of Filtered Rain Water with Pump. Lot 4 has the right of side draught from the Tank. These are in the occupation of Miss Field (the owner) and Mrs. Pates, a very respectable tenant.

LOT 3

IS A VERY DESIRABLE

PLOT OF BUILDING LAND,

CONTAINING ABOUT 4,400 FEET SUPERFICIAL.

Now used as a Garden, and well enclosed with Walls and Fence, possessing a Frontage of 44 feet or thereabouts, and well adapted for building a respectable residence

LOT 4

CONSISTS OF

TWO COTTAGES,

IN THE REAR OF LOT 2,

Containing each Two Rooms on the Ground Floor, and Two Bed Rooms, with small Yard and Out Offices for the use of both, also side draft to Tank on Lot 2, with Pump.

These are let to respectable weekly tenants, at a rental of 4s. 10½d. per week.

Sales Particulars for 7 Hitchin Hill Path (with large Tank of Filtered Water with Two Pumps), 5 & 6 Hitchin Hill Path, and two cottages (now the Coach House) 1858. (Will Warburg)

the British School), specialist occupations such as a Drawing Master and School Master and eleven heads of household of independent means. There was also a clutch of tradesmen such as bakers, a grocer, tailors, a blacksmith and a butcher. The pattern looks somewhat pre-industrial in that people of widely differing means lived not too far apart with the better-off mainly in the area of larger houses between the Stevenage and London roads.[8]

Or a centre of smoky industry?

In addition, however, there was also an emerging industrial component to the settlement – brickmaking. It seems likely this was initiated by the need to provide materials (mainly red-brown bricks) for the new houses themselves in a pre-railway age when it made sense to source such supplies as locally as possible. By 1838 there were over 30 mainly smaller houses along the north side of Stevenage Road, again it seems built piecemeal. The 1841 Census here includes a range of poorer occupations such as nine agricultural labourers, a shepherd and a washerwoman. There is only one "journeyman brickmaker" but five "labourers" could have been so employed and, as the activity was seasonal, some of the agricultural workers could also have worked at the claypit and kiln.

It is clear that, once established, this local activity expanded steadily even allowing for the national depression of 1840–41. By 1841 Benjamin Bolton (a relation of Thomas Field) and Thomas Gorham Pierson were respectively owner and occupier of the original brickworks. Their activities coincided with the end of brick production at Maydencroft and Abel Sharpe, formerly proprietor brick-maker there, moved to a new house on Hitchin Hill where it seems likely that he was engaged in supervising Pierson's works. Later in the 1840s George Jeeves, of the Hitchin building dynasty, also established brickmaking on Stevenage Road, but at a site much further to the southeast of Hitchin Hill's New Town.[9]

A mixed community in miniature

The 1851 Census gives more detail of the inhabitants as its enumerators asked about subsidiary individuals and occupations within households. Hitchin Hill still retained a wide social mix divided, mainly, between the main villa triangle and the generally smaller houses on Stevenage Road. There continued to be an important body of householders of "independent" means plus a segment of retirees, including three Chelsea Pensioners. One such retiree – Mr Clark, formerly a shoemaker of Sun Street – fell victim to a *"daring highway robbery"* between Gosmore Road and the Moorhens while returning home one dark evening in November 1855; the alarm was raised and *"our policemen fell in with three men near the station who had been applying for tickets to get off. The biggest of the three knocked the Inspector down and got safe off, but the other two were taken."* [10] The professionals and tradesmen were still there such as the Registrar, an Inland Revenue Officer, some schoolmistresses (who may have run a school there) and several small businessmen including three bakers and a grocer. There was also a good number of artisan workers such as a coach-smith, three tailors, a painter and two shoemakers; there were some bricklayers and one brickmaker. The poorer inhabitants comprised a clutch of agricultural and railway labourers (these latter, unsurprisingly, included incomers from both Scotland and Ireland, five of whom lodged in one house); there were also thirty-two straw-plaiters who traditionally worked to eke out lower family incomes.

As the 19th century wore on Hitchin Hill maintained its character as a "tale of two communities". The main core of 1830s building in Thomas Field's triangular plot still seems to have remained home to the more prosperous inhabitants; for example Butcher's Lane recalls Thomas A Butcher, the District Road Surveyor, who was living at Hitchin Hill in 1871. The properties

Above: The Reverend Bamlet Neptune Switzer 1904. (NHM LTS Vol 3A p5)

Left: Hitchin Hill: houses mostly built in the 1820s on the north side of Stevenage Road (now demolished) *c.*1900. (NHM)

7 Hitchin Hill Path.
(Scilla Douglas 2010)

on Stevenage Road generally housed more modestly provided townsfolk. This area does not, however, seem to have had the problems of deeply established poverty found along Queen Street and in some of the town centre yards; a photograph of Stevenage Road taken in the early 1900s shows mainly smaller but tidy houses and neat gardens.

But a local contrast remained and the career, between 1895 and 1904, of the young, *"very popular"* and evangelical Curate, Bamlet Neptune Switzer, exemplifies it. He lived comfortably, with his wife and family, on Hitchin Hill Path (in No.7) but worked hard and effectively to recruit the younger inhabitants of the smaller Stevenage Road houses into the Established Church. Alice Maud Carter, grandmother of one of the authors and a pupil at the Hitchin British Schools, lived in the Stevenage Road houses where her father was described as both carpenter and insurance agent. She was poached, along with her younger sisters, from a lapsed Methodist tradition and given an adult baptism in her late teens at St Mary's Hitchin on 14 May 1901, by which time she was in service with Walter Millard, churchwarden and architect, on Benslow Lane. The records of the parish church show that Alice was not alone in her baptism and confirmation; Switzer was particularly successful in this more modest part of Hitchin Hill, no doubt honing skills (such as in youth activities) that he later put to good use in a long career in London's under-privileged East End.[11]

Hitchin Hill absorbed by the wider town

Hitchin Hill survived little changed into the 1940s, despite post 1919 pressures to build further and further from the town centre. By 1926, the area between the Stevenage and London Roads was designated for future housing and classic ribbon development began. In 1913 the Tudor style Dower House designed by Geoffry Lucas was built on the spare land immediately north of the 1830s New Town suburb for the Phillips family; 1933 saw Conquest Close constructed to the south and, about the same time, Coach Drive was built up to the west. The new mid 1920s council housing at Sunnyside was also not far away. The brickworks had closed by the early 1920s. The Wellington was lost in 1922 when its licence renewal was refused, perhaps because of a reputation for disturbances[12].

It was after 1945 that the major changes came. A desire for improved living standards was translated into an antipathy towards modest "Victorian" housing. The smaller houses along Stevenage

Road were demolished in the late 1950s; the William IV went too with its licence being transferred in 1960 to The Fountain at the heart of the new Oakfield housing estate.[13] The site of the smaller houses, now designated The Maples, was redeveloped with the blocks of flats that stand there today. There was also additional 1960s and 70s housing infill in the wider Hitchin Hill area. The post-war years witnessed an inexorable rise in road traffic particularly on Stevenage Road and in 1981 the consequent opening of Park Way and its huge new roundabout transformed Hitchin Hill's link to the town centre. The Dower House was demolished shortly after and replaced with Dower Place flats. Happily, however, the earliest and better quality housing of Thomas Field's triangle, grouped around Hitchin Hill Path, survived and now forms a Conservation Area that was designated in 2010–11 and which recognises the historic and architectural distinctiveness of this special Hitchin area, hopefully preserving it for future generations.[14]

A house in detail: Montserrat by Peter Ellis

Montserrat is an imposing Grade II listed late Georgian house on the corner of Hitchin Hill Path and London Road. The stucco render to the exterior walls was originally mock ashlar, the illusion of masonry joints being scored into the stucco surface. This marking has long since disappeared under decades of paint coatings. Three blind window recesses on the west elevation and one on the north add symmetry to the exterior without impact on the interior

The door knocker design was used on at least three other early 19th century properties in Hitchin, presumably a product of local ironworks. (Peter Ellis 2017)

Montserrat at the corner of Hitchin Hill Path. (Peter Ellis 2017)

The porch over Montserrat's front door has cast iron treillage supports with a zinc concave hipped roof. (Peter Ellis 2017)

The timber staircase rises to the first floor, with a polished mahogany handrail, with wreathed turned termination on the ground floor.
(Peter Ellis 2017)

layouts. The parapet also reflects the fashion to hide the roof from view at street level.

Internally, although small in plan, the hall and the connecting drawing room have a grandeur that reflects the exterior presence, but this does not extend into the rest of the house. The front door width of 3 feet 3 inches is matched only by the drawing room door, all the other doors in the house are 2 feet 6 inches. The hall and drawing room have decorated plaster cornices and a central ceiling rose. The first floor landing, visible from the hall, has a simpler plaster cornice but the remainder of the first floor landing, not visible from below, has no cornice. This underlines again the intention to provide a grand entry, whilst the remainder of the house remains plain.

It is difficult to trace the earlier occupants of the house because Hitchin streets were not numbered before 1890[15] and the first mention of the name "Montserrat" only occurs in the 1901 census. We do know that in 1839 the house was owned by Joseph Margetts Pierson and occupied by James Coleman, the Registrar of Births and Deaths. Joseph Margetts Pierson probably built the house between 1827 and 1834 as an investment. He was a wealthy Hitchin banker and brewer, living with his large family in Lewesford House, Upper Tilehouse Street. Sadly his speculative investment in an alkali works in Brussels ended in his bankruptcy in 1841, resulting in the sale of all his property.[16]

The house was then owned by members of the Wright family until 1928. In 1841 George Wright, a farmer, was living at Montserrat with his wife and mother-in-law, but the following year, his father's death led him and his wife to take over the tenancy of Preston Hill Farm, and his widowed mother moved to Hitchin Hill. George seems to have been a man of intemperate disposition because in 1870 he appeared in court charged with assaulting his 11 year old plough boy whose arm was *"very much injured"* and just over two years later he was summonsed for assaulting a young woman. George moved to Graveley where his family had a long connection, dying in 1890.[17]

From at least 1861 Montserrat was the home of William Cox, a landowner, who remained there until his death in 1909 aged 77. William was described in his obituary as being *"a cripple almost all his life, owing to a spinal complaint"*. He attended the Brand Street Methodist Chapel *"where a special seat was reserved for him"*. Interestingly, the small yard to the north of the house enclosed by high masonry walls contained a coach house and a stable for one horse.[18]

By 1911 Montserrat was the home of George Archibald McKay, a travelling salesman, and his sisters. In 1928, now living in The Avenue and Secretary of Wirksworth Quarries Limited, he bought Montserrat where his unmarried sister Nellie still lived. Montserrat remained in that family's ownership and occupation until 1975.[19]

1   1841 census; 1818 copy of 1816 map and schedule of Hitchin NHM
2   1818 copy of 1816 map and schedule of Hitchin NHM; Notes from deeds to 7 Hitchin Hill Path made by Will Warburg – the original deeds are in NHM; William Urwick. *Nonconformity in Herts.* (Hazell, Watson and Viney 1884) p644; Bridget Howlett, *Hitchin Priory Park. The history of a landscape park and gardens* (HHS 2004) pp56–58
3   Bargain and sale from Robert Parris to John Andrewes 1565 HALS 87587; Map of Purwell Field c.1770 HALS DZ/72/P121605: Hitchin Board of Health OS map 1851 10 feet to 1 mile sheet XIII HALS; OS 25 inches to 1 mile 1st edition Herts XII.1 1881
4   1818 copy of 1816 map and schedule of Hitchin NHM; Hitchin rate book 1825–1827 HALS DP/53/11/7
5   Notes from deeds to 7 Hitchin Hill Path made by Will Warburg
6   Hitchin manor court book 1827–1841 TNA CRES5/309 pp60,130,320; Pat Gadd, "Hitchin Inns", 1987 typescript, pp41, 63; Hitchin tithe apportionment 1841 HALS DSA4/53/1
7   Hitchin rate assessment 1838 HALS DP/53/11/9; Hitchin tithe map 1844 HALS DSA4/53/2A: Urwick. *Nonconformity in Herts.* p64
8   William Ranger, *Report to the General Board of Health – Hitchin* (HMSO, 1849) p5; 1841 census; Jacky Birch, Scilla Douglas et al, *Educating Our Own* (British Schools Museum, 2008) pp32-36
9   Hitchin rate assessment 1838 HALS DP/53/11/9; Hitchin tithe apportionment 1841 HALS DSA4/53/1; Bridget Howlett, *Maydencroft. A Manor, hunting park, farm and brickworks Near Hitchin* (HHS, 2012) pp90–91; Tony Crosby, Priscilla Douglas, Steve Fletcher et al., *Jeeves Yard. A dynasty of Hitchin builders and brickmakers* (HHS, 2003) pp44,54–55
10 G E Bryant & G P Baker ed. *A Quaker Journal Vol II*, 1933, p493
11 NHM LTS Vol 3A pp14–15; 1901 census; Hitchin British Schools admission register; St Mary's Hitchin baptism register 1885–1904 HALS DP/53/1/10
12 HUDC minutes 8 Apr 1913 HALS; Pat Gadd, "Hitchin Inns", 1987 typescript, p41
13 Pat Gadd, "Hitchin Inns", 1987 typescript, p45
14 *Hitchin Hill Path: Conservation Area and Character Statement*, North Hertfordshire District Council, 2011
15 Hitchin Local Board minutes 22 October 1890 HALS Off Acc 1417
16 Hitchin rate assessments 1838–1839 HALS DP/53/11/9,11; Allan Whitaker, *Brewers in Hertfordshire. A historical gazetteer* (University of Hertfordshire, 2006) p143; Anthony M Foster and Lionel M Munby, *Market Town* (HHS, 1987) pp172–175
17 Deeds to Montserrat in possession of owners; 1841 and 1851 censuses; Philip J Wray, *A History of Preston in Hertfordshire* (Privately published 2015) pp45,51,70; National Probate Index https://probatesearch.service.gov.uk/#calendar ; Wright family memorials in Graveley churchyard
18 1861–1901 censuses; NHM LTS Vol 3A p49; Hitchin 1913 Project www.hitchin1913.org.uk using Inland Revenue Valuation Office Field Books (TNA IR 58) and maps (HALS IR1). Montserrat is plot 2461
19 1911 census; deeds to Montserrat in possession of owners

St John's Road and the surrounding area

4

CHRISTOPHER HUBBARD

Stone plaque on 31 St John's Road. (Alan Fleck 2017)

S t John's Road, known as Bethel Lane up to the early 1920s, runs from the top of Whitehill Road to the top of Hitchin Hill, opposite the Three Moorhens public house. The 13 red brick terraced cottages on the left-hand side going down from Whitehill Road, now numbers 25 to 37, were originally numbers 1 to 13, Providence Terrace, Bethel Lane. The original landowners were Edward Ransome Allen and William Clarkson Allen, drugmillers of 7 Cowper Street, City Road, also Metford Warner, paper stainer, of 44 Highbury Park, Islington. The land had been willed to them by William Allen, a Quaker, son of Samuel Allen of West Mill and his wife, Phebe Lucas. On his death in 1897 the land passed to the above as executors. They sold the plot in 1898 to a local builder named John James, who constructed houses and named them Providence Terrace. A stone plaque above what is now number 31, shows this and the date of 1898. When I first moved to number 28 (formerly 4 Providence Terrace), in November 1972, purchased then for £8,400, I set about repointing the brickwork as one of my first major projects. My efforts were commended by an old chap, Percy Simmons, who lived around the corner in Wedmore

Bethel Lane (now St John's Road) in 1910. (Excerpt from Valuation Office Survey map HALS IR1/90d)

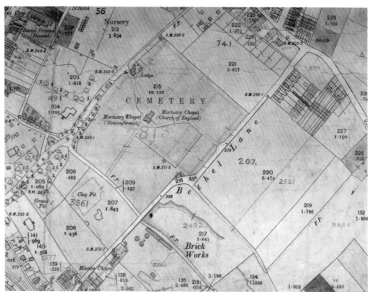

Road and was probably then in his 80s, and he informed me that his father helped to build the terrace, at a cost of about £100 for each house.

Local building materials

Although there is no proof, it would have made sense for the local builders to use ready to hand materials, which, in this case would have been the bricks made at the brickworks, which were situated opposite the cemetery, and where there are now football pitches and playing fields. In the

Cemetery Road (now Standhill Road) constructed in 1870 through a former sand and gravel pit to provide work for the unemployed. Postcard *c*.1900 (Terry Knight)

1880s the brickworks were owned by the Ransom family, Alfred (who incidentally also owned the lime quarry in Benslow Lane), then by his son Theodore, where seven men and two boys were employed. The bricks were apparently handmade from the brick earth, and were of a red brown colour. In much later years, the locals referred to the site as "The Mounds" and there are memories of a brick building and chimney, which must have been the works and kiln. Another source of material would have been Theodore Ransom's sand and gravel pits situated between St John's Road and Standhill Road. This road was originally known as Cemetery Road, and the section running into St John's Road is still called that. In what is now Passingham Avenue, around the corner from the top of St John's Road, were two gravel pits which are now two grassed areas set with trees, and that area was owned by the local Worbey family, of whom more later. Incidentally, the pay office for the pits was situated at 83 Whitehill Road, where, until his recent passing, lived Alec Worbey, a well known local landowner, chimney sweep, and steam railway enthusiast. Some may remember the big "King's Cross" enamel sign kept in the extensive barns at the rear of the property, which also housed a good amount of railway memorabilia. For timber, there were two local sawmills, one was Sunnyside Sawmills, owned by Mr Massey, and the other being the sawmills in Hermitage Road, owned by Mr Barker.

Providence Terrace, Bethel Lane

The first property, number 24, was actually not part of the terrace, as it stood in its own grounds at the junction of Whitehill Road and Bethel Lane, and was, it seems, originally a First World War hut. A Mrs Golby lived there in the 1950s, although I remember Miss Montgomery, who was either her sister or sister in law. Their heating and lighting was by paraffin and to do their washing, they would withdraw rainwater by hand pump, from two sunken tanks, which were housed in a corrugated outhouse. Next door, at number 25, originally 1 Providence Terrace, lived Mr and Mrs Read, and their son John. Bill and Gwen met as Sunday school teachers, at what was, although now sadly demolished, Queen Street Congregational Chapel, which stood next to the British Schools, and it was at the chapel they married in the 1940s. When first built none of the cottages had a bathroom, although in time these were added in the place of the coal barn at the end, but Bill and Gwen decided against this, and so John remembers the tin bath coming out on Saturday evenings. Bill had worked for Mr Barker at the sawmill in Hermitage Road, first in the workshops, and later as his gardener. His skills were reflected by the wonderful annual display of chrysanthemums in his own back garden. Bill was very lucky to escape with his life when gardening at number 24, which he'd done for years. When digging, his spade carried on going, which he just managed to retrieve by smartly stepping backwards. Had he not, he would have fallen down a 60 feet deep well, the wooden cover of which was sunk in the ground and over time, had rotted. Clearly no one had any idea why the well was there, but whoever had sunk it, had brick lined it. It took some filling!

Highbury Studio, 26 St John's Road

Next door at number 26 lived Mr Herbert Minnis and his wife. He was a well-known Hitchin photographer who had a studio and dark room in a wooden building, just away from the back of his house. John Read remembers the old photographic equipment, made of hardwood and brass, also the Edwardian hand-built seat that Mr Minnis used for his customers' photos that I now have in my back garden courtesy of John, also the aspidistra, which must be at least 100 years old. Mr Minnis was in business from 1908 to probably the 1950s.

Moving down to number 29 where Maurice Foster lived. He'd been a train driver in the steam days, and recalled when Sir Ralph Delmé-Radcliffe of the Priory, who worked as a stockbroker in the City, would sometimes ride a short distance with Maurice on the

Brian Worbey aged four in his "Christmas Car" outside 15 St John's Road, June 1940. On the left is Farrow's shop with Pulters Way beyond. (Brian Worbey)

footplate. All very unofficial! Maurice, who was a bachelor, was a big horse racing man and was well known in racing circles by both jockeys and trainers, and a very successful chooser of the winning horses. From an old Hitchin family, he possessed the old local accent that you rarely hear now.

At number 37, the last house on the terrace, was a small shop, like a general stores, which was housed in the front room run by a Mr and Mrs Farrow. It was very small with labelled drawers for things like rice, raisins and such, and where the sugar was weighed and bagged individually and the butter cut and patted into blocks. After the Farrows, Mr & Mrs Winch, then Mr & Mrs Hammond ran it, although by the time I arrived in 1972, trading had ceased.

Beyond Pulters Way

Crossing Pulters Way and a little further on were, as already mentioned, the brickfields. At the bottom end, where the houses in Eynsford Court face up the playing field, was originally a smallholding owned by Albert Westwood, where he kept pigs in an orchard. The fallen apples provided them with a ready meal. Just about where Latchmore Close is situated stood three old cottages, numbered 40, 41 and 42, which by the early 1960s were uninhabited and, it seems, ready for demolition. A short distance further on, just where the road narrows, was a parcel of land on which stood wooden barns. These were owned by Johnny Howard, who some may remember, had a small greengrocery shop at the bottom corner of Radcliffe Road and Nightingale Road. Brian Worbey remembers that he kept his lorry at these barns which he used for storing vegetables for sale at his shop. On this land now stand three more recently built houses, numbered 42, 44 and 46.

Coming back up the road

The first property is the Lodge House to Greyfriars, the big house at the top of Hitchin Hill, and then follows St John's Path, which has eight cottages, and leads down to Standhill Road. Next are three cottages, numbered 1–3, which, until the early 1960s, were followed by 4–6, probably demolished to make way for the Cheshire Home. Then came Robin's Hill, the home of Hitchin's first lady doctor, Dr Winifred Symonds, who was apparently an authority on birds.

St John the Baptist Mission Church

The original building was occupied for many years by the Particular Baptists, during which time it was known as Bull's Barn or Bethel Chapel, and had a small graveyard attached to it. What happened to that? At least, we now know the reason for the original name for the road, Bethel Lane. It was sold in 1868 and the use of it was

Above left: Memorial to Graham Vinicombe Winchester Clowes in St Mary's Church. (Bridget Howlett 2017)

Above right: St John the Baptist Church c.1910. (NHM LTS Vol 3A p.83)

granted to the clergy of St Mary's. The Rev Claude Lewis was in charge of the church for eight years, during which time the building was enlarged to nearly twice its size and the interior decorated and re-furbished. A new font was presented to the church by the family of Mr Winchester Clowes, as a memorial to the family's association with the church. Apparently, the memorial was dedicated on Easter Day 1901, and was made of Caen stone with coloured marble pillars, and bore the inscription on a brass plate *"To the glory of God and in memory of Graham Vinicombe Winchester Clowes, Lieutenant 1st Battalion Gordon Highlanders, born October 3rd 1880, killed in action near Doorn River, Cape Colony, South Africa, January 30th 1901"*. Local people who used to attend St John's Church remember the church hall next door, run as a youth club, and recall in particular a very popular curate, Denys Graebe, well liked throughout the area of St John's and Sunnyside for his involvement in the community. The church ceased to be used in 1963 and was demolished in 1974.[1]

Next to the hall, in the time of the Second World War, was an air raid siren, allegedly one of the first in the country. Interestingly, there was also a pill box that stood alongside numbers 36–38 Whitehill Road which looked down St John's Road.

The Cemetery

The newer section of the two sides of the cemetery which was started in the mid 1960s, was originally a piece of rough ground, former site of a disused brickfield. This was, I was told, owned by Johnny Howard, but was used by Joe Dearman, to graze his horses, Joe being what was then termed a rag and bone man. Running between the two sections of cemetery is Cemetery Road, an extension of the original Cemetery Road, now known as Standhill Road. The original cemetery was opened on 3 May 1857, and, with the Mortuary Chapel, was consecrated by the Bishop of

Rochester, whose diocese included Hitchin at that time. Additional land was consecrated by the Bishop of St Albans on 11 July 1900. The Mortuary Chapel, still occasionally used, had two sections, one Anglican, and the other Non-conformist. My own family grave is situated not far from the double gates in St John's Road. Here my paternal grandfather was buried in 1925, and the ashes of my grandma and my mother and father are laid. My grandfather worked for the Moss family at Elmside and Westbourne as their gardener. He and grandma, my dad, and his sister Lillian, came to Hitchin in 1915, and so, we are, compared to the real old Hitchin families, just interlopers.

Mortuary chapels in the recently opened Hitchin Cemetery looking towards St John's Road and the fields beyond. (NHM 365–05)

Insert: Henry Hubbard's memorial card 1925. (Christopher Hubbard)

Clubland

Next to the cemetery wall was Hitchin Clubland, founded as Hitchin Girls' Club in Queen Street in 1915 by Miss Aillie Latchmore and Miss Jessie Buck. Following the demolition of the original club as part of the Queen Street clearances in 1926, a wooden hall was erected in St John's Road and opened by Lady Cecil. The club provided members, mostly from the Sunnyside area, with the opportunity to learn many skills and to enjoy the friendship and companionship of others. Miss Latchmore possessed a strong sense of social justice, in accordance with a Quaker upbringing, and this is highlighted in her book, *A Venture of Faith*, foreworded by Baroness Shirley Williams, a frequent visitor, as was her mother Vera Brittain, to Miss Latchmore's house at 18 St John's Road. Clubland closed in 1973.[2]

Hitchin Clubland, St John's Road. (E Aillie Latchmore, *A Venture of Faith. The Story of Hitchin Clubland* frontispiece)

Day's Store. Golden
Jubilee Tea Party
1954. (*From Day to
Day an autobiography
by Edie Day*)

Day's Shop

Next door to Clubland, and also opened in
1926, was Day's Stores. built by Joseph Day
from materials he acquired following the
demolition of the Mission Hall, in the Queen
Street clearances. The shop, as described in
Edie Day's book, *From Day to Day*, was a
butcher's, grocer's, and general store, and was
numbered 9/10 St John's Road. It was open
seven days a week, from 8 a.m. until 8 p.m.,
until, sadly in 1958, Miss Day was forced,
because of ill health, to give up the business.[3]
The end of an era! Subsequently the shop was
taken over by the Letchworth, Hitchin and District Co-operative
Society Ltd, then by Brian Worbey and his cousin Len Springett. It
is now a private house.

11–18 St John's Road

These were built in the mid 1930s by Mr Fred Pettengell of
Brampton Park Road, on land he purchased from Charles Worbey.
Brian Worbey, who used to live at number 15 and was Charles'
grandson, told me that the first pair of houses, numbers 11 & 12,
were built at a cost of £300 each, and the price of the subsequent
pair of houses increased by £50 each so the last two, 17 & 18, were
£450 each, a 50% increase. Interestingly these had a porch with
a stained glass window above, something the others didn't have.
Number 17 was at one time owned by the parish church and housed
the curate responsible for St John's Church.

The fire station, Newton's Way

Named after Isaac Newton of the building firm, who became
involved in the town's fire brigade from the late 1830s, Newton's
Way was built in the early 1960s following the compulsory
purchase by Hertfordshire County Council of land owned by
Charles Worbey. This new fire station replaced the former one in
Paynes Park and included houses for both police and firemen.

Orchard House

Charles Worbey's house, known as Orchard House, was purposely
built at the top end of Kershaws Hill, as it was planned that Standhill
Road would be continued to meet up with Hollow Lane at the top,
which, of course, never happened. The materials used to build
Orchard House were recycled from the demolition of properties in
the Queen Street area. Brian Worbey recalls that there was an unmade
wide path from St John's Road leading up to Orchard House, with

a good amount of the land used for orchard, the remnants of which are still there today, in the form of five pear trees and one rather sad looking plum tree. Brian Worbey tells me that his father Bob lived at 38 Whitehill Road, known as Joyner's House, and he and his brothers between them owned the land on which the Passingham Avenue estate was built by Wimpey's in the 1960s. The last house at the junction of St John's Road and Whitehill Road is number 19, a bungalow built in the 1960s in what was, I think, part of the garden of Mr Lucas' house, 31 Whitehill Road, which has a rather curious finial in the shape of a terracotta dragon on the gable end.

I am indebted to the following friends for their time and good advice: – Brian Worbey, John Read, John Joshua.

Kendale Road, Sunnyside

I'd like to finish this chapter with some personal recollections from John Joshua. Although he lived in Kendale Road, this is just yards from St John's Road and I think that his recollections are of interest. John lived with his mother Cath, and later her sister Ethel. The family name was Day, and John's grandparents ran a pub in the old Queen Street area, by the name of The Bushel and Strike. The pub's small back garden ran down to what was in those days called the Stream, which is now the much widened River Hiz. I remember John's mum, and aunt, both of whose vocabulary would have been widely heard once upon a time throughout Hertfordshire Bedfordshire and Cambridgeshire, and which frequently included the words "goo" and "duck". In fact John recalls that his mother would write down words exactly as she would have said them. It does remind me of an alleged remark by a local, who was trying desperately to get something rather unsuccessfully to work properly *"I can't git it a goo, duck"*, he said in exasperation.

Terracotta dragon finial on the gable end of 31 Whitehill Road. (Simon Walker 2018)

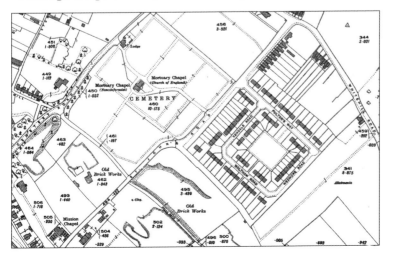

The newly built Kendale Road, Wedmore Road, Waltham Road and Pulters Way from the 1923 OS map. (HHS Scilla Douglas Collection)

Mrs Degan and John
Joshua. (John Joshua)

John Joshua's recollections

I suppose I was around three years old as I was born in March '39, near the beginning of the war. My mother had two evacuees. Glad of the money she was paid. Also Aunty Degan lived with us. She was French, her husband was a chef at, I think, the Dorchester Hotel. They had a flat in Brixton.

There were many evacuees living on the estate. There were also air raid sirens going at certain times to warn us of an impending attack. My childhood was filled with people everywhere. There were Canadians, relatives of my granny's from London. These were "company" – my mum used to say *"we've got company staying"*.

Moving on to 1945 VE Day and VJ Day, the public holidays to celebrate victory in Europe and victory in Japan

A huge party on St Mary's Square, with a searchlight on the Windmill Hill. I should say parties, there were more than one. By this time I was six, and would have been at Queen Street Junior and Infant School. The headmistress was Miss Whitehead, and she had a head of grey/black hair. Whenever she walked through the playground, we would all suddenly stop, until she had gone into the school building. This also happened with Miss York. A very strict matriarch, who usually had a trail of "teacher's pets" trailing behind her, as they came from the canteen, which was in The Hall, the building on Storehouse Lane.

There were two cinemas, The Hermitage and The Regal in lower Bancroft, where Regal Chambers are now. These were patronised by many from the Sunnyside area as we were called. I always disputed living in Sunnyside. Quite right, because I lived in Kendale Road. My granny, and Aunt Ethel, lived in Sunnyside.

At 11, I took the 11 plus exam. There were two parts to this. First the written part, and if one passed this, then there was "the interview". I didn't pass the written test, which was basically English and maths, plus an intelligence test. Very few people on the estate passed the first exam. Of those that did, very few passed "the interview". The reasons, in hindsight, were that *"they would only leave at 14"* (the school leaving age) and with the girls *"Well …. they were only girls, and why waste an education on them, when they would only get married at 19 to 21"*!!

1   St Mary, Hitchin, parish magazines
2   E Aillie Latchmore, *A Venture of Faith. The Story of Hitchin Clubland* (Privately published c.1970); E Aillie Latchmore, *People, Places and Past Times of Hitchin* (Privately published 1974)
3   Edie Day, *From Day to Day an autobiography by Edie Day* (Privately published n.d.)

Hitchin's Victorian Photographers 5

ALAN FLECK

In 1839, the world suddenly changed. It's hard now to imagine a world in which we did not know what the monarch looked like for certain. In which we could only remember what our grandparents looked like: a world where you might hear a Beethoven symphony just once in a lifetime. Where news of the outcome of a distant war might take weeks to arrive.

1839 was a tipping point where suddenly, we could see the past, exactly as it was. From then on we could hold in our hand a photograph of a loved one, a landscape, an event. Two people invented different photographic processes with different outcomes. And after these came other inventions which enabled us to hear, again and again, a piece of music, and soon to see, again and again, a celebration in which people moved and rushed across a screen in front of us. Suddenly a message could stutter across the surface of the planet down a wire, and we'd know about a distant event on the same day, rather than waiting for a ship to return, bearing news.

T.B.Latchmore, studio self-portrait, 1866. (NHM LTS Vol 1A p94)

The photographers of the Victorian era led the way. Hitchin's photographers were not leaders or innovators, they were people who learnt the processes, and then marketed their output. Hitchin's photographers were a microcosm of a changing world. The unusual thing about one of our photographers is that we can track the development of photographic processes along his career.

The first practical process was the daguerreotype: it involved sensitising a highly-polished silver-plated copper sheet with light-sensitive silver iodide salts, exposing the plate in the camera for several minutes, and then developing the image with mercury vapour and fixing it with common salt. The image was laterally reversed, as if in a mirror: this could be remedied by photographing the subject with a mirror. A major problem with the process was one exposure = one image. The image was highly detailed, but very fragile, as it consisted of very tiny globules of condensed mercury vapour amalgamated with the silver surface. To protect it, the image was always placed behind a glass cover, inside a shallow book-like box. Since the image sits on a silver plate, the silver is prone to tarnishing, and the distinctive tone of tarnish can sometimes help to distinguish between a daguerreotype and some other processes. The daguerreotype image could be hand coloured, by finely dusting

Hand-coloured
daguerreotype of
unidentified members
of the ?Lucas family.
(NHM)

with watercolour pigments and gum arabic: a gentle breath would fix both in place.

Early photographic exposures were not instantaneous. There were several solutions to this difficulty. Photographic studios resembled, or in some cases were, modified greenhouses, to let in as much light as possible. Given the vagaries of the English climate, this was not always the perfect remedy, and the exposure would still be a matter of minutes, so the subject or victim would stand or be seated up against a weighty metal stand, from which extended a shaped prong to keep the neck and head steady.

William Lucas records having his likeness taken in 1851:

> *"[we] had our likenesses taken by an American Daguerreotypist. We had to wait a long time and felt a good deal spent. The operation was not a pleasant one."*[1]

The town's new Corn Exchange opened for business on 22 March 1853: the Shambles in front of it are noted by William Lucas in 1854: *"A subscription is set on foot towards pulling down the houses in the Market Place which now stand in front of the new Corn Exchange. £1,600 or more is required, a large sum certainly for a mere local improvement."*[2]

We'll return to this image later.

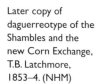

Later copy of
daguerreotype of the
Shambles and the
new Corn Exchange,
T.B. Latchmore,
1853–4. (NHM)

William Henry Fox Talbot invented in 1841 an alternative process which did produce what we all know as a negative, where blacks are white, and whites are black. The image is formed on

and in a sheet of good quality writing paper, hence the very grainy image. Whatman's Turkey Mills paper was recommended. The process does produce a negative, from which many positive prints can be made. Again, it's a long exposure.

The Museum Service holds two local calotypes, one of the Shambles in the Market Place, demolished in 1854. It's a print, and the image has faded to pale primrose on white. The image can be enhanced and reveals the overall shape and texture of the building not visible from Lucas paintings or maps.

The other image is a calotype negative in good condition with a rich dark-brown hue. It shows The Croft, in Bancroft as it was before James Hack Tuke occupied it in 1859 and converted a group of late mediaeval buildings into one large Gothic revival house.

Lastly – for now – there was the wet-plate collodion process. This was apparently simultaneously invented by Gustave le Gray and Frederick Scott Archer in 1851. It combines some of the disadvantages of the daguerreotype process with some huge advantages. The disadvantages are the toxicity and hazard of the chemicals involved. Where the daguerreotype process used vapours of iodine and mercury, the collodion was pyroxiline, also known as gun-cotton, dissolved in ether: an explosive dissolved in an anaesthetic. The silver salts were mixed into this liquid in the dark and then poured over a sheet of glass to form an even coating. The plate was then put into a wooden, light-tight 'dark slide'. Once the plate was in the dark-slide, and the dark-slide was in the camera, the exposure and development had to be completed before the ether evaporated, which meant a window of about 15 minutes.

The advantages of the process were trivial grain, meaning high detail, and a glass negative allowing almost limitless copies off the same exposure, though this brought a weight penalty. Think of this when you next take out your 5 megapixel, no-bigger-than-a-credit-card camera: in 1861 Auguste Bisson (and 25 porters) took 20" x 16" glass plates up Mont Blanc; he successfully exposed and

Above left: Calotype of the Shambles, T.B. Latchmore, 1853–4. (NHM)

Above rght: Calotype of The Croft, Bancroft, T.B. Latchmore, assumed 1853–4 but before 1859. (NHM)

Wetplate print of
High Street, T.B.
Latchmore. Before
1868. (NHM)

developed three and came down again successfully three days later. In 1867 Carlton Watkins exhibited his 20 x 16 images of Yosemite Valley at the Paris Exhibition.

These three processes began our obsession with photography. They were also an obsession for Thomas Benwell Latchmore, the son of a Quaker grocer in Hitchin High Street. Thomas was fascinated by chemistry and experimented with the three processes. The daguerreotype image of the Shambles is a later copy, but it was taken from the roof of his father's grocery shop.

The calotype of the Shambles was taken less than 30 yards away, and the view of the High Street is a contact-print from the 10" x 8" wet-plate glass negative which is held in the Museum collections, and which came from Latchmore's studio. So Latchmore had tried out the major processes before setting up in business.

He wasn't the town's first photographer: that was Samuel Debenham. He set up a studio initially at 23 Tilehouse Street in 1862, and moved to Brand Street the next year when he was bought out by George Avery. Both men – and Latchmore – worked to satisfy a craze for cartes-de-visite portraits, the same size as the conventional visiting card. Cartes-de-visite from Avery and Latchmore feature the same rather unusual floor covering, and the same studio furniture is identifiable too. Debenham took a portrait of William Ransom and his family as a carte-de-visite.

Cartes-de-visite were extraordinarily popular. John Thompson, a Quaker and High Street tailor, compiled a series of large scrapbooks; five pages, each approximately A2 size, are covered with the little portraits, all identified and mostly dated, and other pages have additional cartes.

Latchmore set up his studio in 1864 at the home of William Dawson, a local polymath and autodidact, in Bancroft, and many Latchmore cartes clearly show this. Portraits were popular but the local well-to-do also commissioned views of their homes and gardens: the earliest is an unidentified snowy garden firmly dated "TBL Phot Feb.17 1865".

Carte-de-visite portrait of William Ransom and his family, Samuel Debenham, 1862–3. (NHM)

Prompt processing of negatives remained an issue, but Latchmore had a portable darkroom, a handcart with a large box on the back which would accommodate the upper torso of the standing photographer in darkness. This worked: the photograph we have of it was taken in Essendon, just west of Hertford. Beside the darkroom stands a young man, leaning on a camera, which has two lenses: Latchmore had an assistant, and was taking stereo photographs.

Several of these survive, and many others betray their existence by an edge which includes details of the other edge – they've been crudely cut in half, to gain two images for the price of one.

Latchmore's portraits and commissioned work brought him success. He too was a Quaker, and the Quaker banker, academic and philanthropist Frederic Seebohm built for him a shop, house

Wetplate print of a snow scene, T.B. Latchmore, 17 February 1865. (NHM)

Wetplate print of Essendon, Herts., showing Latchmore's portable darkroom. (NHM)

Above left: Half of wetplate stereo print of Priory Park, Hitchin. T.B. Latchmore, undated. (NHM)

Above right: Latchmore's studio, shop and home in Brand Street. T.B. Latchmore, 1870. (NHM)

and studio at the top of Brand Street, just west of the 1840 Town Hall. Latchmore bought out Avery, whose output ceases in 1870.

In the Herts. Express issue of 5 March 1870, Latchmore advertises *"Having purchased Mr Geo. Avery's Photographic business, together with all the Negatives taken by him at Hitchin and in the neighbourhood, will continue to take Photographs on the same premises in Brand Street."*

Avery tried to continue in business: the Herts. Express for 2 January 1864 contains a plaintive advertisement:

"To houseowners etc. in Hitchin Wanted, a House or part of a House near the Market; must have a yard with a good light from the north, or a roof capable of being converted into a Photographic room. A good supply of water is also necessary. Apply to Mr. G. Avery, late Debenham, Brand-street, Hitchin."

This may explain the appearance of a greenhouse on the roof of a property in Churchyard, about this time, though no photographs taken by Avery after 1869 have been found.

The dry-plate process was invented by Dr Richard L Maddox in 1871, and by 1879 it was so popular that the first dry plate factory had been established: the portable darkroom was no longer needed, and exposure times were now shorter too. Latchmore adopted the new process.

The Lawson Thompson Scrapbooks in the North Hertfordshire Museum Service contain several town views attributed to one Nichols: all are dated 1876. George Albert Nichols worked from Croydon House, Station Road (now Walsworth Road), Hitchin from 1876 to 1878. Thereafter he worked in Stamford until his death in 1897. Were his photographs not attributed to Nichols in the scrapbooks, it would have been assumed they were the work of Latchmore. Apart from the use of a different lens and slightly less concern with converging verticals, there's little to distinguish these from Latchmore's work.

Latchmore married and had a son, Thomas William, and two daughters. His obituary notes that he held no public office in the town, though he served for a time as secretary to the Hitchin Mechanics' Institute, and was also a teacher in the Friends' Adult School for some years after its foundation in 1860. Thomas Benwell died in 1908 and is buried in the Quaker Burial Ground on Paynes Park, a few yards from his home and studio. Thomas William took over the business at some point - the 1911 Census records Thomas William as a Photographer's Manager - but it's not clear when: he may simply have done more and more, whilst his father did less and less. Some postcards exist with a T.W. Latchmore blind-stamp across the bottom-right corner. He was a Conscientious Objector during the First World War, and died in 1946. Almost immediately after his death the premises were cleared, and all bar a handful of negatives were smashed. A few albums also survive in the Museum collections.

Henry George Moulden, on the other hand, ran a thriving business based on the Biggin Studio in Biggin Lane. The son of a

George Nichols, dryplate print of High Street, Hitchin, 1876. (NHM)

23378 Hitchin. High Street.

Postcard of H.G. Moulden's High Street shop, dated c.1906. F.C. Sharp carried on the business here until 1926. (Gerry Tidy)

shoemaker and sometime publican of The George in Bucklersbury, H.G. Moulden was born in 1861 and worked with Latchmore as an informal apprentice. In 1884 he set up the Biggin Studio, adding a shop at 8 Sun Street from 1895 until 1899, finally working from 27a High Street from 1906 until his death in 1916.

He was an active portraitist, but also contributed significantly to the growing market for postcards of local views.

Moulden, like his father, was very musical and involved with many local music groups: he was organist and choirmaster of St Mary's Church from 1892 until his death, enabling him on at least one occasion to play the organ for a wedding, and take the photographs afterwards. Before he died he sold his business to Frank C. Sharp, a member of St Mary's Church choir. Sharp carried on the business until 1926 as "F.C. Sharp, late Moulden."

Victorian Hitchin did not support many photographers, but those who did work in the town give us examples of the major photographic processes: it is sad that so much of Latchmore's output was destroyed after his son's death.

1   G E Bryant & G P Baker ed. *A Quaker Journal Being the Diary and Reminiscences of William Lucas of Hitchin (1804-1861) A Member of the Society of Friends Vol II* (Hutchinson, 1933) p.452
2   Bryant & Baker ed, *A Quaker Journal Vol II*, p.481

Oughtonhead, Oakfield and the Lucas Family

JOHN LUCAS

T he Lucas family is perhaps best known in Hitchin for its ownership of the brewery whose premises were on the corner of Sun Street and Bridge Street. However, although the brewery provided the family's main source of income, by the mid-19th century many of its members were known to have been unhappy with their involvement in the trade, largely because of the conflict with their Quaker faith.

In 1841 William Lucas VI* recorded in his journal:

"I often feel such misgivings as to the propriety of holding Public House property that I wish we were fairly out of the business; but

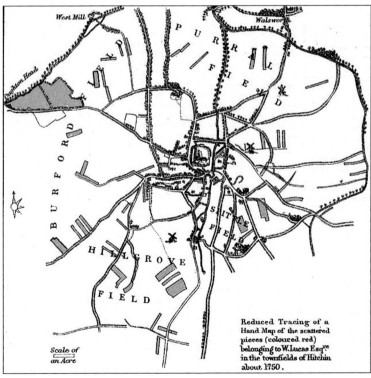

Lucas Lands – Land occupied around Hitchin by William Lucas III in about 1750. (From *The English Village Community* by Frederic Seebohm)

Reduced Tracing of a Hand Map of the scattered pieces (coloured red) belonging to W.Lucas Esq.re in the townfields of Hitchin about 1750.

Scale of an Acre

* There were eight successive eldest sons called William in the Lucas family, the first being born in 1675 and the last dying (childless) in a road accident at Cheltenham in 1940. To distinguish them, they were later assigned 'regnal' numbers I to VIII.

then again it seems necessary to provide for the settlement of my six sons.''[1]

The salve was farming. In 1736, William Lucas II who was variously a miller, draper, woolstapler and brewer, had obtained from the Draper and Conquest families 42 acres of land at Oughtonhead, in addition to the brewery premises in Sun Street. *The Terrier and Rental of the Manor of Hitchin 1727*[2] lists several other pieces also obtained from the Drapers and Conquests, some freehold and some copyhold. Other pieces were acquired and in *The English Village Community* discussed in Chapter 1 "The Fields Beneath", Frederic Seebohm shows the land occupied by William Lucas in about 1750.[3]

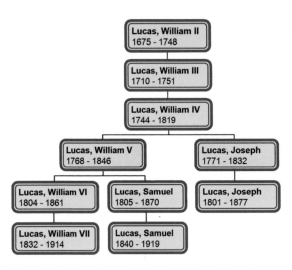

Above: A family tree showing the Lucas family members who are known to have been active in farming in the Hitchin area in the 18th and through into the 19th centuries. Most were primarily involved in the brewery management but some decamped to concentrate on farming in later life. Samuel Lucas, the artist, listed his occupation jointly as brewer and farmer in the mid 19th century censuses. His son, also Samuel, took a different path. He was recorded as a farmer in his earlier years but later concentrated fully on brewing.

Right: The 1818 map of Hitchin annotated to show the land in which the Lucas family had an interest. Their efforts were already being concentrated on the land held to the west of Hitchin. Several of their scattered pieces held to the east were being leased to others. (Does not show Lucas properties held in Hitchin Town)

1818 Hitchin tithe map showing land which the Lucas family had an intere

Leased from others

Leased to others

Owned and occupied

By 1844, the Lucas holdings had been concentrated in the west of Hitchin although there were still considerable gaps. Most of the scattered pieces elsewhere had been released.

More land was acquired over the years and by the time that the 1818 rate assessment map was published, the land owned or occupied by William Lucas IV and his sons William V and Joseph, some individually and some in partnership, was as annotated on the map on pages 52–53. The "patchwork quilt" arrangement of the land had been dictated by the medieval open field system which had been sustained for many hundreds of years. But by the time of the 1844 tithe survey there had been considerable consolidation of Lucas holdings into larger blocks in the Gaping Hills areas, as shown on the map above.

The family had another significant holding further out to the south-west of Hitchin. In her *Recollections of my Childhood*[4], Phebe

Lucas mentions visits to the Offley Grange estate (in the 1820s) in which her father had an interest. It would appear that The Grange was held in partnership by the Lucas's but that they withdrew from Offley in 1834 in order to concentrate on their land nearer to Hitchin.

The Lucas Windmill

William Lucas V recorded his land holdings in a small notebook[5]. In one of the entries he records: *"A piece of land bo[t]. of James Creasy on which a windmill lately stood but now removed."*

This simple sentence underlies an interesting event. In a journal entry for 12 February 1820, George Beaver, the Hitchin Borough Surveyor, reported the move of a windmill owned by Joseph and William Lucas V. He wrote:

> *"Bodily removal of J. & W. Lucas's windmill standing in open field land between Manley Highway and Offley Road, at about 100 yards from S.W. corner of Mount Pleasant plantation to a new site on Gaping Hills (approx. 450 yds)."*[6]

The event was also described by Reginald Hine:

> *"The ground from point to point was cleared and levelled of all fences, banks and ditches; and then the mill, being raised by screwjacks and a frame on four wheels being built under it, was pulled in full working order (stones, machinery, sails and all) by thirty-six horses, harnessed in six rows of six abreast. The schools were allowed a holiday to see this wonderful feat."*[7]

The reason for the move is not entirely clear but it may have been that having acquired the mill in a land deal, it was decided to move it to a more convenient location on Gaping Hills, where the family was concentrating its holdings. Cyril Moore described the mill as *"a relatively primitive post windmill and no doubt built well before*

William Lucas and his son Herbert. Orton Head Farm.

William Lucas VI and his son Herbert at Oughtonhead Farm, with the windmill on Gaping Hills visible in the distance. A drawing by Samuel Lucas from the late 1840s. (*A Quaker Journal* Vol II p.350)

The Lucas windmill on Gaping Hills, from a watercolour by Samuel Lucas (date unknown). (Photographed and digitally enhanced by Simon Walker and reproduced here by permission of Tim Dye and Charlotte Ransom)

1820".[8] Moore surmises that the mill must have been dismantled by 1850 as it is not shown on the local Health Board map of that date.

There were, no doubt, good reasons for moving the structure intact although one cannot but feel that the operation was fraught with danger – successfully concluded however, much to the relief of all concerned!

The Ladies' Copse

In 1842 a piece of land at Oughtonhead was acquired in an exchange with the Court Leet of the Manor of Hitchin who regulated the common. William Lucas VI wrote in his journal:

> *"11th Month 7th, 1842: "Met the Leet Jury at Orton Head Common and they marked out a piece of ground to be given up to us in lieu of the cartway from the lane to our seven-acre piece. This piece I intend to plant.*

> *"12th Month 5th, 1842: "Finished planting my new clump at Orton Head. The ladies have all taken their share. J. Lister planted all the Poplars, Christiana Lucas all the Chestnuts, Sarah Lucas the Mountain Ash and Phebe Lucas the Abel Poplars.*

> *"12th Month 24th, 1842: ... and I have been planting Elms about Orton Head and Hungry Hill, also the small piece of land taken from the common, which should be called Ladies' Copse"*[9]

Two Ladies in the Ladies' Copse at Oughtonhead. Scilla Douglas and Bridget Howlett on 29 November 2013. (John Lucas)

The copse survives and is again part of Oughtonhead Common but beech now predominates.

Natural History

The Lucas enjoyment of the land manifested itself in another way – a love of natural history. William Lucas V was particularly noted for his observations and had a special interest in geology and ornithology. When his relative Joseph Lister* was due to visit Hitchin, he would be reminded to bring *Thy Thor's Hammer* so that the two might explore the geology of Hitchin's pits and quarries. William was often a companion of Joseph Ransom whose notebooks covered the period 1804–1816 and were transcribed and edited by Val Campion and published by Hitchin Historical Society in 2004.

Lucas reported many sightings of birds that were rare, even for those days. Unfortunately the term, *preserving wildlife,* had a wholly different meaning at the time. It is ironic that many of the species noted as being rare were shot in order to mount them as trophies in order to preserve them for posterity! Even the 'enlightened' Lucas was not above shooting them, but later he did forego the sport on the urging of his wife. His nephew, Charles Lucas, was an avid collector of specimens for his taxidermy hobby and became known as "*The Bird Stuffer*".

Undoubtedly the "Jewel in the Crown" was the river at Oughtonhead. William V, who was always reclusive, is known to have spent long periods there; quietly watching and communing with nature even after his health began to fail. William VI recalled

* *The Quaker Lucas and Lister families were related by marriage. Joseph Jackson Lister (1786–1869) was a wine merchant based in the City of London but became a noted natural historian who is credited with perfecting the optical microscope. Despite his amateur status, he was made a fellow of the Royal Society. His son was Joseph (later Baron) Lister, famed for his work in antisepsis.*

the old man *"...it was painful to see him return from his daily visits to the Orton Head very much exhausted."*

William V's son Samuel was also an *habitué*, sitting for hours observing and sketching for his works such as *Our Small Birds* which was exhibited at The Royal Academy.

Oughtonhead (Orton Head) Farm

Acquisition of land by the Lucas's continued apace for in his journal entry for *12 month 2nd, 1843,* William Lucas VI recorded *"We have now received the penalty of gratifying our desire for purchasing land etc., in the lawyer's bills which amongst us all amount to between five and six hundred pounds. The expense of conveying both Freehold and Copyhold property is scandalous."*[10] A conservative estimate of the *"five to six hundred pounds"* in today's values is in the order of £50,000!

The large conveyancing costs probably arose as a result of the acquisition of land in the Oughtonhead and Gaping Hills areas, filling in to allow the development of Oughtonhead Farm in the mid-1840s. Until that time, the Lucas farming activity had been based at Wratten Road and Grays Lane, where their barns were situated. The creation of Oughtonhead Farm allowed their activities to be centralised there. William's cousin Joseph was evidently tasked with managing the family's farm, for in the same journal entry as above, William recorded an apparent rebuke: *"Our partner, Joseph, who manages our farming matters, has taken all at once to keep a large number of sheep. For some years we had none. I fear he has gone from one extreme to the other. Farming paid nothing last year."*

This was in a climate of uncertainty over the future of the Corn Laws* which were repealed in 1846. Why the family chose to risk investing so much in farming at this time must remain a matter of speculation but, thankfully, there was always the income from the brewery upon which to rely!

The farmhouse at Oughtonhead, which was built in about 1846, was never intended to be a family residence. It was to be used to provide accommodation for the farm bailiff. At that time the three family members active in farming; William Lucas VI, Samuel Lucas and Joseph, were living at their respective houses: Wratten Cottage in Wratten Road, The Tilehouse in Tilehouse Street and the Brewery House in Sun Street.

---

* *The Corn Laws were initially enacted in 1815 as a protectionist measure for British farmers, imposing a tariff on imported cereals. They were repealed in 1846 in the face of food shortages exacerbated by the Great Irish (potato) Famine. William Lucas VI was an advocate of a free market and made many references to this in his journal – A Quaker Journal.*

A tender survives for The New Farm – for the construction of Barns and Chaff House, Cattle Sheds and all other buildings at a cost of £735 10s 11d with an additional £144 for 12 Rods of Brickwork. The tender is dated April 1846 and was submitted to William Lucas Jnr. (William VI) by H & W Butterfield of Hitchin[11].

In 1851 the Oughtonhead Farm Bailiff was John James, a native of Irthlingborough in Northamptonshire. He was at the farm with his wife and family until at least 1871.

William Lucas VI died in 1861 and in the 1871 census his son, William VII, was recorded as a brewer and farmer of 370 acres employing 11 men and 12 boys. He made no mention of farming in subsequent censuses.

In the 1881 census, Leonard Moules was the Bailiff, with responsibility for 388 acres and employing 13 men and 8 boys. He was the son of Benjamin Moules, a Baker and Corn Merchant of the High Street, Stevenage.

The Lucas's appear to have withdrawn from active involvement in farming at about this time as by 1891 Leonard, a well respected member of the local community, had taken on the full tenancy at Oughtonhead and farmed it in his own right. He lived at Oughtonhead until at least 1913 as he's shown as being the occupant in the "Domesday" Survey of that date. [12]

The owner of the farm was then William Lucas VII of "The Firs" (now The Firs Hotel) in Bedford Road Hitchin. It is thought that the final Lucas disposal of Oughtonhead Farm took place in about 1914 when William Lucas VII died, by then a widower. In his will, a very simple document, he divided the whole of his estate equally between his son and daughter, both of whom lived away from Hitchin. To achieve this it would have been necessary for his assets, including the farm, to be sold and thus would have ended Lucas ownership of the land after nearly two centuries.

The farmhouse survives, as do the barns, in which much of the original fitted equipment is still to be found.

Joseph Lucas and Oakfield House

The Lucas family had owned the brewery on the corner of Sun Street and Bridge Street since 1736. The Brewery House in Sun Street was rebuilt in the early 1780s and became the family home for several generations. The final members of the family to live there were Joseph, grandson of William IV, and his wife Deborah. All of their eight children were born at the Brewery House and spent their formative years there, continually exposed to the odour of hops and fermenting yeast!

By the 1850s there had been a parting of the ways between William Lucas VI and his cousin Joseph, each to concentrate

Joseph Lucas and his house at Oakfield in the 1870s. The house now forms part of Kingshott School.
(Both – NHM LTS Vol 1B p.124)

on their individual farming interests, William on the farm at Oughtonhead and Joseph on his estate at Oakfield.

Joseph had a house built at Oakfield. George Beaver reported in his journal that in 1857 he had conducted a survey of land owned by Joseph Lucas beside the Stevenage Road in Ippollitts, in order to assess its suitability for building a family residence [13]. Then in 1858 he noted that he took levels for the new house. Lucas ownership of land in the area can be traced back to at least 1805 when Joseph's father acquired from the Manor of Hitchin the copyhold on a small coppice beside Ippollitts Glebe (Lot 4 on the plan on page 62). The first part of Lot 1 was acquired by Joseph himself in 1824 and the final acquisition, from the Beaver family, was not until December 1876.

The house was completed in 1859 and the family then moved there from Sun Street. At about that time, Joseph relinquished his

Oakfield House with Scilla Douglas and Pauline Humphries studying a finer point of the architecture. Incised brickwork, dated 1859, containing the initials of the family of Joseph and Deborah is to be found high up on the ground floor of the south-east elevation.
(Photographed by John Lucas, 24 September 2014, by kind permission of the Headmaster, Kingshott School)

role in the brewery management and passed the mantle fully to cousins William VI and Samuel Lucas. After the family's departure the Brewery House was occupied variously by brewery employees and then others not connected with the brewery, until being sold in 1923. The building is now (2017) occupied by Mevan Restaurant and The Secret Garden.

At the time of the 1871 Census, Joseph, described as a landowner aged 69, was living at Oakfield with his wife, their three unmarried daughters and four servants. Deborah died there later that year and Joseph died on 14 June 1877. In his will he directed his trustees to sell all of his property. After payment of his funeral expenses, debts and legacies, the trustees were to divide the residue of the money equally among all of the children.

All seemed to be going well, with the executors methodically working through the actions. The estate sale was scheduled for 6 September 1877, the house contents on the 11 October and the farm live and dead stock on 18 October. On 21 August the executors were advised that Joseph's eldest sons, Joseph John and

Sale notice for Oakfield Estate 6 September 1877. (HHS Scilla Douglas Collection)

Frederick, had initiated proceedings to have the estate placed in Chancery, but they subsequently agreed that the sale could proceed, providing that the *"whole of the Oakfield Estate shall not be sold for less than £19,000"*, but the minimum amount was not to be achieved.

The estate was initially offered as one lot, the reserve being £17,100, but was withdrawn when bidding reached just £15,000. The property was then divided into 14 lots, in accordance with the plan on page 62. Perhaps the market was depressed as woodland and arable land on either side of the Hitchin to Stevenage road failed to sell. The lots that did sell, including the house, raised a total of £15,597 with an additional £994 from sale of properties in Tilehouse Street and Arlesey. The house and 77 acres were bought by George Jeeves, a Hitchin builder.

The value of the unsold lots was £2,690 at the reserve price. Lots 7 and 8 were sold to Alfred Ransom for £950 and Lots 3 and 4 to Matthew Foster, another Hitchin builder, for £750, both by private treaty. As a result of the under-selling Joseph

---

HITCHIN, HERTFORDSHIRE,

A Junction on the Great Northern, Midland, and Hitchin, Royston, and Cambridge Railways, within about 40 minutes ride of London.

Particulars and Conditions of Sale of the very

Choice Estate, known as "Oakfield,"

Situate in the Parishes of Hitchin and Ippollitts, comprising a substantial White Brick-Built and Slated

COMMODIOUS FAMILY RESIDENCE,

WITH GREENHOUSE OR VINERY.

Delightfully situate on an Eminence, in the midst of Park-like Grounds, approached by a Carriage Drive from the Road leading from Hitchin to Stevenage, from which it is screened by a Plantation, about 1 mile from the Town of Hitchin, and 1½ miles from the Railway Station, commanding extensive and varied views, with

Lawn and Pleasure Grounds, Vegetable and Fruit Garden, and Paddock Orchard,

At a convenient distance from the above is a very

COMPACT & SUBSTANTIALLY-BUILT FARMERY,

Comprising a Red Brick-Built & Slated BAILIFF'S HOUSE, Court Yard, with Brick and Slated Dairy and Granary, 2 enclosed Farm Yards, with numerous

WELL-ARRANGED & BRICK-BUILT AGRICULTURAL BUILDINGS,

(The whole of the above has been erected within a few years, by the late Joseph Lucas, Esq.) ; together with about

155 ACRES OF GRASS, ARABLE, AND GARDEN LAND,

In the highest state of cultivation, a portion of which is

VALUABLE AS BUILDING GROUND,

Without interfering with the comfort and privacy of the Family Residence ;

At the extremity of the Property are 2 Brick-Built and Slated COTTAGES with Frontage to the Hitchin and Great Wymondley Road; also

DWELLING HOUSE, GROCER'S & DRAPER'S SHOP,

And GARDEN GROUND, in the occupation of Mr. John Fletcher, and

TWO COTTAGES adjoining, situate at Arlsey, Beds.;

TO BE SOLD BY AUCTION, BY MR.

GEORGE JACKSON,

AT THE SUN HOTEL, HITCHIN, IN CONVENIENT LOTS,

On Thursday, September 6th, 1877, at Two for Three o'clock,

BY DIRECTION OF THE EXECUTORS OF THE LATE JOSEPH LUCAS, ESQ.

May be Viewed by Cards only, to be had of the Auctioneer, and Particulars with Lithograph Plans and Conditions obtained of Messrs. Hawkins & Lindsell, Solicitors, Hitchin, Herts. ; at the Auction Mart, London ; the Inns in the Neighbourhood ; Place of Sale ; and of Mr. George Jackson, Auctioneer and Appraiser, Hitchin, Baldock, and Royston, Herts.

PATERNOSTER AND HALES, MACHINE PRINTERS, HITCHIN.

Plan of

THE

OAKFIELD ESTATE,

In the Parishes of

HITCHIN AND IPPOLLITTS,

To be Sold by Auction by

Mr GEORGE JACKSON,

At the Sun Hotel, Hitchin, Herts.

On Thursday, September 6th, 1877.

Scale of Chains.

John initiated a further action in the Court of Chancery so as to prevent the sale of the remaining lots. However, in February 1878, an order was issued by the Court that the rest of the land should be sold.

The Executors minutes record: *"November 1st 1877 – Keys to house and premises given over to Mr. G. Jeeves on that day.*

"November 3rd – Bartlett (an Executor of the estate) to Oakfield. Paid bailiff, gardener and woman in house. All dismissed from today. Executors last visit to Oakfield."[14]

Thus, the Lucas occupation of the house was ended after some 17 years.

Jeeves immediately sold the estate to Thomas Dashwood, a barrister and respected Chairman of Hitchin Magistrates. Dashwood enlarged the house and lived there with his family until at least 1901. He subsequently retired to the Isle of Wight, which is where he died in January 1909.[15]

Opposite page: The plan which accompanied the sales particulars when Oakfield was auctioned after Joseph's death in 1877. The land to the north of Ippollitts Brook was developed in the 1950s as the Oakfield Estate. See Chapter 7. (HHS Scilla Douglas Collection)

HERTFORDSHIRE,

about a mile from the TOWN OF HITCHIN, one-and-a-half miles from Hitchin Railway Station, and within 40 minutes' ride of LONDON.

PARTICULARS, PLAN, VIEWS & CONDITIONS OF SALE

OF AN EXCEEDINGLY DELIGHTFUL

Freehold Residential Property,

KNOWN AS THE

"OAKFIELD ESTATE,"

SITUATED IN THE

Parishes of Hitchin and Ippollitts,

COMPRISING

AN EXCELLENT FAMILY RESIDENCE,

Standing in Beautiful Pleasure Grounds,

with Carriage Approach, STABLING FOR THREE HORSES, KITCHEN AND FRUIT GARDENS, GARDENER'S COTTAGE, &c. Also capital

FARM-HOUSE with FARM BUILDINGS,

RICH PASTURE & Productive ARABLE LAND,

including HARKNESS'S ROSE GARDENS, several Enclosures forming

Accommodation Holdings with Building Frontages,

to Good Roads. The whole containing an Area of nearly

100 Acres.

POSSESSION WILL BE GIVEN OF THE HOUSE AND GROUNDS, which are in Hand, and the remainder is Let to excellent Tenants at Rents amounting to £176 6s. per Annum.

Which will be Sold by Auction,

BY MESSRS.

FAREBROTHER, ELLIS, EGERTON, BREACH & CO.

At the Mart, Tokenhouse Yard, London, E.C.

On THURSDAY, the 24th day of JUNE, 1909,

AT TWO O'CLOCK PRECISELY—IN ONE OR MORE LOTS.

May be Viewed by Orders only, and Particulars obtained of Messrs. PARK NELSON & Co., Solicitors, 11, Essex Street, Strand, W.C.; at the Auction Mart, E.C.; of the principal Hotels in the neighbourhood; and of the Auctioneers, MESSRS. FAREBROTHER, ELLIS & CO., 29, Fleet Street, London, E.C.

NOTE.—For Order of Sale see "The Times" or "The Standard" of the day preceding the Auction.

Dryden Press: J. Davy & Sons, 8-9, Frith-street, Soho-square, W.

Sale notice for Oakfield Estate 24 June 1909. (HALS DE/Ry/B275)

Between 1895 and 1918 the Harkness family cultivated roses on the farmland at Oakfield, as shown in this postcard which was postmarked in 1904. (Kindly supplied by Terry Knight)

The estate was inherited by Dashwood's son who immediately put it up for auction in June 1909. The estate was bought by John Joseph Chapman of Whitby, whose executors owned it in 1913. Between 1895 and 1918, the land at Oakfield and the farmhouse were leased to the Harkness family of rose cultivation fame. In the 1911 census the main house is recorded as being "untenanted", but in 1913[16] the occupant was Mrs Georgina Pollard. She was the wife of William Pollard, a government scientist. His father, Joseph Pollard of High Down near Pirton, was one of Joseph Lucas' executors back in 1877. Later directories show the Pollards in residence at Oakfield until at least 1926.

Nothing is known of any occupants between 1926 and 1931, which is when Kingshott School was founded by Mr G. B. Stafford, initially as a preparatory boarding school for boys. The house now forms the main building of a thriving co-educational day school.

Joseph's land on the north side of Ippollitts Brook was developed in the 1950s as the Oakfield housing estate.

1   *A Quaker Journal being the Diary and Reminiscences of William Lucas Vol. I* (Hutchinson, 1933) p. 238
2   HALS 64356 Terrier of the Manor of Hitchin 1727
3   Frederic Seebohm, *The English Village Community* (Longmans, 1890) Frontispiece
4   John Lucas, *Phebe's Hitchin Book* (HHS, 2009) pp. 35–36
5   NHM: Lucas papers
6   NHM M265: Journal of the Life of George Beaver of Hitchin Land Surveyor 1809–1895
7   Reginald L Hine, *The History of Hitchin Vol. II* (Allen & Unwin, 1929) pp. 423–424
8   Cyril Moore, *Hertfordshire Windmills and Windmillers* (Windsup, 1999) pp. 91–92
9   *A Quaker Journal Vol I* pp. 287–289
10 *A Quaker Journal Vol II* p. 322.
11 NHM: Lucas papers
12 HALS IR3/44/1 Valuation Office Survey 1910–1915
13 NHM M265: Journal of the Life of George Beaver of Hitchin Land Surveyor 1809–1895
14 Bartlett's notebook in author's possession; HALS DE/Ha/B1202 Executors' minute book 1877
15 NHM: Lawson Thompson Scrapbooks Vol. 3A p. 80 Thomas Dashwood obituary
16 HALS IR3/44/1 Valuation Office Survey 1910–1915

The Oakfield Estate

7

NIGEL CLAYDON

The Oakfield Estate is a 75 acre area on the south east side of Hitchin between the railway, Stevenage Road and the Ippollitts Brook. This chapter is about how it was built, how my parents moved here and about growing up here in the late 1960s and 1970s. I was told that if the Great Northern Railway's plan to build its railway works in Hitchin had succeeded, it would have been a much larger town than now and the National Railway Museum might now be where the Oakfield Estate is!

My parents first came to Hitchin in 1956 for a day trip to look at houses and bungalows on the Oakfield Estate. Dad's new job was going to be based in the Hertfordshire, Bedfordshire and Suffolk area. He was leaving the London Ambulance Service to work for the union NUPE and his office would be in Bury St Edmunds. He had been told by a friend about the Oakfield Estate, so on his way back to London he stopped off to get the details. The builder was Sir Lindsay Parkinson & Company and the head office was at the bottom of Whitehill Road, near where Daniel Monk lived in a Romany caravan at the back of a cottage. It is said that he was a pipe layer, did odd jobs and may have worked in the rose nursery on the other side of the Stevenage Road. It is not known what happened to him, but it seems he was moved when Sir Lindsay Parkinson built the sales and site office on this field.

Oakfield Avenue under construction c.1956 looking towards Oakfield House now Kingshott School. (NHM 10090–335)

Right: Sir Lindsay Parkinson
Sales Brochure c.1956.
(Nigel Claydon)

Delightfully situated in the
beautiful Hertfordshire
countryside this Estate is a
model of careful planning,
offering a wide range of modern,

Oakfield Estate

White Hill Road, Hitchin, Herts. Telephone: Hitchin 2005.

ideally planned, houses and
bungalows at a reasonable
price, within easy reach of
London. We will not weary
you with a catalogue of sales
features as we are confident
that the quality of our work-
manship will commend itself to
the discerning purchaser. The
Oakfield Estate provides an
ideal environment for people of
all ages. Visit the Estate.
See for yourself and make a
Parkinson home your choice.

Oakfield Estate is within easy walking
distance of Hitchin Station, and Green
Line and local bus services pass by.
The charming town of Hitchin offers
excellent market and shopping facilities
and most traders operate a delivery service.
A number of shops will later be built on
the Estate. There are several excellent
schools in the area.

We have our own mortgage department to
help you with any problems and we can arrange
for 90 per cent. mortgages to approved clients.

Parkinson homes are constructed to the
highest standards and all materials
used comply with the British Standards
Specification where applicable. Cavity
walls, back boilers and tongued and grooved
flooring ensure warmth. Felt lined
roofs have colourful interlocking concrete
tiles. A bituminous damp-proof
membrane is in all walls and window
and door openings. Door thresholds
are of oak with weather bars. Flush
doors are fitted throughout. Pipes
are lagged for all year round protection.
Power points are provided in all
main rooms. Decorations are to the
choice of the purchaser. A coal
bunker is provided.

Sir Lindsay Parkinson & Co. Ltd.

Parkinson

Above: Show House in
Oakfield Avenue.
(NHM 10090-335)

The Charlton . . . . . type 3H. 13

Similar in design to type 3H10 but with
alternative elevation in fair face brickwork
to suit individual taste, this semi-detached
house offers the following accommodation:
Principal Bedroom, 11' 0" × 12' 0", fitted
power point: Second Bedroom, 11' 0" ×
11' 0", fitted power point: Third Bedroom,
7' 9¾" × 8' 11½", with hanging cupboard:
Bathroom, with modern panelled bath and
a lavatory basin: Separate W.C. with low
level suite: Dining Room, 11' 7¾" × 10' 0",
with fire place and fitted back boiler for
domestic hot water: Living Room,
12' 9" × 12' 0" with fitted fireplace:
Modern labour-saving Kitchen,
8' 9¾" × 8' 7", with sink unit, dresser
unit, larder and broom cupboard: Entrance
Hall and space for garage. Colour scheme
to choice. Really excellent value for money.

First Floor

Ground Floor

built by Sir Lindsay Parkinson & Company Limited

Above: Mr & Mrs Claydon looking at a chalet
bungalow in Broadmead priced at £2,425 in
1958. (Nigel Claydon)

Left: Sales particulars for "The Charlton"
3 bedroom semi-detached house available for
£2,420 in 1957. (Nigel Claydon)

Sir Lindsay Parkinson bought the land for the Oakfield Estate on 29 June 1955. Before this the Worbey's farmed barley, wheat and potatoes. They would drive their tractors from Highbury down Riddy Path to Oakfield. Retired horses from Orchard House Farm were also kept here. It's hard to imagine today but you could stand in the paddock behind Highbury Post Office and look across the fields to the tree line of the brook. We just need to look at the 1950 local Ordnance Survey map or the map on page 62 to see the area before the Oakfield Estate was built.[1] This map shows the Riddy Path joining up with the walk at the back of Ninesprings Way. I am told that there was a hedge to the left of the path with a gate and stile. The path now comes out at Manor Crescent, but it once curved to the right in line with Manton Road and down the hill to the gap by 60 Ninesprings Way, which leads through to the rural walk by the brook. Local people say Riddy means "path to the fields", but the usual explanation is that "Riddy" derives from the old English word "rith" or "rithig" meaning a small stream. The previous chapter describes how after Joseph Lucas' death in 1877, his Oakfield House estate was broken up and sold at auction. For one of the purchasers a right of way 12 feet wide leading to Wymondley Road was established next to the Ippollitts Brook. This became the rural walk by the brook at the back of Ninesprings Way.

Sir Lindsay Parkinson set about building nine styles of houses and bungalows after first pegging the area with white pegs that could be seen from the Wymondley Road. Each design of the 754 homes to be built was given a name:

Oakfield Estate under construction c.1956. The Riddy Path ran downhill between the hedges and trees towards the Ippollitts Brook in the near distance. The railway embankment can be seen in the far distance.
(NHM 10090–325)

The Benslow   3 bed semi house
The Charlton   3 bed semi house
The Minsden   3 bed detached house
The Waltham   3 bed detached house
The Hampden   2 bed bungalow semi
The Highbury   2 bed detached bungalow with study
The Walden   2 bed chalet bungalow with study
The Warren   2 bed detached bungalow
The Wellbury   2 bed semi bungalow with study

From the price list and invoices the Hampden Bungalow in Ninesprings Way with taxes paid in February 1958 was £2,125. This was considered to be the less expensive part of the estate because of the noise and smoke from steam engines on the railway.

The twelve roads were named Broadmead, Lindsay Avenue, Manor Crescent, Oakfield Avenue, Ninesprings Way, Manton

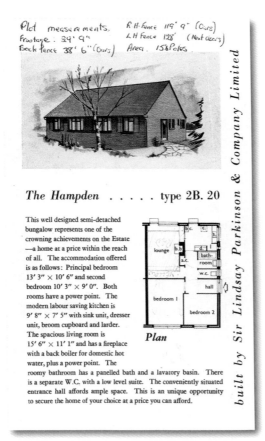

Plot measurements.
Frontage: 29' 9"
Back fence 38' 6" (Ours)
R.H. fence 119' 9" (Ours)
L.H fence 128' (Next door)
Area. 156 Poles

The Hampden . . . . . type 2B. 20

This well designed semi-detached bungalow represents one of the crowning achievements on the Estate —a home at a price within the reach of all. The accommodation offered is as follows: Principal bedroom 13' 3" × 10' 6" and second bedroom 10' 3" × 9' 0". Both rooms have a power point. The modern labour saving kitchen is 9' 8" × 7' 5" with sink unit, dresser unit, broom cupboard and larder. The spacious living room is 15' 6" × 11' 1" and has a fireplace with a back boiler for domestic hot water, plus a power point. The roomy bathroom has a panelled bath and a lavatory basin. There is a separate W.C. with a low level suite. The conveniently situated entrance hall affords ample space. This is an unique opportunity to secure the home of your choice at a price you can afford.

Plan

built by Sir Lindsay Parkinson & Company Limited

Sales particulars for "The Hampden" bungalow. There were five different designs of bungalow available. (Nigel Claydon)

The "Hampden" bungalow 106 Ninesprings Way under construction in 1958. (Nigel Claydon)

106 Ninesprings Way completed in 1958 with its telegraph pole, the first on the estate. Mr Claydon needed the telephone for his job. (Nigel Claydon)

Advertisements for two of the new shops opened in Ninesprings Way in 1960 at the same time as The Fountain Public House (now demolished). (Nigel Claydon)

Road, Aston Rise, Uplands Avenue, Linten Close, Bell Close, Brook View and Poplar Close. 136 to 164 Wymondley Road were also built by Sir Lindsay Parkinson and are therefore part of the Oakfield Estate. There was a pub called The Fountain and shops in Ninesprings Way which opened at the end of May 1960. The shops were a butcher, newsagent, general store, hardware, grocer and hairdresser. Building was finished in June 1960, although many houses and bungalows have been added to and extended since. There is always building on the estate!

I was born in Hitchin, in the fruit and veg aisle of Waitrose; well at that time it was North Herts Maternity Hospital, when you were taken home after two weeks and not two hours like now! My first memories are the trains on the railway line that runs to the north and to London, I just remember a few steam trains, most trains were the new diesels. The pig farm and the shunting yard were still the other side of the railway, so there was no route from Walsworth to Oakfield like now. Before the Poets Estate was built, the only way to drive to the Walsworth area or to get to the station was along the Wymondley Road, down the Avenue, then along Walsworth Road to or past the station and under the bridge. Or with a good pair of boots in the winter, you could walk along two paths over the fields off Wymondley Road, very muddy in wet weather.

Above left:
The garden of
106 Ninesprings Way
in the hard winter
of 1962/3.
(Nigel Claydon)

Above right: "Along
the back". The rural
walk along the
Ippollitts Brook
behind the gardens
of Ninesprings Way
1973. (Nigel Claydon)

This was a time when there were no mobile phones and only two channels on the TV and very few cars in the area. At home there was only a small fridge and no freezer so on special occasions if mum had made jelly, I would run up the shops in Ninesprings Way to buy ice cream. I would play in the fields and the "rec" with friends and only come in for dinner. There were no computer games to play so I spent many hours outside. There is a small park at the end of the walk along by the brook known as "along the back". The park was the "rec", much time was spent playing on the swings and at football, cricket, and hide and seek. With wellies on, a gang of us would try to dam the brook without getting "booties" in the process and the squelch of the water in your boots walking home. We would make camps in the trees and play in the fields at harvest and would be chased by the farmer a number of times. There is a large black poplar tree in the old Worbey's field by the Ash Brook, many branches have broken off in storms over the years and it has been hit by lightning a couple of times. This tree I would have climbed with friends in my childhood without knowing it is over 250 years old. The black poplar may be one of the oldest trees in the Hitchin area.

1 Six inch map Hertfordshire XII NW can be viewed online at http://maps.nls.uk/view/101579025

Fruit, Veg. or a Privet Hedge

Home-Grown Wisdom in Hitchin

8

DEREK WHEELER MBE

Everyone loves a garden centre, yet few people now have either an allotment or a productive garden. For half the 20th century, F.A. Wheeler and Son, of 55 Nightingale Road, Hitchin, supplied fruit and vegetables to the town, seeds to the aspiring gardener and roses to the leisured classes.

My grandfather, Frank Arthur Wheeler, was born in 1882 to landscape gardener George Wheeler and his wife in a cottage in Pin Green in Stevenage. George Wheeler travelled under contract from one country estate to another, living in tied cottages. One of his sons was born on the Rothschild estate in Tring, but by the 1890s, the family was living at the top end of Victoria Road, Hitchin, in a house rented from Mr Fowler, the Master of Hitchin Workhouse.

Frank Arthur left St Mary's School in Hitchin, almost certainly at the age of 12, to be trained as a gardener's boy, working for the Lucas family who lived at what is now the Firs Hotel in Bedford Road. By 1906, when my father Frank Carrington Wheeler was born, the family was living on the corner of Garden Row, off Nightingale Road, in a house which was rented from Mr Fells, their next-door neighbour. Mr Fells ran a nursery in Whinbush Road. It is worth assuming that Frank Arthur worked for Mr Fells after leaving the Lucas family. By my father's birth, grandfather had turned the front room of the house into a greengrocer's shop. It is also reasonable to suppose that he took over Fells' nurseries, since in the inter-war years he had a small nursery with glasshouses in Whinbush Road along with other land in the town.

Receipt from John Fells' Nurseries for quick thorn (hawthorn) for hedging 1861. (Terry Knight)

In 1925 he purchased a former timber yard on the corner of Kings Road, next to the 1844 Nightingale Cottages and had a shop and outbuildings constructed there. That building is now the John Myatt music shop. My father, his brother Bob, and their three sisters all worked at some time in the business. Frank Arthur must

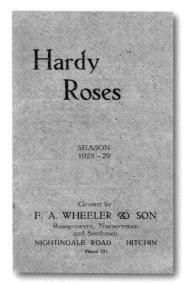

Catalogue for Hardy Roses grown by F.A. Wheeler & Son 1928–29. (Derek Wheeler)

The Wheeler family attending the public viewing of the R101 Airship at anchor at Cardington, October 1930. Left to right: Frank A, Gwen, Kathleen, Frank C. and Bob Wheeler. (Derek Wheeler)

have been well-established in trade because he sent my father to Oaklands College in St Albans to learn his skills professionally.

Bob became a nurseryman and Gwen, the eldest sister, trained as a florist. My grandfather was a Fellow of the Royal Horticultural Society and was so respected in the town that he gave advice on amateur food production during World War I in the Herts. Express newspaper and spent the next half century judging at horticultural shows throughout the Home Counties. He was in his element when exhibiting and judging with Bill Harkness at the Hitchin

Queen Mary viewing F.A. Wheeler's roses at the National Rose Show in 1932. (Derek Wheeler)

F.A. Wheeler judging at a village flower show in 1962. (Derek Wheeler)

Horticultural Show on Butts Close. He even exhibited the firm's roses at Chelsea Flower Show. Grandfather laid out gardens for most of the local gentry and was still having horticultural conversations with their widows when I came to travel with him as a teenager. He was obviously once prosperous, since in 1930 he purchased the left-hand Nightingale Cottage as a home for my parents, later purchasing the other cottage for his eldest daughter, Gwen, to live in.

Before my time, the firm had land at Westmill (later covered by housing development) and during my early years, there were glasshouses in Whinbush Road adjacent to the river and rented land along the Bedford Road between Ickleford and Holwell. The biggest plot was at the end of Benslow Lane, adjacent to Pinehill Hospital. This land had once been Ransom's property and poisonous plants such as belladonna could sometimes be seen appearing between the lines of roses.

This land originally stretched from the railway cutting to flank both sides of the narrow track leading from Benslow Lane to what is now the William Ransom School field, but F.A. Wheeler sold the eastern plot to his younger son Bob just after World War II. This was known as Hilltop Nursery for many years. Originally the track

An invitation to *"visit our Benslow Rose Gardens at any time"*. F.A. Wheeler's catalogue 1928–29 (Derek Wheeler)

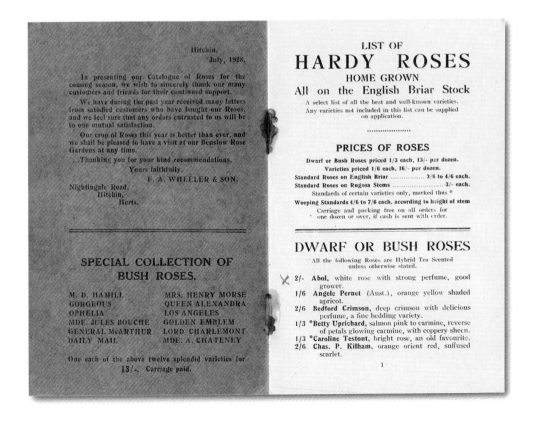

Hitchin,
July, 1928,

In presenting our Catalogue of Roses for the coming season, we wish to sincerely thank our many customers and friends for their continued support.

We have during the past year received many letters from satisfied customers who have bought our Roses, and we feel sure that any orders entrusted to us will be to our mutual satisfaction.

Our crop of Roses this year is better than ever, and we shall be pleased to have a visit at our Benslow Rose Gardens at any time.

Thanking you for your kind recommendations,

Yours faithfully,

F. A. WHEELER & SON,

Nightingale Road,
Hitchin,
Herts.

SPECIAL COLLECTION OF BUSH ROSES.

M. D. HAMILL	MRS. HENRY MORSE
GORGEOUS	QUEEN ALEXANDRA
OPHELIA	LOS ANGELES
MDE. JULES BOUCHE	GOLDEN EMBLEM
GENERAL McARTHUR	LORD CHARLEMONT
DAILY MAIL	MDE. A. CHATENEY

One each of the above twelve splendid varieties for
13/-. Carriage paid.

LIST OF

HARDY ROSES

HOME GROWN

All on the English Briar Stock

A select list of all the best and well-known varieties. Any varieties not included in this list can be supplied on application.

....

PRICES OF ROSES

Dwarf or Bush Roses priced 1/3 each, 13/- per dozen.
Varieties priced 1/6 each, 16/- per dozen.
Standard Roses on English Briar .... 3/6 to 4/6 each.
Standard Roses on Rugosa Stems .... 3/- each.
Standards of certain varieties only, marked thus *
Weeping Standards 4/6 to 7/6 each, according to height of stem
Carriage and packing free on all orders for
one dozen or over, if cash is sent with order.

DWARF OR BUSH ROSES

All the following Roses are Hybrid Tea Scented unless otherwise stated.

2/- **Abol,** white rose with strong perfume, good grower.
1/6 **Angele Pernet** (Aust.), orange yellow shaded apricot.
2/6 **Bedford Crimson,** deep crimson with delicious perfume, a fine bedding variety.
1/3 *****Betty Uprichard,** salmon pink to carmine, reverse of petals glowing carmine, with coppery sheen.
1/3 *****Caroline Testout,** bright rose, an old favourite.
2/6 **Chas. P. Kilham,** orange orient red, suffused scarlet.

1

The site of F.A. Wheeler's nursery at the end of Benslow Lane with the disputed footpath leading diagonally to Benslow Bridge. Valuation Office Survey map c.1910. (Extract from HALS IR1/91)

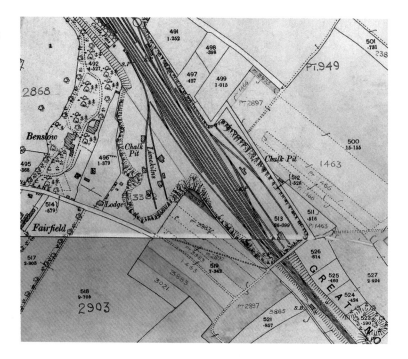

led diagonally from Benslow Lane to Benslow railway bridge, but my grandfather was constantly at odds with predatory pedestrians who stole his produce and trampled his field. He decided to divert the path to its present position in the late 1920s, thereby causing a furore which resulted in a court appearance, each side trying to find ever-older maps to establish where the track went before even the railway was built. Contemporary accounts refer to angry protesters pursuing Mr Wheeler and his son Frank as they left the site one Saturday morning in a Model T Ford under the avuncular eye of a police constable. If ever that little path receives a name it should surely be "Wheeler's Folly"!

That Ford features in family lore more than once. Apparently when my father was courting my mother, he was out delivering in Whitwell and he parked the Model T facing towards the river on Horn Hill, leaving her in the passenger seat. The handbrake mysteriously released itself and the Ford gathered speed as it descended towards a watery grave. My father managed to leap aboard and avert a catastrophe. On another occasion, he was turning the corner from Benslow Lane into Walsworth Road and a wheel came off the Ford and gently came to rest against the public bar of the Radcliffe public house!

I never saw my grandfather drive but allegedly he owned a French Gladiator car before World War I. Perhaps either the gearbox or the instruction manual defeated him and he subsequently bought

Model T Fords which were pedal controlled and could be mended with a hammer. During my early years his favourite steed was an ancient Cyclemaster power-assisted bicycle which owed its very existence to the copious quantities of florists' wire which held it together.

The Whinbush Road glasshouses were semi-derelict by the 1950s, later giving way to flats, but the firm's remaining Benslow land was still in cultivation up to 1960. All the Benslow site which once had Wheelers working the soil is now under housing development. From the top of Benslow Hill, to the south, could be seen the land of Mr Bill James, another nurseryman. His land disappeared under William Ransom School. To the north east could be seen the fields of William Harkness. At one time, this nationally-famed enterprise had land which is now under houses both in Walsworth and the Oakfield estate. On the other hilltop, to the west of Hitchin, stood Cannon's Nurseries, along Lucas Lane (again under houses), opposite the Workhouse wall. They had a shop in High Street which could be seen as one came down Brand Street.

At the other end of Bancroft, behind the Skynners' Almshouses, stood Bill Upchurch's nursery. He had a shop almost opposite the almshouses. His water came from the Capswell Brook which runs under Bancroft. He pumped it up to a small water tower and fed his glasshouses by gravity. A car park now stands on this land. Halfway down Grove Road, almost hidden from sight, was where Bill Abbiss had his nursery, directly adjacent to the Hiz. As I remember, this was the last town nursery to go.

J. Cannon 'The Hitchin Fruitery' 16 High Street. (NHM 264–06)

Not only did these firms supply plants for the garden, they supplied fresh fruit and vegetables for the table as well as flowers for every occasion. Wreaths, crosses and bouquets were once big business in Hitchin, but florists and greengrocers can now be counted on one hand. In the 1950s, there were four greengrocers in Nightingale Road: John Howard at the bottom of Radcliffe Road, F.A. Wheeler almost opposite, Gregory's opposite Berry House and Rainbow's a bit further down towards the Florence Street junction. Within a short distance was Day's in Walsworth Road with another shop in Churchyard. There were other fruiterer's shops too. There was one in Queen Street and a tiny shop next to the Red Hart in Bucklersbury. There was Brown's in Bancroft and Tomlin's in the Arcade. W.H. Church also had a shop in the Arcade opposite Tomlin's. This specialised in seeds, garden sundries and at one time it was the only pet shop in the town. There were possibly other specialised shops on the outer perimeter of the town, but after half a century, perhaps memory lets me down. We must also consider the numerous produce stalls on Hitchin Market. They all survived because there were no supermarkets and they all sourced their produce locally. F.A. Wheeler once had a market stall, but this did not survive the market move to St Mary's Square prior to World War II.

"Wreaths, Crosses and Bouquets made to Order", "Gardens kept in Order", and "Advice Gladly Given" as well as Fruit Trees, Spring Bedding Plants etc. advertised in F.A. Wheeler's catalogue 1928–29. (Derek Wheeler)

FRUIT TREES.

Apples, Pears, Plums, Damsons, etc.

In all the leading varieties.

MAIDENS .... 2/- each; 21/- per doz.
BUSH, two years .... 3/- each; 33/- per doz.
DITTO, two to three years ... 4/- each; 42/- per doz.
STANDARDS (according to age and size) .... 4/- to 7/6 each
TRAINED TREES, for walls .... 6/- to 10/- each
SINGLE CORDON APPLES .... from 2/6 each

Currants.

RED AND BLACK .... 9d. each; 8/- per doz.
EXTRA STRONG .... 1/- each, 10/- per doz.

Gooseberries.

TWO YEARS OLD .... 9d. each; 8/- per doz.
THREE YEARS AND OVER 1/- each; 10/- per doz.

Raspberry Canes.

FIRST SIZE, strong .... 3/- per doz.; £1 per 100
SECOND SIZE, strong ... 2/- per doz.; 16/- per 100

Strawberry Plants.

EXTRA STRONG PLANTS (in small pots) .... 4/- per doz.
OPEN GROUND PLANTS ... 1/- per doz. 7/- per 100

Loganberries and similar Hybrid Berries
                                    1/6 and 2/- each
Rhubarb Roots of sorts .... 9/- to 12/- per doz.

8

Spring Bedding Plants.

Wallflowers . Forget-me-nots
Sweet Williams
Canterbury Bells
etc.

HIGH-CLASS SEEDS.

Catalogues Free.

BULBS IN GREAT VARIETY.
HEDGING PLANTS.
SHRUBS & FOREST TREES.

WREATHS, CROSSES AND BOUQUETS
MADE TO ORDER.

GARDENS KEPT IN ORDER BY THE DAY,
WEEK OR CONTRACT.

ADVICE GLADLY GIVEN ON ALL
MATTERS IN CONNECTION
WITH THE GARDEN

T. Dunnill Sykes (Printers), Limited, London and Letchworth.

The Worbey family were also represented in the town by Alec Worbey's nursery in Whitehill Road, where Whitehill Junior School now stands, and Alf Worbey's smallholding in Blackhorse Lane, now largely covered by The Paddock housing development. Alf sold most of his produce on Hitchin Market, although he took some in his immaculate Austin K4 lorry to Covent Garden where he also purchased other fruit and vegetables, not grown locally, to sell on his stall and to supply Alice Grimes' (*née* Worbey) greengrocer's shop in Queen Street, next to the Bricklayer's Arms. Alf, his wife Elsie and their two children, Robina and Alan, lived further along the street in Nursery Villas. Alf was a hard worker and fastidious with the maintenance of his land and buildings. One of Alan's school friends remembers them being used as ballast on the harrow hauled around the field by Alf on his 'Fergie' tractor!

F.A.Wheeler and Son lost staff due to military call-up in 1939 and it would appear the family had a hard time during the conflict, since my grandfather was obliged by law to take on inexperienced Italian prisoners of war and unemployed bombed-out workers from London. He took on such a refugee one Wednesday and found that there was nothing in the till with which to pay him the following Saturday morning. A court appearance and a fine was the result.

With the constant post-war expansion of the town, all useable pockets of land were surrendered for house building, and if the land was rented anyway (as was the remaining Benslow plot from Howard Ansell, a retired councillor who lived in the West Country), no compensation was expected. Perhaps mail order horticulture and the rise of the garden centre also contributed to the demise of the family firm. The growing of roses was scaled down, as the business could not compete with nationally-famous firms like Harkness and Wheatcroft. Pot plants were bought from local nurseries and cut flowers were purchased from the old Covent Garden Market.

Grandfather used to catch the first train from Hitchin in the morning and by 8 a.m. he was eating his breakfast in Drury Lane, having made all his purchases. They were already on their way by van or cart to King's Cross. My father would then meet the train at Hitchin station with the firm's ancient Austin Heavy Twelve car, sometimes towing a trailer, to pick up dozens of cardboard flower boxes from the guard on a passenger train and take them down the road to the shop. Grandad would already have come home and walked to Benslow to work on his rose or chrysanthemum cultivation. Sometimes my father had to take the car to nurseries as far afield as Esher or Chesterfield to satisfy a particular customer's demands, leaving the shop to be managed by my mother or his youngest sister.

The shop was very old-fashioned. To the left of the front door was the fruit and veg department, protected by a large counter upon which stood an ancient fretted cast-iron-and-marquetry till and a push-operated brass bell to attract attention. The floor was dominated by an enormous set of scales with weights, the biggest of which was a challenge to a child. To the right of the door was the flower and seed department, where bucket after bucket was filled with the most exotic cut flowers. The large-paned window on this side of the shop had faded ceramic or enamel signs advertising "Clay's London Fertiliser", "John Innes Compost", "Derris Dust"; the whole atmosphere being suffused with the mixed odours of daffodils and DDT.

The counter here had a tiny set of brass scales for weighing seed envelopes and a primeval Oliver typewriter with letter strikers which rose up either side like organ pipes. In the corner of this department was a faded white wooden kiosk with tiny paned windows which contained a daffodil-like telephone, with the number Hitchin 331 marked on it. Effectively this was the office, with scribblings all over the rear wall. The whole back wall of the shop from floor to ceiling was covered with exquisite mahogany drawers which contained seeds and their relevant envelopes. Above the door leading to the domestic quarters, was the circular wall clock which had the Gatward name on it and Hitchin twice, the latter spelled differently each time!

The outbuildings to the rear of the shop were a veritable cornucopia of construction materials for me in my childhood: silver wire, iron wire, tissue paper, silver paper, cellophane, wooden boxes, sacks and an old toolbox filled with army-surplus

Left: Bob Wheeler about to "scuffle" the ground at Hilltop Nursery, Benslow Lane, 1950s, now the site of 79–125 (odd) Benslow Lane. (Janet Swan & John Wheeler)

Right: Friends helping Bob Wheeler outside his glasshouses c.1960. (Janet Swan & John Wheeler)

Bob and Gladys
Wheeler pricking
out plants 1960s.
(Janet Swan & John
Wheeler)

nails, screws and nuts and bolts. Grandfather would buy anything
which he thought would be useful at Jackson's Sale Yard. Those
sheds were to me as the wrecked ship was to Robinson Crusoe. At
the end of World War I one purchase was an army-surplus horse
which proved to be useless at ploughing as it would only respond to
commands in Russian!

My mother resisted all my grandfather's blandishments for
me to go into the business. My parents lived a hard life, since rose
growing, wreath making and the creation of bouquets all play havoc
with the hands. Holly leaves, rose thorns and florists' wire show no
mercy. The seasonal demand for holly wreaths brought pleasure to
many, but pain to those who crafted them. I have spent Christmas
Eve in the grounds of Benslow Nursing Home gathering holly for
customers who insisted on picking their orders up on Christmas
Day.

When my grandfather died in 1963, everything had to be sold.
Sherriff's of Hatfield, one of the firm's long-term suppliers of seed
potatoes, purchased what was left of the business and kept my
father on as shop manager. They subsequently sold the shop, my
father becoming manager of "Floral Gardens" in Hermitage Road,
working for Mr C.E. Chapman, another long-term supplier from
Whitwell.

It was the end of an era. Bob Wheeler's Hilltop Nursery survived
for a number of years but this site is now under houses. Home-
grown wisdom has to be found elsewhere. There is no Wheeler left
to lead you knowledgeably up the garden path.

Justice in Hitchin

9

STEPHEN BRADFORD-BEST

Until recently local justice was administered in Hitchin, both civil and criminal, at the County and Magistrates' Courts. Now you need to go to larger towns further afield! My forty plus years career with the Lord Chancellor's Department gave me an insight into the workings of these courts, particularly Hitchin County Court where I spent my early years as a clerk (1964–1984). But when were these courts created?

Collecting debts through the Court of Pleas, or the old county courts, had become expensive or centralised in London. New local courts, known as courts of request, had been established in some areas but successive governments, in the early 19th century, strived to reform the courts to make them more accessible and affordable. As a result, the new County Courts, dealing solely with civil cases, were created under the County Courts Act 1846. Their jurisdiction covered debt and damages and, in some towns, also bankruptcy and later divorce proceedings. The then Lord Chancellor, Lord Cottenham, divided England and Wales into 60 circuits, with a total of 491 county courts within these circuits. He wanted everyone to be within seven miles of a court and the final

The old Town Hall in Brand Street where courts were held until the new police station was built in 1885. (NHM LTS Vol 1A p84)

scheme came close to that aim. Hitchin County Court was one of those original courts. County Courts are controlled by the Lord Chancellor's Department, now known as the Ministry of Justice.

In the early years, court hearings in provincial towns were often held in the town hall. This was the arrangement in Hitchin, at the old town hall in Brand Street, until the new police station was built in Bancroft, in 1885, which incorporated a courtroom. In the mid-19th century, the court in Hitchin was held every other month, increasing to monthly by the end of the century. The judges in this period, who were always salaried, included John Koe Q.C., John Collyer and William Gurdon, a first-class cricketer. However, the administration of the court by the registrar was often a task carried out by a local solicitor. Initially he received a share of the court fees but later he also became salaried. In Hitchin the first registrar was believed to be Hitchin solicitor, Charles Times, who had an office for the administration of the court in Bancroft with Mr Gripper as his treasurer and Mr Impey as his sub-bailiff. Times also had the title High Bailiff. A couple of years after his death in 1876, he was replaced by his son, William Onslow Times, at the early age of 25 years. He had an office at 90 Bancroft, on the corner of Portmill Lane, with, in later years, E H Grellet as his clerk. The registrar's clerk gradually took over the daily administrative duties of the court giving the registrar more time for his judicial responsibilities at court hearings. Times, a partner in the solicitors' firm of Hawkins & Co in Portmill Lane, was a powerhouse of a man who remained registrar for several decades, as well as holding many other civic offices in the town until his death in 1934. The judges in this period included Edmond Beales, Shortt, Wheeler and William Bagshawe Q.C., who gave the altar for the new Roman Catholic church that opened in 1902.

Above left: Charles Times, who became the first registrar of Hitchin County Court in 1846. (NHM LTS Vol 3A p116 NHM)

Above right: The office of W O Times from where the County Court was administered around 1900. (T N Thomson)

Details about the County Court from the Hitchin Household Almanack for 1915. (HHS Scilla Douglas Collection)

Hitchin County Court.

Judge—His Honour Judge Wheeler, K.C.   *Registrar and High Bailiff*—Mr. W. O. Times.   *Clerk*, Mr. E. H. Grellet ; *Bailiff*, Mr. H. H. Harding. Office—90, Bancroft.   The Registrar disposes of all actions in which the plaintiff's claim is admitted, and of all actions in which the defendant does not appear either in person or by someone on his behalf.   The Judge takes the Judgment (Commitment) Summonses first, and afterwards the other business of the day, in the order of the entries in the Cause List, and in all cases in which the plaintiff does not appear, either in person or by Solicitor, are struck out.   Judgment Summonses are taken on alternate Court Days.

By the 1930s, the offices had moved to larger premises on the first floor of 107 Bancroft, in part of the old Hermitage buildings, the former home of Frederic Seebohm, accommodating a staff of clerks, bailiffs and a typist. The new registrar, following Times' death, was Donald Scott Anderson McMurtrie, by now taking mainly a judicial role, and the judge was W Lawson Campbell. Whilst working at the court during World War 2, a young Kathleen Pettengell married John Melot but was requested to leave a few years later when she became pregnant with her daughter, a requirement in those days. The ground floor beneath the office provided Dr Marshall Gilbertson's surgery, later converted to Furr's fishmongers and Kirby's mens' outfitters and more recently a variety of restaurants. Next door, where the County Court offices spread on the floor above, was Burgess' Library and later estate agent's offices. Further next door, on the first floor, was the

His Honour Judge W Lawson Campbell, presiding County Court judge from the 1930s to the 1950s. (Peter Crofts)

solicitor's partnership of Hartley & Hine, one of the partners being the noted local historian Reginald Hine; they had their own private door into the court offices!

In this period, the courtroom was still shared with the Magistrates' Court using the one within the police station until, from the 1930s, the courtroom of their new purpose-built building situated behind the police station was built. Post World War 2, Connolly Hugh Gage, a former Ulster Unionist MP and award-winning rose grower, was appointed the judge and Alfred Arthur Hunt, a larger than life character known to many as Mick, who had joined the court before the war, was promoted to be the man in charge, now called the Chief Clerk. His second in command, or Staff Clerk, was Patrick Ritchie, and one of his six bailiffs, who drove him around the district as he was unable to drive, was Bert Blott from Campton. The bailiffs frequently had previous careers in the services or the police force. In 1963, a new young and enthusiastic registrar, Bruce John Elliott, was appointed to replace Registrar McMurtrie who had died in office; every member of his staff was required to attend his funeral, without exception. Hitchin County Court also staffed the part-time offices of the Royston and, later, the Biggleswade County Courts, until their closures.

By 1970, the County Court needed larger accommodation and they moved to occupy the top (2nd) floor of the newly built Station House in Nightingale Road, formerly the site of the Hitchin Bacon Factory, but they still used the courtroom of the Magistrates' Court, now an inconvenient drive into the town. They also shared the services of their usher, the imposing figure of Cyril Freeman. The lower floors of Station House were occupied by the Institution of Electrical Engineers. The Chief Clerk, who oversaw this move, was Victor Teague, who hailed from Bodmin in Cornwall; he retired in 1983. Although Bruce Elliott continued as registrar, he later shared this duty with several other members of the judiciary, including Andrew Myers and Mark Le Mesurier, together with local solicitors appointed temporarily as deputy registrars, necessary to cope with the increasing workload. A significant increase in work resulted from the Divorce Reform Act 1969 when, in 1971, Hitchin gained jurisdiction to deal with matrimonial proceedings. This act simplified the divorce procedure by defining the sole grounds for the divorce as the breakdown of the marriage.

Above left: The County Court occupied the top floor of Station House in Nightingale Road from 1971. (NHM)

Above right: A staff group in the bailiffs' office of Station House on the retirement of Senior Clerk, Bill Pipe, in 1975. (Robert Germany)

In 1984, the court offices moved again, this time to Park House, 1–12 Old Park Road. The big advantage of this new building was that it was specifically designed to provide all the facilities required to administer the court including, for the first time, its own integral courtroom. The Chief Clerk who oversaw this move was Yorkshireman, Peter West. One of the judges was local man John Farnworth whose father, George, had owned Morgan's Garage in Sun Street. Registrars were re-named district judges in 1990. Station House was later demolished and replaced by an Audi car showroom and garage.

Hitchin County Court finally closed in 2010. Its district was absorbed by Luton County Court

Park House built for the County Court in 1984. (Alan Fleck 2015)

and the staff were transferred to other offices. The court building became the headquarters of the All England Netball Association until 2018 when it was converted into apartments.

Next, we deal with the court which dealt with criminal misconduct, the Magistrates' Court. There had been locally based 'keepers of the peace' to enforce the law since the medieval moot and manorial courts, with the title Justice of the Peace (JP) introduced by the Justice of the Peace Act 1361. The JPs had powers to restrain offenders and to chastise them according to their offence. By the 18th century, the JPs were usually appointed from the landed gentry but, in the 19th century, JPs were appointed from a wider spectrum of residents, including the professional classes and leaders of industry. As the centuries passed magistrates had increasingly become local administrators, but they were relieved of these duties when, from 1888, elected county councils were created to administer local services. Those crimes that could not be tried summarily by the magistrates without a jury in petty sessions were heard by the quarter sessions, with the most serious crimes being tried by the periodic assizes. In the early 19th century, hanging and deportation were still punishments for minor crimes, like theft.

John Hawkins, Clerk to the Justices. (NHM LTS Vol IA p20)

Whereas the Times family, particularly the redoubtable 'W.O', seemed to control the civil court in Hitchin for decades,

it was the Hawkins family, and their successors in the firm of Hawkins & Co solicitors, established in the town since 1591, that administered the criminal court. The Clerk to the Justices in the mid-19th century was John Hawkins, operating from his office in Portmill Lane. A separate entrance, on the corner of their building, gave access to the office from where the court was administered. In provincial towns like Hitchin, the Magistrates' Courts were controlled by the Magistrates' Courts' Committee, who employed the staff, but they were paid by the county council, including the Clerk to the Justices, the senior court official. However, unlike the County Courts, the Magistrates' Courts were overseen by the Home Office, although in recent years, that responsibility has passed to the Ministry of Justice. The first female magistrate was not appointed until 1919 but, today, most magistrates are women.

Left: Frederick Peter Delmé-Radcliffe, a long serving magistrate until his death in 1875. (NHM LTS Vol 1A p20)

Right: Justice off duty! W O Times (left) and E B Lindsell (right) in discussion with Lawson Thompson (centre) outside Barclays Bank in the High Street photographed by H Moulden in 1909. (NHM LTS Vol 3A p153)

In Hitchin, in the early years, the petty sessions were held at noon on a Tuesday, Market Day, and, as used by the County Court, the venue was the old Town Hall in Brand Street. In 1853, the Chairman of the Bench was Andrew Amos, joined by many eminent Hitchin worthies like Frederick Delmé-Radcliffe of Hitchin Priory, Henry Bland of Temple Dinsley, Preston, and William Carling of Bancroft. By 1870 they had been joined by Marlborough Pryor of Weston Park, Francis Lucas, a banker, of Tilehouse Street and Thomas Dashwood who bought Oakfield House in 1877 and who, by 1886, had become Chairman. By this date the clerk to the Justices was Edward Barber Lindsell, also a partner of Hawkins & Co. Common offences resulted from theft, acts of violence and excessive drinking.

The move of the police station from Silver Street (the name formerly given to the lower part of Bancroft) to a new red brick building further up Bancroft, in 1885, marked the inclusion of the first purpose-built court room in the town. In 1910, the duty of chairman was undertaken by Francis Delmé-Radcliffe and, in 1917, by William Tindall Lucas, both familiar dignitaries in the town, with Arthur Lindsell as their clerk. By this time the punishment of hard labour for those convicted of minor crimes had been replaced by imprisonment or fines. A hatch was added in the court office in Portmill Lane through which fines could be paid. There were further changes of chairman in the inter-war years, but the major change was the building of a new separate Magistrates' Court building, in the Art Deco style, with an impressive wood panelled courtroom – not unlike the furnishings of an ocean liner.

In the post-war period the court continued with Kenneth Lindsell as the clerk and Donald Christmas as his deputy; his secretary was Adeline Darvill. The staff of four included Historical Society

Above left: The new police station and courtroom built in Bancroft in 1885. (NHM 373–01)

Above right: The new Magistrates' Court building behind the police station in Bancroft opened in the 1930s. (Stephen Bradford-Best)

member Vicki Lockyer. The magistrates included more notable local names including Powell-Davies and Seebohm. Each March the magistrates heard applications from the landlords of public houses for licences to sell alcohol on their premises. They also dealt with domestic violence and motoring offences, adoption applications (as did the County Court) – they even dealt with exemptions from holding a licence for a farm dog. The juvenile court, dealing with young offenders, was held each Friday. From 1971, serious cases were referred to the newly formed Crown Courts, replacing quarter sessions and assizes, usually in St Albans or Bedford and later in Luton. Many local solicitors regularly represented defendants in the Magistrates' Court, including Bob Boulton and Roger Crabtree. Common offences still included theft, acts of violence and excessive drinking, now joined by drug related crimes.

Hitchin Magistrates' Court had also administered Letchworth, Royston and Stevenage Magistrates' Courts but, in the 1990s, this role, including the control of the Hitchin court, was transferred to Stevenage Magistrates' Court, although hearings still took place in Hitchin until around 2000. In those later years at Hitchin, the Clerk to Justices, who was the senior court official, was Paul Fellingham; Andrew Staples was one of the Court Clerks at Hitchin shortly before it closed.

With the creation of combined court centres in large towns or cities, and the use of new technologies, the notion of locally administered justice is a thing of the past – you can now even sue online!

Sources

Patrick Polden, *A History of the County Court 1846–1971* (Cambridge University Press, 1999)
Hitchin Town Guides (HALS)

St Michael's Mount and the Poets Estate

10

DAVID HOWLETT

Soulless Suburbia?

All areas have their local history. That modern source, Mumsnetlocal, has assessed the "Poets area": a potential resident Mum noted many of the houses on estate agents' websites had *"attractive insides"*. But our Mum continued *"..wandering around ..we found the area very quiet and maybe a bit 'soulless'.."*. The townscape we see today, covering almost 75 acres, was built mainly between about 1973 and 1984 by construction giant George Wimpey with housing designs similar to many of its sites across the country. But first impressions – and Mumsnetlocal – are misleading.

Landscape established: two millennia of continuity

The Poets Estate, linked today by St Michael's Road, sits on centuries of local history. In Roman times it was probably within the agricultural estate (possibly a thousand acres) of the nearby Purwell villa, accessed by what is now Gypsy Lane. The villa flourished from about AD 250–375 but may well have had earlier origins. The land is varied, with higher portions to the north being chalky and dry mixed with lower areas in the south of deeper moister clay soils; villa estates needed different land types to provide both for grazing animals and arable crops.[1]

After Roman rule the Poets land was included in one of the large open fields – Purwell – that grew around the new Saxon township of Hitchin. Tracks linked it, and Purwell Mill, to the town. Purwell Field was divided into individual "strips" but cultivated collectively. A basic pattern of land organisation was established which lasted into the 20th century. There was gradual change as some adjoining strips were enclosed with hedges or fences, but the main framework of Purwell Field survived.[2]

From the 1600s documents gradually give us more detail. The strips had local labels such as Beggarly Shot after poor soils and Long and Short Shadwell (roughly where Coleridge Close stands today) after nearby springs. Some key names, such as the Shadwells and Purwell, probably have very early origins. Others names, such as Ninesprings, Skimpot (sometimes Pisspot) and St Michael's Mount, are only recorded during the 19th century. Documents

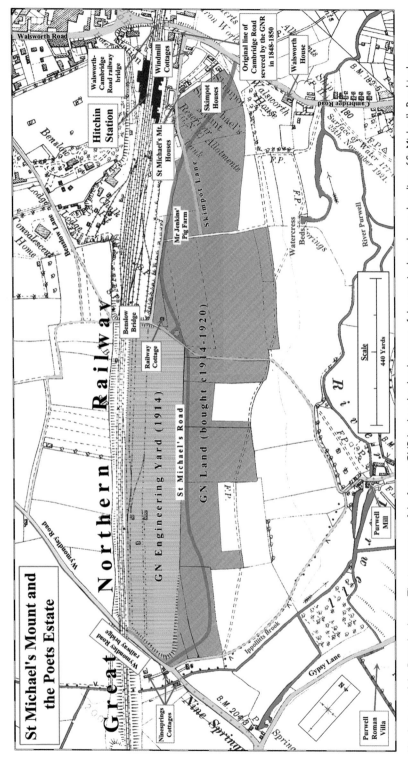

Key features of the Poets landscape. The importance of the former GNR land to the development of the area is clear; the modern line of St Michael's Road is shown. Composite plan, based on the 1925 edition 6" OS map augmented by GNR Landholding Plans with LNER and BR amendments (Haygreen Collection). Mapwork by John Lucas.

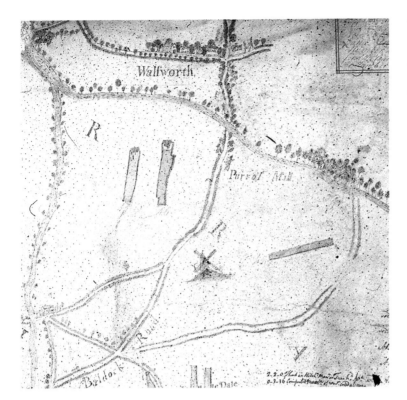

Walsworth Windmill in c.1770. It lay immediately north east of the present railway station. Built and operated in conjunction with Purwell (water) Mill. (Excerpt from map of Hitchin c.1770 NHM)

also give evidence of the first buildings. For example, by 1728 a windmill, owned by William Malein (then miller at Purwell), is recorded near Skimpot. By 1838 this mill had gone but was recalled by Windmill Cottages overlooking Cambridge Road: these survived into the 1960s. Several small houses appeared at Skimpot after 1816; by 1851 there were about a dozen. Some cottages were also built about 1816 at Ninesprings, owned by the Nash family, by then owners of Purwell Mill. Ninesprings had further dwellings by 1844 but these had gone by the 1960s; today the only survivors are on Wymondley Road just east of the Ippollitts Brook. There were likely also some small agricultural buildings scattered across the area; for example a plan of 1914 shows what looks like a cluster of pig-pens on allotments belonging to Hitchin Grammar School.[3]

Landscape severed: the original railway impact

Constructing the Great Northern Railway (GNR) between Peterborough and London in 1848–50 made the biggest single impact on the local landscape since Roman times. The new line severed the Poets piece of Purwell Field from its larger portion to the west with a new 'hard' boundary; the deep chalk railway cutting sliced through the hill. To preserve Hitchin's access to Purwell Mill a brick bridge – Benslow Bridge – was built over the railway. The long established routes of Wymondley and Cambridge Roads were provided with underbridges.

The upheaval of railway construction was significant but short-lived and the bulk of the Poets land continued in agricultural use. Chalk extraction – lime for both fertiliser and mortar – was undertaken on both sides of the railway. Immediately north of Benslow Bridge the new cutting accommodated the station and engine yard. For much of the rest of the 1800s not much else happened. Formal gardens at Walsworth House (to the northeast of the site) expanded alongside the wet marshy edge of Purwell Meadows and their watercress beds. But Hitchin's major suburban expansion remained west of the main line.[4]

The only area of significant habitation was at Skimpot, augmented soon after 1850 by St Michael's Mount. Here new dwellings probably replaced a row of earlier cottages owned by the Upchurch family which were demolished to make way for the railway cutting in 1848–50; an Upchurch still lived in the successor houses into the 1950s. The brick and slate houses of both Skimpot and St Michael's Mount were mainly small two-up two-downs. Census details between 1871 and 1901 reveal households whose heads were mainly labourers of various sorts but also included a

Skimpot and St Michael's Mount in 1898. (Excerpt from HALS IRI/91)

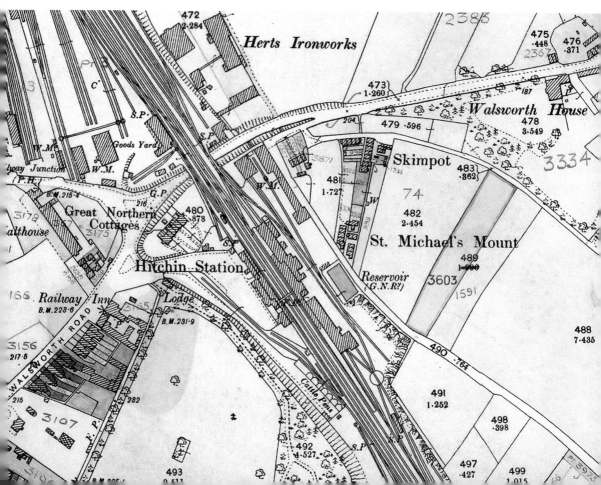

scattering of skills such as gas fitter, groom, coal dealer, bricklayer, tinman and carpenter. The area did not have "railway houses" but was still home to numbers of working railway men (such as labourers, a shunter, a steam raiser and a porter) and an engine driver's widow. Most houses were densely occupied; for example a railway labourer at Skimpot – John Hill – lived in one with his wife and six children. The area had likely never been particularly prosperous; in 1909 some country walkers from the pristine Garden City nearby observed *"..a row of neglected-looking cottages bearing an ineffaceable mark of poverty and attendant squalor..."*.[5]

The late 19th century was a heyday of big railway business. By 1910 the GNR planned the consolidation of its southern engineering and maintenance work (hitherto mainly at King's Cross and Southgate) in a new yard at Hitchin. Local tradition has it these plans also included a new locomotive works but, so far, no clear evidence of this has surfaced. The GN scheme certainly involved *"planned new shops"* but, although significant, these seem connected with maintenance. In 1914 the GNR sponsored a Parliamentary Act which included plans for the new engineering facilities to the east of the mainline at Hitchin: this had implications for the Poets area.[6]

The Act allowed the GNR to demolish Benslow Bridge provided a new road was constructed (the origins of today's St Michael's Road) between Cambridge Road and Ninesprings. Removal of the bridge would allow easier connection of the engine shed area to the new engineering yard planned immediately to the south (today the Hillview Estate) and allow the engines of longer trains to take water without obstructing the running lines. The Act also empowered the GNR to buy the land it needed, compulsorily if necessary, *"in connection with the transfer of the Engineer's yards for the South District to that place"*.[7] The Company began buying land late in 1913 and started work prior to its Act, but purchases were complicated given the area was still divided – medieval open field style – with inter-mixed holdings of several separate owners who each had their own tenants.

The original Benslow Bridge looking south not long before its demolition in 1974. (Terry Wilson)

The land the GNR wanted belonged to six owners including James Albon, Miss Lovell, Miss Wilshere and Hitchin Grammar School; Albon in particular was unhappy at the pressure applied by the GNR to secure his land. Contracts for work (including to Hitchin firms J Willmott and Innes & Co) were also let before the Act received Royal Assent in August 1914. The GNR plan included *"the consequent necessity of arranging for additional housing accommodation in the district"*, perhaps accessed by the new road, to provide for the staff moved to Hitchin.[8]

Landscape saved: plans shelved

The British Government declared war on Germany on 4 August 1914 but the conflict was not expected to last long. The GNR's Hitchin work, therefore, continued. The new south yard was almost finished by July 1915, although Benslow Bridge was not demolished and the full range of buildings was not completed. But soon wartime conditions did impinge such as contractors demanding pre-payment. The GNR, despite buying some extra property in 1915–16, deferred further work until hostilities ended, including delaying purchase of further land owned by Miss Wilshere, Theodore Ransom and William Onslow Times to the east and north of the new yard. After the war this extra land was finally purchased in 1920; a small slice went back to Miss Wilshere the same year to 'protect' her adjoining grounds at Walsworth House although she soon sold this to the Hitchin Urban District Council. The GNR's precise reasoning behind these additional land purchases remains unclear but the prospect of main line modernisation, including a new marshalling yard and possibly an electric locomotive depot at Hitchin, might be factors.[9]

After 1919 the HUDC became prominent in plans for the Poets area. It queried GNR intentions and asked if the company would sell it about 15 acres of its newly acquired land at cost. The council was pondering, in the context of Queen Street slum clearance, a St Michael's Mount council housing scheme, in addition to that at Sunnyside, and had bought from six separate owners almost 22 acres in readiness, including Miss Wilshere's piece. About 300 'cottages', designed by local architect Frank Selby, would be built along the access road originally planned by the GNR in 1914. This would start from Cambridge Road with the potential of being extended to Ninesprings. Councillors suggested an attractive format with dwellings facing over the Purwell valley and that three 'representative' Hitchin women be allowed to comment on the detail of the house plans (including Mrs Reginald Hine of the Hitchin Women Citizens' Association) – they understandably criticised the pantries which faced south (!).[10]

The GNR initially agreed in 1920 to let HUDC have 15 acres for about 100 houses, but was slow in confirming help with the new road and not willing to sell further land. Miss Lovell also owned land affected by the council's plans and objected to any compulsory purchase. The result was the St Michael's Mount plans stalled and the HUDC considered another site for council housing, at Westmill. Tussles ensued with the Ministry of Health (which supervised local authority housing) on the costs incurred and what might be done with the land already bought. Ironically, in 1925, Miss Lovell offered up her holding *"near St Michael's Mount"*. The council deferred even though discussions still continued *"with the object of constructing a road on this site [for 200 houses] which would greatly enhance its value"*. But by now the London and North Eastern Railway (LNER) had succeeded the GNR and made clear it was not much interested in collaboration with the council, including buying any of its land no longer required for housing.[11]

Yet, in 1927, the LNER still noted an agreement with the council could be reached, including previously proposed exchanges of land, and that it did not propose to drop its powers allowing closure of Benslow Bridge *"although they were not in a position at the moment to say when the work was likely to be carried out"*. About 1922 Railway Cottage was built adjacent to Benslow Bridge on land bought by the GNR in 1914. It had no electricity or gas but John Pateman, whose father was later a crane driver based in the Engineering Yard, recalls it was warm and cosy because of numerous fireplaces fed by engine coal. The cottage sat on a distinctive triangular plot, the tiny remnant of a medieval field strip that once stretched west over the

Plan *c.*1920 showing land already bought by HUDC for council housing (blue) and that offered by the GNR (red). Also shown is the proposed new route from Cambridge Road to Ninesprings. (NHM)

Alec Worbey driving his Minneapolis Moline tractor c.1948 near where Chaucer Way is today. The attached planter was of his own devising. (Mervyn Spokes)

land removed by the original railway cutting in 1848–50 and its subsequent enlargement soon after. The long gestated road between Cambridge Road and Ninesprings was also by now included in Hitchin's first systematic Town Planning Scheme. HUDC next weighed disposal or use of its land at St Michael's Mount; part was occupied by allotments and part was of interest to local farmers, the Worbey brothers. The LNER also allocated some of its land, already allotments, to be administered by the HUDC. In 1932 the Worbeys took up an annual tenancy of about 19½ acres.[12]

Little happened during the 1930s. The HUDC remained undecided on what might be done with the area. Mr Flint of Purwell Mill submitted plans for about 100 houses on his land at the eastern edge but the council had decided this should remain open space. The plans for railway modernisation at Hitchin faded and another World War came and went. Between 1949–51 a revised local authority planning framework proposed "*the land between St Michael's Mount and Ninesprings …be specifically reserved for railways and railway land in view of the proposed electrification of the London–Hitchin railway*". The Railway Executive (responsible for the newly nationalised British Railways) was noted as owning "*a considerable amount of land to the south of the railway station*" originally purchased for a large marshalling yard and that it "*is still required for this purpose*". But yet again railway investment did not materialise and the Poets land slumbered through the 1950s in agricultural use. Small scale pig production existed on the St Michael's Mount allotments by the Second World War, although it seems to be 1952 before formal permission was sought; by then several of the plots were vacant and neglected. A larger pig unit, sited east of Benslow Bridge at the top of the chalk cliffs, was run by Ron Jenkins and accessed along Skimpot Lane; another free range pig operation was also established near Purwell Mill and the land between the two remained under arable, grazing and some chicken farming.[13]

In 1949 ten of the freehold cottages at St Michael's Mount were sold at auction. The HUDC was concerned at the declining quality of housing here and at Skimpot. Amidst rising post-war aspirations and more interventionist planning policy, these houses were identified as 'slum' dwellings ripe for replacement or improvement; several were designated 'overcrowded' or as 'unfit for human habitation' as the costs of improvement were judged 'unreasonable' by 1957. Terry Wilson, who used to deliver milk and papers in the area in 1958, recalls that the Windmill Cottages were better looked after.

In the late 1950s railway electrification plans surfaced once more. This revived interest in the GNR Act of 1914 because demolition of Benslow Bridge would be required for overhead wiring, underlining the need for a Cambridge Road-Ninesprings route. This was now to be linked to A505 widening from near the station entrance to Stotfold Road. In turn, questions were reopened about the use of the Poets area through which the new road would pass. Much of the land was still owned by British Railways (the GNR's purchases of 1916–20) and by the HUDC, although the holdings remained intermixed.

By 1963 St Michael's Mount, after over forty years, was once more under consideration for council housing, including possible acquisitions of adjacent plots in private or railway hands, as part of a comprehensive scheme for the whole area. Most of the allotments were now vacant, the pace of declaring houses at St Michael's

Hitchin Engine Yard in 1939 looking north. Some of the cottages at St Michael's Mount can just be seen top right. (Terry Wilson)

Mount 'unfit' quickened and the council moved to buy some for demolition. Following an agreement in 1961 between its owners and the County Council, a Further Education College was planned for Walsworth House. About 8 acres of adjoining HUDC land – still tenanted, either as allotments or 'short term' since the 1930s (!) by the Worbeys – were added to the college site. At one point, land at St Michael's Mount was also considered as a possible location for a new Lister Hospital before the decision was taken to move it to Corey's Mill.[14]

Landscape developed: at last

In 1964 the final phase began. The HUDC continued efforts to tackle the 'problem' housing at St Michael's Mount and Skimpot, where over 20 dwellings were still occupied; it bought Windmill Cottages that year *"with future redevelopment in mind"*. The council now decided that *"joint arrangements be made for the development of the land between Cambridge Road and Wymondley Road which has been zoned in the revised Development Plan for residential development"*. The idea was to involve the several landowners in a comprehensive scheme for the whole area, providing about 500 dwellings, shops and a junior school. By 1965 national builder George Wimpey was prepared to negotiate consolidation of the land and deliver such a scheme, including public housing on a portion of the site that would be sold to the council. The HUDC accepted in principle though *"it will not be possible to consider proposals for the future redevelopment of this area until the Cambridge Road improvement scheme is carried out"*. In 1967–69 detail was worked up for three segments: first a central one – council housing accessed mainly from Purwell Lane plus a school; next a southern area and finally a northern area, both of private housing. Included was a new footbridge to give *"access from the estate to the railway station"*, a new road from Kingswood Avenue to Wymondley Road and through traffic was to be prohibited on the new St Michael's Road until improvements had been made to Cambridge Road.[15]

In 1970 the HUDC approved outline plans for about 240 council houses and flats on 17 ½ acres accessed from Purwell Lane. The council already owned 9 ½ acres, purchased an additional 8 acres from Wimpey and sold its remaining 3 ½ acres within the planned private northern sector of the development to the company. The start was delayed to 1973 for several reasons: by further planning discussions; Wimpey's involvement with *"protracted negotiations which had been necessary for the acquisition of the various landholdings"* (note how the involved medieval pattern of land-holding still had a grip!); and a *"national fuel crisis"*. In June 1973 it was decided to take Poets as the theme for the new street names. The first houses were soon complete on Chaucer Way; Hardy Close followed. The County Council proposed, then abandoned, plans for a mental health unit within the scheme, but did confirm arrangements for Mary Exton primary school which opened in 1976. Meanwhile Wimpey had begun to construct St Michael's Road from Wymondley Road to supersede the track by the Ippollitts Brook as the southern entrance to the Poets; they also developed the first private houses (around Tennyson Avenue) under the label of Chilterns Estate. Further plans were devised in 1975–76 for the area around Keats Way.[16]

By now too, after over fifty years of false starts, railway electrification between King's Cross, Hitchin and Royston was at last in hand. With the demolition of the Benslow Bridge finally approved (being replaced by a footbridge), more of the length of St Michael's Road was needed for access to the railway yards. Its northern portion was, therefore, now completed opening the way for the building of private houses off Cambridge Road. These were marketed as the Cottage Meadow Estate and completed by 1984, including the

Avon
Two Bedroom
Semi Detached
House

Please note that the housetype illustrated overleaf is shown for general guidance only. It may be featured on this estate with varied external materials and architectural treatments particularly when on corner positions, as it is our aim on all developments to enhance the visual appearance and offer purchasers the benefit of new or improved materials. Details of all types are available for your inspection at our estate office.

Ground Floor   **First Floor**

Above: Nos. 14–15 Coleridge Close, two bedroom semi-detached houses, under construction April 1980 being inspected by Kathleen Cook, the author's aunt. (James Cook)

Left: Wimpey sales particulars for Avon two bedroom semi-detached houses on the Cottage Meadow Estate 1979. (Bridget Howlett)

The GN Engineering Yard in 1992 not long before its redevelopment as the Hillview Estate. (David Howlett)

St Michael's Mount Community Centre. This appeared on the triangular site of Railway Cottage which had been demolished in the late 1960s. Four 19th century houses at St Michael's Mount survived to be refurbished at the same time as the land surrounding them was built on by Wimpey to form Burns and Byron Closes. The lane that is today called St Michael's Mount preserves the original line of Cambridge Road before it was diverted below the railway. It also connects to the original Skimpot Lane, which was itself partly realigned by railway construction in 1848–50.[17]

By 1984 St Michael's Road was open throughout, almost seventy years after it was first planned (!) though without the promised Cambridge Road improvements or eastern access to the station. The final portion of the Poets (Gibson Close) was constructed by McLean Homes in 1991. Last of all, between 1996–98, housing appeared on the 1914 railway engineering yard (now redundant) as the Hillview Estate, with its own spine road of Wedgewood Way (incorrectly spelt!), to commemorate Sir Ralph Wedgwood, a Chief General Manager of the LNER. Sadly, suggestions of railway names with closer Hitchin and GNR links were ignored to the frustration of at least some local historians interested in this modest, but far from "soulless", area.

1   William Ransom, "An account of British and Roman remains found in the neighbourhood of Hitchin", *Transactions of the Hertfordshire Natural History Society Vol IV* 1886; K J & T Fitzpatrick-Matthews, *The archaeology of Hitchin from prehistory to the present* (NHM & HHS, 2008) p13

2   See Terry Slater & Nigel Goose ed. *A County of Small Towns. The development of Hertfordshire's urban landscape to 1800* (University of Hertfordshire, 2008) pp188–9

3   H S Merrett, Hitchin Map & Schedule 1818 NHM; The Town, Fields, Hamlets, Roads & Waste 1816, typescript extract 1379/40 NHM; Frederic Seebohm, *The English Village Community* (Longman, 1884 ed) p2; Cyril Moore, *Hertfordshire Windmills & Windmillers* (Windsup, 1999) p90; Hitchin Board of Health OS Plans 1851 HALS; GNR Act 1914 Ch clvi 7 August 1914 Plan Sheet 19 HALS Off Acc 1024

4   See Phil Howard, *Take the Train From Hitchin* (HHS, 2006) and Valerie Taplin & Audrey Stewart, *Two Minutes to the Station* (HHS, 2010); Richard Holton, "The Great Northern Railway at Hitchin", *Hertfordshire Past & Present No 14* 1974 p12;

Janet Walker & Margaret Watson, *A Stroll Around The Old Village of Walsworth* (Privately published 1997), illustrations 6–11

5   See for example 1881 census for Hitchin Urban; Hitchin Directory 1956–57; *Letchworth Citizen*, 22 March 1909

6   R Holton, "The Great Northern Railway at Hitchin", *Hertfordshire Past & Present*, No 14 1974 p28; GNR Way & Works Committee 6 March, 7 November 1913 TNA RAIL 236/64; Ways & Works Committee 27 January 1921 TNA RAIL 783/557; GNR Act 1914 Ch clvi 7 August 1914; Priscilla Douglas & Pauline Humphries, *Discovering Hitchin* (Egon, 1995) pp116–9

7   GNR Ways & Works Committee 6 March 1913 TNA RAIL 236/64

8   GNR Ways & Works Committee 5 March, 23 July, 5 November 1914 TNA RAIL 236/189; Hitchin 1913 Project www.hitchin1913.org.uk using Inland Revenue Valuation Office Field Books (TNA IR 58) and maps (HALS IR1); letter to W O Times 15 May 1913 TNA RAIL 1189/1890; *Great Northern News 153* May/June 2007 p15

9   GNR Landholding Plans Sheet 8 Hatfield to Huntingdon, Haygreen Collection; GNR Ways and Works Committee 8 January 1915 TNA RAIL 236/65; Andrew Everett, *Visionary Pragmatist: Sir Vincent Raven* (Tempus, 2006) p172; GN Electrification Minute 16 October 1923 TNA RAIL 390/265

10 HUDC Housing Committee 24 June, 8 July 1919 HALS; Solicitor to GNR, 25 October 1920 TNA RAIL 783/557; *Hertfordshire Express* 5 March 1921; GNR Board Note 5 April 1921 TNA RAIL 783/557

11 HUDC Housing Committee 22 June, 9 November 1920; 10 February, 16 August 1921; 31 March, 15 September, 24 November 1925 HALS; GNR Ways & Works Committee 6 January 1921 TNA RAIL 236/190; Nigel E Agar, "Homes Fit for Heroes", *Herts Past & Present* Autumn 2013 p3ff

12 HUDC Housing Development & Town Planning Committee 8 March 1927, 12 December 1932, 24 January 1933 HALS; GNR Landholding Plans Sheet 8 Hatfield to Huntingdon, Haygreen Collection; Hitchin Registers of Electors 1922–1923 HALS; Hitchin Town Plan No.2 1926 HALS DE/Ws/P24

13 HUDC Housing Development & Town Planning Committee 10 December, 19 December 1934; Allotments Committee 25 March 1933, HALS; GN Electrification Minute 19 September 1929 TNA RAIL 390/265; HUDC Housing Development & Town Planning Committee 6 March 1950; Public Health & Markets Committee 12 September 1952; Allotments Committee 11 December 1953, HALS; HUDC Development Plan 1951 p25

14 Shilcocks sales particulars 1 November 1949; HUDC Housing Development & Town Planning Committee 10 September 1957, 9 May 1961, Minute 772 1962; General Purposes Committee 6 July, 31 August 1961; Allotments Committee 3 December 1962; Housing Committee 20 November 1962; Highways Committee 14 October 1963 HALS

15 Hitchin Directory 1965; HUDC Housing Committee 9 June 1964, 15 June, 7 September 1965 17 October, 14 November1967; Plans & Licensing Committee 8 April 1969; Housing and Public Health Committee 24 June 1969 HALS

16 HUDC Housing & Public Health Committee 22 December 1970, 22 February, 25 April 1972, 26 June, 28 August, 18 December 1973; Management & Finance Committee 11 January 1971, 8 May 1972, 3 July 1973; Highways Sewerage & Markets Committee 19 June 1973 HALS; Keats Way deeds, N Claydon.

17 John N Young, *Great Northern Suburban* (David & Charles, 1977) p150–9; HUDC General Purposes Committee 19 August 1971 HALS; NHDC Official Opening of the St Michael's Mount Community Centre programme, 8 December 1984; Janet Walker & Margaret Watson, *A Stroll Around The Village of Old Walsworth* illustration 4; H S Merrett, Hitchin: Map & Schedule 1818, NHM; Hitchin Board of Health Plans OS 1851 HALS

Walsworth

11

JANET WALKER

W̱alsworth is a settlement of some antiquity. It sits astride the River Purwell, which rises at Ninesprings and flows through Purwell Mill, across the meadows and Walsworth Common to meet the River Hiz at Grove Mill. The Purwell is a chalk stream, and internationally important: there are only 210 chalk streams in the world, and 160 of those are in England.[1]

The name Walsworth is believed to be from the Old English, thought to mean either *"the settlement of the Welsh"* or perhaps *"the settlement of Wealh"* (a personal name). For centuries it was little more than a rural hamlet on the outskirts of Hitchin; but its position on Cambridge Road (the A505), the coming of the railway in the 1850s, expansion and population growth changed all that.

Walsworth School was built on the British Schools model in 1852 by Mary and William Exton, on ground given by Mr William Wilshere; other local people contributed funds. Mary was the daughter of John Ransom who built Grove Mill House which stood adjoining Grove Mill. Sadly, William died before the project was completed, but Mary and the other subscribers saw it through.

Nineteen children attended on the first day, and it remained in use as a school until 1957; it subsequently became Walsworth Community Centre, the role it fills today. The playground at the rear of the school is still there. Nellie Smith, born in 1909, recalled

A postcard view of Walsworth c.1908, with local schoolchildren on the bridge over the Purwell to Walsworth Common. On the right is the Sailor Boy; further down is the Thatched Shop and Walsworth School. The buildings in between ("the Side-on House" and Titmuss Cottage) have been demolished. (Janet Walker)

that the school was divided into three rooms, each with a coal fire. The school bell was rung in the street by a favoured pupil to announce the start of the school day, which was from 9am–4pm (earlier in winter). Two hours for lunch! The School Log Book from the early days reflects the rural nature of Walsworth:

September 9, 1878: School open today. Very poor attendance owing to the fact that gleaning is not nearly over. All the elder children still being employed in the harvest fields.

July 28, 1893: Closed school for harvest holidays about a fortnight earlier than in previous years because the gleaning has commenced.

Gleaning is the practice of collecting leftover crops from fields after they have been commercially harvested. Other entries from the logbooks are impossible to omit, they are so interesting:

October 22, 1917: The Children very much upset on account of the Air raid and the dropping of bombs in the village on Friday night. Several panes of glass in the School windows were smashed.

March 22 1918: The children were very much disturbed at their lessons; because of the number of Aeroplanes passing over the School.

It isn't clear exactly where the bombs landed. There was a Zeppelin raid on the night of 19–20 October 1917, as recorded in the diary of

The plaque that now graces the front of the building. (Simon Walker)

Walsworth School/ Community Centre. Still a popular venue for clubs and parties. (Simon Walker)

the Hitchin South Signal Box: *"Air raid by Zeppelins. Bombs dropped on Walsworth."*[2] The late Fred Swadling remembered that *"two bombs fell on a field on the left side of Highover Way."* Fred was under the impression that this was at about 9pm one night in October 1916, but he was only eight years old at the time. Two more bombs fell in what was then a field between what is now Purwell Lane and Desborough Road, opposite the cottages in Willian Road, breaking windows and slates of the cottages. *"After the mess was cleared up in the field and on the following Sunday, there was someone with a money box collecting subscriptions for the hospital from anyone visiting the field to see the craters where the bombs had dropped."*

In 1894, at his own expense, the Reverend George Bernard Gainsford built St Faith's Church, transforming Walsworth from hamlet into a village in the process. The church remained in the possession of the Gainsford family until 1931, when it was passed to the Church of England.

As Hitchin grew, Walsworth was absorbed, and its rural status and nature was eroded; it became part of Hitchin Urban District in 1921; and in the 1930s HUDC built social housing on the land opposite Walsworth Common, and began using the Common itself as a rubbish tip.

During the Second World War, Orchard Road saw the only fatality due to direct enemy action in Hitchin, when Miriam Simms (née Pepper) was killed with her unborn child by a German bomb on 12 August 1941. Another bomb damaged the bridge over the river next to the Ship (now renamed the Millstream), but repairs were possible without closing the road completely. The old bridge still exists beneath the latest iteration.

The house in Orchard Road in which Miriam Pepper lost her life. (*Hitchin Pictorial*, NHM)

Osbourne's bakery.
Mr W E Osbourne
is the bearded
gentleman in front of
the railings.
(Evelyn Osbourne)

Also in Orchard Road was William Everit Osbourne's Hygienic Bakery. It was built in 1908 to meet the needs of local people. It was still in operation until at least the 1960s, and the building still stands, retaining much of its character, though it has been converted to apartments and renamed 'Baker's Mews'.

After the War there was further development. There was more housing, on both sides of Cambridge Road: the Purwell and Highover estates, and Purwell and Highover Schools. In 1964 the dump on the Common was closed and levelled, and covered with topsoil, returning it to a more pleasing appearance.

Near to the former Sailor Boy pub stands what is now the only thatched house remaining in Hitchin, coincidentally itself once a public house – the Red Cow. It was later a shop, locally known

The Thatched Shop
in the winter of
2007, by then a
private house. The
two buildings, though
very different in style,
today form a single
property.
(Simon Walker)

The river Purwell, with the Thatched Shop in the background. The large willow was used by local people, some of whom had very small gardens, to tie their washing lines to; it bore the marks in its bark until the sad day of its collapse. (Richard Whitmore c.1960s)

(unsurprisingly) as the Thatched Shop, but is now a private house. Behind it stands the Long House, which is quite – well, long, and believed to date from the 17th century.

Of the mills of Walsworth, two still stand, both water mills: Purwell Mill, and (most of) Grove Mill. According to one local source, one of the doors now in the Purwell Mill came from the original Angel Vaults public house in Sun Street which was demolished in 1956.

Unsurprisingly, Grove Mill is in Grove Road. It is on an ancient milling site, dating back at least until the 15th century. The current building dates from 1814; it replaced an earlier building, the thatched Shottling, Shooting or Shoting Mill, that had been destroyed by fire following a lightning strike. The new mill came

Purwell Mill in 1915. It looks very much the same today, more than 100 years later. (From a contemporary postcard)

Grove Mill goes up in smoke in 1889. The damage was clearly extensive, but the walls are very thick; the lower storeys survive, with a new roof, to this day. The building now houses Kinder's Mill Day Nursery. (NHM Loftus-Barham Scrapbook)

close to suffering the same fate in 1889, but the lower two storeys were saved by Hitchin Fire Brigade. The building stands today, and is now a day nursery.

Grove Mill was at one time owned by Joshua Ransom, and it was he who, in 1855, took Hitchin Local Board (the equivalent to the district council) to court for discharging sewage into his mill pond, turning it into a cess pool. The ongoing litigation resulted in the Local Board collapsing, leaving the entire Hitchin area without local government for fifteen years.

On Cambridge Road there still stands Walsworth House. It is now part of North Hertfordshire College. It stands to the right as you enter the main gates. It was at one time owned by the Wilsheres, a prominent local family. Like so many old houses, it has been added to and altered many times over the years. Parts of the structure are thought to date from the 16th century – perhaps even earlier – and as a result the building is listed Grade II. The house as we see it today presents a rather higgledy-piggledy appearance, with some sections seemingly out of kilter with others, almost as though several buildings have been cobbled together, which, indeed, they have.

The accommodation of Walsworth House was extensive, with thirteen bedrooms (several allocated to live-in domestic staff), several reception rooms, and an extensive cellar. The gardens ran to some seven acres; there were wide lawns, herbaceous borders, a rose garden, tennis courts, a vegetable garden, a piggery, and a hen-house; and an avenue of substantial beech trees, some of which still stand.

The buildings were refurbished by North Hertfordshire College in the 1990s, and present a similar aspect to their appearance in

Cambridge Road, looking towards Hitchin, in about 1900. Walsworth House is the buttressed building in the centre of the photograph. The buildings on the right were demolished in 1932; those on the left, sometime in the 1950s. (Pat Gadd)

On the left is the Ship, which has now fallen prey to the trend for renaming pubs. It is currently called the Millstream. The Anchor is just visible on the far right, and Walsworth Crossroads is in the distance on the right. Note the pub sign: an ironclad of the late 19th century. (From a contemporary postcard)

their heyday, though the thatched stables and the barns, which once stood near the entrance in Cambridge Road, have sadly disappeared.

Not far from Walsworth House stands the Anchor pub. It dates from at least 1736, and has been considerably altered; but the building retains much of its character. More recent is the Ship, which has also been much changed. The earliest reference for these premises we have is 1769, though that building was later demolished. The current building has been remodelled and extended several times.

Incidentally, there is an enduring myth about the public houses in Walsworth: it is said that their nautical names – the Anchor, the Ship and the Sailor Boy (sadly damaged by fire in May 2015) – were

so named because there had once been a canal that ran all the way from the River Ivel to Grove Mill. This is quite untrue; whilst such a canal was at one time planned, it never got further than Shefford in Bedfordshire.[3] In fact, nautical names for pubs are common in the UK – there are more than 250 "Ships" alone.

Some Walsworth Plaques

A date plaque on cottages in Woolgrove Road, built for Mr Arthur Witney Watson in 1886. Arthur owned several properties in Cambridge and Woolgrove Roads. (Janet Walker)

Wootton Terrace in Woolgrove Road was built for Ernest John Webster in 1906. (Janet Walker)

Florizel Terrace in Cambridge Road. Built by Arthur Whitney Watson, it was named after an 18th century thoroughbred racehorse, one of whose descendants won a race, the winnings of which paid for the project. The plaque is partially obscured by ivy now – this picture was taken almost twenty years ago. (Janet Walker)

Cleveland Terrace, Woolgrove Road. ABNB stands for Alan Bernard Nigel Bridges, who built at least six houses in Walsworth in the late 19th – early 20th centuries. He was a general builder and repairer. His son Bernard sold paint and building supplies from the old building next to the river; it later became the Hitchin Garage, and has now been demolished, and a house built on the site. (Janet Walker)

1   https://en.wikipedia.org/wiki/Chalk_stream accessed 31 December 2016
2   Derek Talbot, *A Diary of Events as Recorded at Hitchin South Signal Box Between 1st January 1906 and 22nd September 1968* (2nd edition Great Northern Railway Society, 2017)
3   TNA LR3/27 31 Oct 1770; www.canalroutes.net/Ivel-River.html accessed 31 December 2016

Highover and Farming in Walsworth

12

BRIDGET HOWLETT AND JANET WALKER

Highover may well be an older settlement than Walsworth itself and certainly was at one time more important. Records of the Manor of Hitchin for the late 15th and early 16th centuries contain several references to the fields and houses at Highover as well as to land and houses at "*Waltonsforth*" (Walsworth). How "*Waltonsforth*" squares with the accepted derivation of the name Walsworth as originating from the Old English, thought to mean either the settlement of the Welsh or the settlement of Wealh, is unknown. Other farms included Walsworth Old Farm and Allwoods Farm; there were others.

History of Highover

The name "Highover", probably meaning "*The high bank or slope*" was first recorded between 1287–1294[1] and aptly describes its situation part way up the steep slope rising from the River Purwell and Walsworth Common towards Wilbury Hill and Letchworth. The present farmhouse is a timber framed building probably dating from the 16th or 17th century re-fronted with brick in about the 1780s and altered and extended in the 19th and early 20th

Walsworth Old Farm, 1875. A watercolour by Samuel Lucas. The farm stood opposite Walsworth Common. It appears on every map after 1767 as either Walsworth Farm or Walsworth Old Farm. (Photographed by Janet Walker).

centuries. Adjacent are barns, one of which contains timber-work dating from the late 16th or early 17th century.[2]

A deed of 1438 records the sale by John Poydras of Almshoe of tenements, lands, pastures and meadows with hedges and ditches in the hamlet of Highover. They were bought by John Pulter and Nicholas Mattok of Hitchin and Thomas Pulter, a canon of St Paul's Cathedral, thus beginning three centuries of ownership by the Pulter family.[3] The fields of Highover rather than the fields of Walsworth are mentioned in the accounts of the manor of Hitchin for 1460. In addition to John Pulter's property, payments for a messuage and a cottage at Highover are listed.[4] In 1556 Edward Pulter owned the farm called Highover with 20 acres of land for which he paid the lord of the manor 4 shillings and 2 pounds of pepper a year. He also held a copyhold tenement at Highover with land attached which John Pulter had bought in 1474. This cottage and its land had by 1676 been absorbed into Highover Farm.[5] It is possible that most of the medieval inhabitants of Highover had gradually moved down the hill to the edge of Walsworth Common. Other Hertfordshire examples are known of settlements moving to sites next to commons where there was easy access to pasture and, in case of Walsworth, abundant water.[6]

An inquisition post mortem for 1488 called Highover a manor, but this may just reflect the Pulter family, who were wealthy wool merchants from Hitchin, seeking to enhance their status.[7] They did not live at Highover; for much of the 15th and early 16th century they resided in the Parsonage House in Hitchin (now the site of Churchgate) which they leased from Elstow Abbey.[8] Edward Pulter, who inherited his father's estate in 1549, moved to Delamere House in Great Wymondley. His son, another Edward, bought the manors of Cottered and Broadfield in the 1580s and took up residence in Broadfield. Edward's grandson, Arthur Pulter, squire of Broadfield, owned Highover in 1676 as well as much other land in Walsworth.[9] In 1690 Martha, the widow of his grandson and heir, James Forester, leased Highover farmhouse with its outhouses,

Above left: Ada Dixon at Walsworth Old Farm, which was demolished in 1948 to make way for the Highover Way Estate. (Janet Walker)

Above right: Allwoods Farm, demolished in 1976, stood at the north-east corner of Walsworth Crossroads. Confusingly this has sometimes been known as Walsworth Farm too. (Janet Walker)

Highover Farmhouse in recent years. (Janet Walker)

The rear of the Farmhouse. (Janet Walker)

Above left: Highover Farm barns. (Janet Walker)

Above right: The farm cottages, built from Arlesey bricks. The bricks of the lower storey are unblemished; those above eye level show the occasional fingerprints from the brickyard workers. (Janet Walker)

barns, stables and 400 acres of land and 36 acres of pasture in the parishes of Hitchin and Great Wymondley to William Maling.[10] In the 1750s Pulter Forester had to sell some of the family's estates.[11] In 1766 his son William sold Highover and his other property in Walsworth to the Reverend Thomas Whitehurst.[12]

Thomas Whitehurst was born in 1733 in London. Though he was ordained, he had no living as a clergyman until 1786, being supported by the property he inherited from his uncle, John Whitehurst, a haberdasher of hats in Hitchin. In 1757 Thomas married an heiress, Sarah, only child of Edward Hitchin, a tanner of Hitchin, who was said to be worth £15,000.[13] As soon as his purchase of the former Pulter estates had made him much the largest landowner in Walsworth, with the support of the other major landowners, he obtained an Act of Parliament to enclose the open fields of Walsworth. Small strips of half an acre or an acre of land were replaced by much larger rectangular fields. Stotfold Road was straightened and diverted from its original course near Highover. On the redrawn map of Walsworth with its new ruler-straight lines, the ancient Highover farm stands out in contrast surrounded by small irregular fields, orchards and ponds. Immediately after

Walsworth was enclosed, Thomas Whitehurst bought more land from smaller owners who would all have had to pay towards the cost of enclosure. His own share was £197 16s 8½d out of a total of £470. He commissioned a surveyor Thomas Bateman to make an attractive map of his estate in Walsworth in 1767 (see page 7).[14]

In 1776 Thomas Whitehurst bought the adjoining manor of Ickleford where he lived in the Manor House (destroyed by fire in 1919). He immediately obtained another Act of Parliament to enclose the open fields and common pasture of Ickleford. This cost him £610 9s.[15] His ambitions outran his means and by the 1780s he was in serious financial difficulties. In 1783 he mortgaged part of his Walsworth estate and in 1786 he mortgaged the rest. Probably in an attempt to improve his finances, in 1786 he became Rector of Colmworth in Bedfordshire. He never lived there, employing curates including his son to perform his clerical duties. In 1788 he sold the manor of Ickleford and moved to London where he had to borrow money from the Hitchin lawyer, William Wilshere, to pay his rent.[16]

In 1791 Mr Christie of Pall Mall auctioned Thomas Whitehurst's Walsworth estate to repay his mortgages and his debts to William Wilshere and other Hitchin residents. The sales particulars described the estate as:

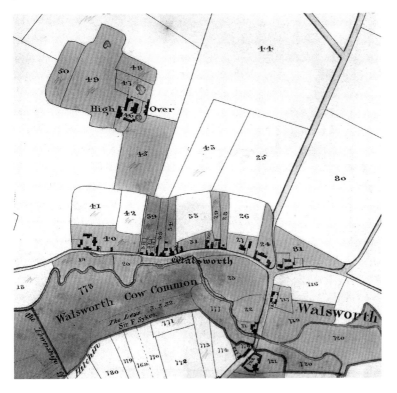

Highover and Walsworth in 1816. (Excerpt from Henry Merrett's copy of map of Walsworth 1818 NHM)

"Three eligible farms" with 605 acres of rich, arable land, meadow and pasture *"in a beautiful and Sporting Part of the Country within One Mile of Hitchin (being one of the first Markets in the Kingdom)"* and *"near a navigable River, which is expected to be continued through Part of the Estate"*. Highover was described as *"the principal Farm House, situate on a pleasant Eminence, and commanding a charming view of the Town of Hitchin"* which has *"been lately rebuilt, and is capable at a small Expense, of being converted into a Gentlemanlike Residence"*.

Highover farm with 319 acres was leased to John Pettengell who paid £200 a year rent.[17]

The purchaser of Thomas Whitehurst's Walsworth estate was Sir John Henniker of Stratford, Essex, a successful London merchant importing timber, leather and furs from Russia and supplying masts to the Royal Navy.[18] After his death in 1803 his Walsworth property was eventually inherited by his grandson, Sir Francis Sykes, whose other grandfather, also called Sir Francis Sykes, had made his fortune in India and built a Palladian mansion at Basildon Park in Berkshire. By 1816 Highover was farmed by Thomas Hailey who married Elizabeth Wilshere, niece of William Wilshere.

Sir Francis Sykes, like previous owners of Highover, was heavily indebted and in 1822 he sold Highover and another farm to William Wilshere. He sold the third farm (later Walsworth House) to William's brother John. In 1838 Sir Francis was forced to sell Basildon Park (which is now owned by the National Trust).[19] The Wilshere family were to retain ownership of Highover and a substantial part of Walsworth for over a hundred years.

A report on Mr Wilshere's land at Walsworth in 1861 stated that *"the Highover Farm has a very fair Homestead and a good House which is conveniently placed, but the land although of good quality has been very much neglected"*.[20] The following year Highover Farm (now with 420 acres) was let to Richard Pedder who was born in about 1817 in Welwyn. His wife, Charlotte, 25 years younger than him, came from Hitchin. In 1881 Richard farmed 422 acres and employed 14 men and 10 boys. Two female servants lived in the house. By the time of his death in 1898, he had retired to 18 Walsworth Road, Hitchin. He is commemorated by a window in the nearby Holy Saviour Church.[21] By 1913 the tenant of Highover was A W Edwards.[22]

More Recent History of Highover

Albert Edwards held the farm between 1902 and sometime in the 1930s. In that time Walsworth villagers played cricket up at Highover, and greyhound racing took place on Saturdays in a field that came to be known as Greyhound Meadows.

Edwards was not shy of an opportunity to publicise his name. This living wagon would have been used by the ploughing team and was, it seems, a chance not to be missed. Unfortunately neither the exact date nor the name of the young man is known. Behind him is what seems to be a portable forge and an anvil. The bicycles date from the first quarter of the 20th century. (Image from the archive of late Malcom Handscombe)

Edwards bought all the latest equipment, and advertised its availability, presumably to defray the cost of the investment. There were at least three other big ploughing contractors in the area: Hailey of Great Wymondley, Oliver's of Wandon End and John Patten of Much Hadham. (Image courtesy of Terry Wilson)

STEAM CULTIVATION

A. W. EDWARDS

Highover Farm, HITCHIN

BEGS TO ANNOUNCE that he has just purchased from John Fowler & Co. a set of their very Latest

Compound Cultivating Tackle

14 H.-P. Compound Engines
6-Furrow Anti-Balance Plough
13-Tine Cultivator
15ft. Turning Harrow, &c.

which will be the most up-to-date tackle in the district and ensure the greatest economy in fuel and water. He will be pleased to quote terms to all Landowners and Farmers who are interested upon application being made to above address.

Edwards was clearly keen to develop his business, advertising the hire of his steam cultivation equipment, as well as horse riding lessons: an advertisement in the Pictorial in March 1930 offered *"Expert tuition for children, on quiet ponies; hunters and hacks for ladies and gentlemen. Ten minutes from station. Trains met. Terms on application to A W Edwards, Highover, Hitchin."*

After 1920, however, Hitchin's population continued to grow. By the 1930s the Chennells family had taken over, and council housing was planned for the area around what is now High Dane, encroaching on Highover's land. After 1945 there was more council building off Woolgrove Road and then the private Rosehill and Grovelands estates in the 1960s and 70s. Most recently, in the 1980s, the extension of Highover Way brought suburbia right up to the gates of the farm; and the latest proposals at the very least seem likely to surround the farm buildings themselves. At the time of writing the Chennells family is still in occupation. The well-preserved late 16th or early 17th century threshing barn has been listed Grade II.

1 J E B Gover, A Mawer, and F M Stenton, *The Place Names of Hertfordshire* (1938) p 10
2 HALS 58488 Sales Particulars 1791; www.historicengland.org.uk/listing/the-list/list-entry/1452743
3 HALS 58331
4 TNA SC6/870/4
5 TNA E315/391; HALS 58314; Bridget Howlett ed, *Survey of the Royal Manor of Hitchin* (Hertfordshire Record Society, 2000) pp107–108
6 Anne Rowe and Tom Williamson *Hertfordshire a landscape history* (University of Hertfordshire, 2013) pp 40–42
7 *Calendar of Inquisitions Post Mortem C. Series II vol 3 (74)*
8 Trinity College Cambridge 42 Hitchin 2–3; TNA PROB2/17 John Pulter's probate inventory 1487
9 Noel Farris, *The Wymondleys* (Hertfordshire Publications 1989) pp238–242, 250; Howlett ed, *Survey of the Royal Manor of Hitchin,* pp107–108
10 HALS 58352
11 Farris, *The Wymondleys* p244
12 HALS 58559–58560
13 Richard Morgan, "The Rev Thomas Whitehurst Rector of Colmworth" *History in Bedfordshire Vol 6 No 2* Spring 2013 consulted online at www.bedfordshire-lha.org.uk/wp-content/uploads/2013/04/HIB-63.pdf
14 HALS 58568, 58882
15 H G Western, *A History of Ickleford* (Privately published 1975) pp30–33
16 HALS 58486–58487; Morgan, "The Rev Thomas Whitehurst"
17 HALS 58488 Sales Particulars 1791
18 HALS 58488; John Henniker-Major, Oxford Dictionary of National Biography; www.discovery.nationalarchives.gov.uk/results/r/7?_ep=John%20Henniker&_dss=range&_ro=any&_p=1700&_st=adv
19 National Trust, *Basildon Park Berkshire* (1991) pp36–39; NHM 1818 copy of 1816 map and schedule of Hitchin; HALS 58666, 58670–58671, 58491
20 HALS 60598
21 HALS 60599; 1881 census; National Probate Index searched at www.gov.uk/search-will-probate
22 HALS IR2/38/3 Valuation Office Survey

Sir Francis Willes and Francis Lovell – from code breaker to landowner

13

BRIDGET HOWLETT

Who was Francis Lovell? And who was Maud Rosalind Lovell? Research into the late 19th and 20th century suburban expansion of Hitchin keeps throwing up references to this family who lived in Brockenhurst in Hampshire. In the 1890s Francis Lovell worked harmoniously with Matthew Foster on the development and sale of his land in Bearton.[1] After the Great War, Miss Lovell's reluctance to sell land in Purwell Field to Hitchin Urban District Council to build "Homes fit for Heroes" helped to delay the development of this area, now part of the Poets Estate, until the 1970s.[2] Francis Lovell also owned land in the Oakfield area and Lovell Close off Passingham Avenue may be named after him.[3] How did this family with no apparent connection with Hitchin acquire all this land which enabled them to influence how and when different areas of the town were developed?

A code breaking bishop

It all began with a code breaking clergyman, the Reverend Edward Willes, who was born in Warwickshire in 1694. While a student in Oxford, he learnt decoding skills from William Blencowe, Queen Anne's decypherer. In 1716 Willes was appointed Decypherer to the Hanoverian King George I who two years earlier had acceded to the throne on the death of his cousin, Queen Anne. Though the first Jacobite rebellion in 1715 had been suppressed, many Jacobite sympathisers in Scotland and England were actively plotting with the rival claimant to the throne, James Francis Edward Stuart, the Old Pretender. Edward Willes's duties, for which he was paid the generous salary of £200 a year, included translating intercepted correspondence as well as decoding encrypted letters. He was fluent in Latin, Spanish, French and Swedish. In 1717 he successfully cracked the code used by the Swedish Prime Minister and his ambassador in London who were plotting with the exiled Jacobite court the invasion of England. His

Edward Willes Bishop of Bath and Wells 1750. Mezzotint by John Faber junior from a portrait by Thomas Hudson. (National Portrait Gallery D4811)

reward was appointment to the valuable Crown living of Barton-le-Clay in Bedfordshire, not far from Hitchin.

Edward Willes married in 1719 and made his home at Barton Rectory where he brought up his family; he had six sons and four daughters. Copies of letters for deciphering were sent to Barton Rectory; special messengers then took his decoded texts to the secretaries of state. From 1719 to 1722 he decoded correspondence between Francis Atterbury, Bishop of Rochester, and the Jacobite court and was chief witness in Atterbury's trial. Further rewards duly followed. His salary was increased to £500 a year and in 1730 he was made Dean of Lincoln. He declined a bishopric until he had trained his eldest son, Edward, to join him as code breaker and share a salary of £1000. In 1743 Edward senior became Bishop of Bath and Wells. His sons William and Francis also joined him in the Deciphering Branch. The French ambassador complained in 1771 that there was in London "*a bishop charged with the decipherment of all the dispatches of foreign ministers who succeeds in finding the key of all ciphers*". He died in 1773 and was buried in Westminster Abbey.[4]

Edward Willes needed to invest his substantial earnings. In 1735 he bought the Lordship of the Manor of Barton. In 1751 he bought a mortgage of land in Walsworth for £1250, though the mortgage was paid off the following year when the land was sold. In 1787 his eldest son, Edward, took over briefly a mortgage of Highover Farm and other property belonging to the heavily indebted Thomas Whitehurst.[5] However it was his youngest son, Francis, who made a major investment in land in Hitchin and Ippollitts.

Sir Francis Willes

Francis, who was born in about 1735, joined his father and brothers in the Deciphering Branch in 1758. In 1772 he wrote:

> "*My present Salary is £300 a year, which I flatter myself will not be thought adequate to a faithful service of about 15 years, during which time I have discovered many & some very difficult Cyphers, attended with infinite Labour & a constant attendance in Town having always endeavoured to deserve that Confidence which has been reposed in me by the strictest secrecy*".[6]

He was appointed to the important post of Under Secretary of State, but in 1775 returned to the Deciphering Branch now with a salary of £700 a year. On his father's death in 1773 Francis inherited £7000. In 1777 he bought a villa on the edge of Hampstead Heath which became his main residence, conveniently close to London for his deciphering work. The following year he married Mary, daughter of Admiral George Clinton.[7]

In 1780, during the American War of Independence, the navy captured a ship carrying a packet of letters from the Marquis de Lafayette to the French government. The letters were thrown overboard, but they were rescued by sailors and deciphered by Francis Willes. Copies of the letters with his transcriptions survive in the British Library. The following year he reminded the Secretary of State, the Earl of Hillsborough, of:

> "the Request, I made some months ago, for some Douceur for decyphering those voluminous letters in Cypher taken on board of a Ship from America, which were sent me from your Lordship's Office, and which being out of the ordinary Line of Business were thought to merit some extraordinary Recompense."[8]

He was indeed rewarded. He was knighted and in 1783 he bought 200 acres of land in Hitchin worth over £220 a year from Thomas Plumer Byde of Ware Park. Thomas Byde had inherited his Hitchin estate from his great grandmother Mary Skynner, only child of John Skynner of Hitchin, who with his brother founded Skynners' Almshouses. Though much of the land was scattered in strips of an acre or less throughout the open fields of Hitchin, his property included Bearton Farm surrounded by small hedged fields.[9]

"Plan of a Farm belonging to the Honourable Sir Francis Willes situate at Bearton" 1787 (W & SA 161/90). The farm on the south side of Bearton Road was let to John Dermer. Other tenants occupied two cottages, one to the east with the Garden Close and the other in Dovehouse Close. By 1816 the whole of Sir Francis' Bearton estate was occupied by Joseph Ransom and the Dovehouse Close cottage had gone.

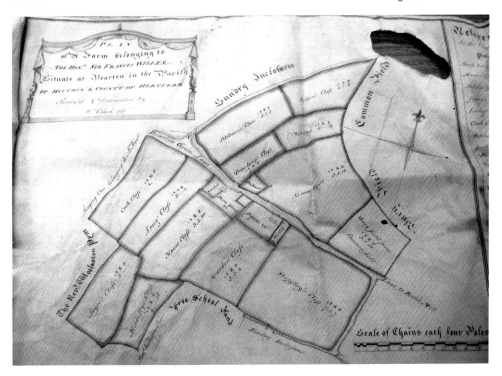

St Ibbs Bush and the Quaker Burial Ground

In 1787 Sir Francis bought two cottages beside London Road in Ippollitts next to the large house called St Ibbs. Sir Francis replaced the cottages with a substantial villa which he called St Ibbs Bush. He acquired adjoining land to create a park like garden of about 9 acres with "*extensive walks enclosed with holly and quick hedge which have been made with infinite labour and trouble*".[10] In 1820 he bought from the trustees of the Hitchin Quakers their original burial ground for £40. This had been established in 1694 on a small piece of land next to London Road immediately to the south of where Sir Francis Willes' new villa now stood. By 1820:

> "*the said piece or parcel of ground hath not for many years been used as a place for burial and by reason that the Society of Quakers have a more convenient spot now in use for that purpose*".

This was the Society of Friends Burial Ground on the corner of Bedford Road and Paynes Park in Hitchin. Sir Francis covenanted that he and his heirs

Excerpt from the Ippollitts Enclosure Map 1816. St Ibbs Bush is 292 and 293 next to the Society of Friends Burial Ground. The Turnpike Road is London Road. (HALS QS/E/45)

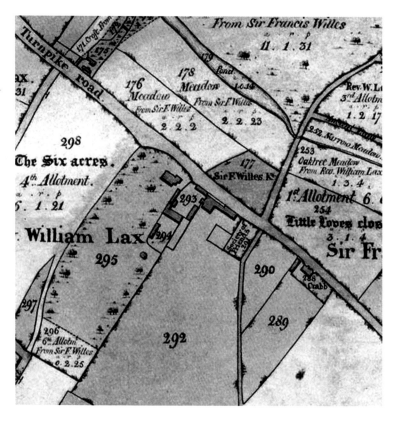

*"shall not and will not wilfully disturb the bones or remains of any
of the bodies interred in the said piece of ground or suffer such bones
or remains to be molested or disturbed".*[11]

The ownership of much of the land in the parish of Ippollitts was
reallocated amongst the existing owners by an enclosure act in
1816. Sir Francis Willes now owned 168½ acres in the parish in two
compact blocks. One was south and west of St Ibbs Bush where he
built a new farmhouse and buildings, St Ibbs Farm. The other was
Home Farm in Preston.[12]

Sir Francis and the Wilshere Family

When opportunity arose, Sir Francis continued to buy or exchange
land in Hitchin and in the neighbouring parishes of Ippollitts,
Ickleford, Pirton and Shillington. In 1807 he purchased the manor
of Biggleswade for £2,180. By 1816 his 210 acres made him the
second biggest individual landowner in Hitchin (excluding
Walsworth), the largest landowner being Emilius Delmé-Radcliffe
of Hitchin Priory with 315 acres. However the combined holdings
of the three Wilshere brothers, William, Thomas and John, were
much greater at about 400 acres.[13]

Sir Francis was still employed in code breaking assisted by his
nephew, Francis Willes, as well as in devising:

*"the sort of Numerical Cyphers which we make use of at the Office,
[which] are of that copious and difficult nature, that no one for a
great length of time (if at all) can possibly make the Discovery".*[14]

This necessitated spending much of his time either in London or
Hampstead. His estates in and around Hitchin were managed for
him by William Wilshere senior, while legal matters were dealt
with by William's son William, the lawyer. Another son, Thomas,
took over the estate management from his father. He and a third
brother John leased much of Sir Francis' Hitchin land, most of
the rest including Bearton Farm being let to the Ransom family.
Thomas named his youngest son who was born in 1814 Charles
Willes Wilshere.[15]

Francis Frederick Lovell

Sir Francis Willes' wife died in 1813 and they had no children.
When he died in 1827, he was buried with his wife and parents
in Westminster Abbey. According to his epitaph, he *"served with
great zeal and integrity in the secret department of the Foreign Office
for a period of 70 years".*[16] He left most of his estates to his great
nephew and godson, Francis Frederick Lovell, who was only six

Francis Frederick
Lovell, Master of
the New Forest
Staghounds
(1883–1893).
Engraving [1888].
(New Forest Centre
LYNHNF 2014.112)

years old. He was the youngest son of
his niece Charlotte and her husband,
Peter Harvey Lovell who owned an
estate at Cole Park near Malmesbury in
Wiltshire. A wise choice of godfather!
Numerous bequests to family, friends
and servants included £50 to Mr
Thomas Wilshere esq. of Hitchin,
and £10 to his gardener at Ippollitts,
William Peacock. Sir Francis wanted his
heir to change his name to Willes and to
come to live at St Ibbs Bush supported
by an estate augmented by purchases
of additional land in Hertfordshire and
Bedfordshire during his minority.[17]

None of this happened. Francis
Frederick Lovell did not change his
name. In 1844 he owned slightly less
land in Hitchin than his great uncle had
owned in 1816. In the late 1840s some
of his land was compulsorily purchased
by the Great Northern Railway Company, including Windmill
Piece on the south east side of Cambridge Road which became the
site of the station. Rather than following his Willes relatives into
the Church or the Deciphering Branch, at the age of 18 in 1839,
Francis was purchased a commission as a cornet and sub-lieutenant
in the 1st Life Guards, a most prestigious regiment. In 1841 he
was lodging in Westminster while St Ibbs Bush was occupied by
his brother, the Reverend William Lovell, who had joined the
Deciphering Branch, and a cousin, William Willes. In December
1842, now aged 21, Francis bought promotion to lieutenant.[18]

"A gallant one-armed soldier" and the Duke's daughter

In 1846 Francis attended a ball where he fell in love with the
seventeen year old daughter of the Duke of Beaufort, Lady Rose
Caroline Mary Somerset. Although the Duke was burdened with
eight daughters and was tottering on the verge of bankruptcy,
Francis was not considered an eligible suitor. Taking advantage of
the speed and convenience of the new railways, the young couple
eloped to Gretna Green where they were married on 4 October.
Their families accepted what they had done and they were swiftly
married again on 11 October at Wroughton Parish Church in
Wiltshire. Francis' brother John Harvey Lovell and his wife, who
lived at Wroughton House, witnessed the marriage. The ceremony
was solemnised by the Rector of Badminton where the Duke of

Beaufort had his principal residence. Francis sold his commission and retired from the army. Their marriage was obviously approved in the highest circles as in 1851, dancing in a French quadrille at Queen Victoria's Restoration Ball, was:

> "Lady Rose Lovell, the young daughter of the Duke of Beaufort, whose elopement at the age of seventeen with a gallant one-armed soldier had been condoned, so that she still played her part in the Court gala".

How and when Francis lost his arm is not known.[19]

Marriage settlements were drawn up in July 1847 nine months after their wedding. All Francis' lands in Hertfordshire and Bedfordshire were vested in trustees for the benefit of himself and his wife (who was to be paid £300 a year from their rents) and their male heirs. In 1873 Francis was reported to own 562 acres in Hertfordshire with an annual rental of £945 7s. He had sold his great uncle's valuable property in Hampstead. This was not really adequate to support a comfortable life as a country gentleman. For instance, Frederick Peter Delmé-Radcliffe of Hitchin Priory owned 3,760 acres in Hertfordshire and Bedfordshire with an annual rental of £5,800 while Charles Willes Wilshere of The Frythe at Welwyn owned 3,342 acres in Hertfordshire and Bedfordshire worth £6,339 a year. Fortunately for Francis and Lady Rose, £20,000 was also settled on them and their children; invested in government securities this would have produced another £800 to £1,000 a year making their combined income more than sufficient for a country squire. Judging by the style in which they lived, they may have had further sources of income.[20]

Life at Hincheslea

Just before his elopement, on 1 September 1846 Francis had leased St Ibbs Bush for seven years to Mrs Fanny Hale, a widow. In 1847 Francis and Lady Rose bought a much larger Georgian house at Hincheslea, near Brockenhurst in the New Forest, surrounded by 86 acres of park land. A son was born in 1848 followed by four daughters. Francis became a Justice of the Peace for Hampshire. Despite his loss of an arm, he served as Master of the New Forest Deerhounds, and during a French invasion scare in 1860, as a captain in the Hampshire Rifle Volunteers. In 1871 the Lovells employed a Swiss governess for the older girls, a nurse for the baby, a cook, a lady's maid, six female servants, a butler, one male servant, two grooms and a gardener.[21]

Their only son, Francis Henry Lovell, at the age of 18 was purchased a commission as an ensign and lieutenant in the

Hincheslea House near Brockenhurst. Oil painting by James Chalmers 1852. (New Forest Centre LYNHNF 2014.111)

Coldstream Guards in April 1867. In November 1868 he retired from the regiment, only to be purchased a commission the following month as an ensign in the 29th Foot Regiment. He was promoted to be lieutenant in 1871, but retired from the army in June 1876.[22] The same year his parents sold St Ibbs Bush including the former Quaker burial ground for £2,840 15s to Mrs Margaret Amos, the owner of the neighbouring house, St Ibbs. They also sold in the 1870s four acres called Fox Holes next to Pirton Road in Hitchin, which became part of the site of William Tindall Lucas's house called Foxholes.[23] If these sales raised money to establish Francis Henry in an alternative career, what this was is unknown. The only other reference to him which has been found is a report in *The Hampshire Advertiser* of his death from pleurisy aged 35 in December 1883 at Avrenches in Switzerland. He is not commemorated with other members of his family in St Luke's Church at Sway, the nearest church to Hincheslea. His mother, Lady Rose, died 15 months later in March 1885. Francis Frederick Lovell continued to live at Hincheslea with his daughters, Maud and Helen. His eldest daughter Edith Rose Alma had married Charles King Francis in 1880. His third daughter Rosalind Ida married her cousin, Peter Audley Arthur David Lovell, in 1890.[24]

Building Plots at Bearton

Agriculture had prospered during the 1850s and 1860s, but from the mid 1870s a run of bad harvests combined with cheap imports of grain from the North American prairies and of chilled and frozen meat from Argentina, the United States, Australia and New Zealand led to a prolonged agricultural depression. In 1878 Francis Lovell's tenant at St Ibbs Farm, William Lake, was forced by debt to give up his tenancy and sell all his farm stock. He disappeared from home and committed suicide. Farmers and landowners hoped at first that conditions would improve. In 1884 Francis Lovell's trustees bought on his behalf for £1,375 Pond Farm at Preston next to land he already owned. But by the mid 1880s several Hertfordshire farmers had become bankrupt and landowners had to drastically reduce rents to enable tenants to survive or to find new tenants when farms became vacant.[25]

Fortunately for Francis Lovell he owned a compact block of 53 acres on both sides of Bearton Road which was now ripe for suburban development. The deaths of his wife and son had left him since 1885 the sole beneficiary of his marriage settlement and made selling land more straightforward. Though his tenant John Ransom had established a brickfield on the site of the ancient Bearton Farm in the 1840s, by 1861 this has been replaced by brickworks in

Bearton in 1851. Sir Francis Willes' farm and cottages have been replaced by John Ransom's brickworks. Another brickworks next to Bedford Road was owned by Joshua Ransom opposite a new Bearton Farm. (Excerpt from HALS Hitchin Board of Health OS map 1851 2 feet to 1 mile sheet II)

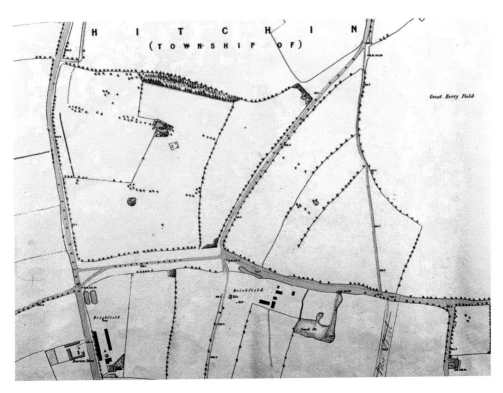

St John's Road. In the late 1890s Francis Lovell auctioned building plots in Bearton and Ickleford Roads and in the newly made up York and Lancaster Roads. In 1906 his field at the top of Benslow Lane became the site of the convalescent home of the German Hospital (now Pinehill Hospital), but most of his property was still too far from the town centre for development. He was able to sell small strips of land to Alfred Ransom and to the Lucas family to allow

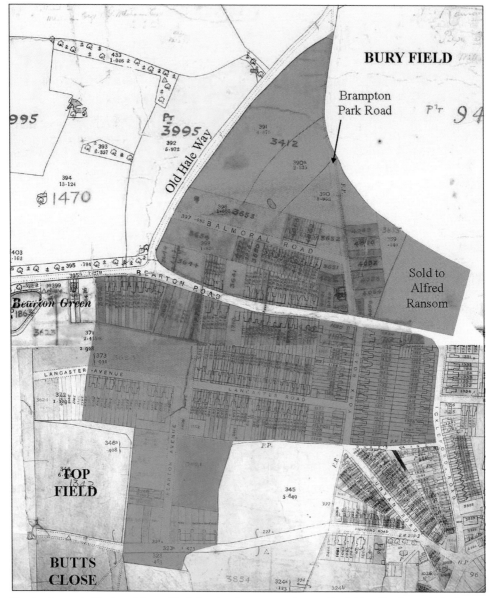

The development of the Lovell Estate (shaded red) at Bearton superimposed by Bridget Howlett and John Lucas on excerpts from 1898 OS maps amended by the Valuation Office c.1915. (HALS IR1/75a & IR1/90b)

them to consolidate their agricultural holdings in Bury Field and at Oughtonhead Farm respectively.[26]

Miss Maud Rosalind Lovell

Francis Lovell died on 1 August 1906 aged 85. He left the bulk of his property, valued at £27,835, to his unmarried daughter, Maud Rosalind. His youngest daughter Helen had died in 1904. His sales of building land must have enriched him as his estate was very similar in value to that of Charles Willes Wilshere, who also died in 1906 (£28,218), and Francis Augustus Delmé-Radcliffe of Hitchin Priory, who died in 1916 worth £27,283. Maud Lovell may have needed to raise money to pay death duties and her father's legacies to her married sisters as she quickly sold the remaining land at Bearton in large blocks. This transferred to the purchasers the responsibility of making up new roads and sewers and then either selling the individual plots or building houses themselves.[27] Chapter 14 "Fine Dry Plots" describes what happened when she sold the Brampton Park Estate. She sold her land between Fishponds Road and Bearton Road, to William Onslow Times, local solicitor and clerk to Hitchin Urban District Council, who with an additional field to the west, developed it as the Fishponds Estate. He laid out Bearton and Lancaster Avenues and built a pair of traditional style houses in Bearton Avenue (nos. 3–5) as well as eight Arts and Crafts style semi-detached and detached houses in Fishponds Road (nos. 50–64). Local builder James Knight constructed three houses at the other end of Bearton Avenue before building was brought to a halt by the outbreak of war in 1914.[28]

Miss Lovell continued to live at Hincheslea. In 1911 aged 50 she was attended by her lady's maid, Sarah Heath, who had been with her for over 20 years, her butler, Robert Bannister, who was to stay in her service until her death, a cook, four maids, a footman,

Arts and Crafts style houses in Fishponds Road built by William Onslow Times 1909–1915 on part of the Lovell Estate. (Alan Fleck 2018)

The Last Harvest Home 1972 before construction of the Poets Estate began. Coleridge Close now stands on this site. Bob Worbey on the combine, Jack Worbey driving the tractor, with his grandchildren, Andrew and Frances Hussey, and two other children on the trailer. Trees lining the River Purwell and the Purwell Estate can be seen in the distance. (Janice Hussey)

and two grooms.[29] After all the sales of land she still owned about 80 acres in Hitchin mostly in Purwell Field, about half of it farmed by Samuel Wallace. She also owned Wellingham Piece on the west side of Bedford Road and part of the brickworks in St John's Road. In the early 1920s when Hitchin Urban District Council wanted to buy some of her land in Purwell Field for council housing, as described in Chapter 10, she initially refused. However in 1925 she changed her mind (too late for the St Michael's Mount scheme) and also offered to sell the Council the site of former brickworks in St John's Road provided that the land was kept open as a playing field. HUDC persuaded her to withdraw her condition, but the land has indeed been used for recreational purposes. In 1937 her London agent queried the density of housing proposed for some of her land in the Hitchin Town Plan, but ultimately accepted the plan.[30]

Lovell Family Memorial in St Luke's Church, Sway, near Hincheslea. Maud Rosalind Lovell is buried in the churchyard with her parents and sister. (Richard Reeves 2017)

To the Beloved Memory of
FRANCIS FREDERIC LOVELL
OF HINCHESLEA (AND FORMERLY OF
THE 1ST LIFE GUARDS)
4TH SON OF P.H. LOVELL OF COLE PARK,
MALMESBURY, WILTSHIRE.
BORN MARCH 4TH 1821, DIED AUG: 1ST 1906.

ALSO TO THE MEMORY OF
THE LADY ROSE C·M·LOVELL
(6TH DAUGHTER OF
HENRY 7TH DUKE OF BEAUFORT)
WHO DIED AT HINCHESLEA MARCH 12TH 1885
WIFE OF THE ABOVE.

ALSO TO THE MEMORY OF
HELEN ROSE LOVELL
BORN OCT: 16TH 1868, DIED FEB: 22ND 1904,
4TH DAUGHTER OF THE ABOVE.

"Blessed be the Lord God of Israel
for He hath visited, and redeemed His people."

The end of the Lovell Lands

Miss Lovell died at Hincheslea in 1941 leaving her estate to her widowed sister, Rosalind Ida Lovell. When Rosalind died in 1946 at the Lovell family home, Cole Park near Malmesbury, she directed that all her property should be sold and the proceeds invested for the benefit of her great nephew, Alec David Charles Francis. Private house building resumed after the war and the suburban expansion of Hitchin absorbed the former Lovell lands. Wellingham Avenue was built on Wellingham Piece in the late 1950s.

Fields on either side of Wymondley Road were developed as part of the Oakfield Estate in the 1950s and Wymondley Park Estate (Halsey Drive) in the 1970s. Finally the land at Purwell, which Miss Lovell was reluctant to sell in 1920, became part of the Poets Estate in the 1970s and 1980s.[31]

Hincheslea House burnt down in 1978, Sir Francis Willes' house at Hampstead "Heathlands" was destroyed by a land mine in 1941, but St Ibbs Bush still stands.[32] The only obvious memorial in Hitchin to Francis Frederick Lovell is the street name, Lovell Close, which ironically does not stand on land once owned by the Lovells.

I am most grateful to Chris Finch, Richard Reeves, Dr Katharine Walker, Alec Coutts, and the New Forest Centre for their help in researching the Lovell family at Hincheslea.

1   See Chapter 14 "Fine Dry Plots for Better Class Houses": the Brampton Park Estate.
2   Nigel Agar, "'Homes fit for Heroes' – the Hertfordshire experience", *Herts Past & Present* 3rd series no 22 Autumn 2013; see also Chapter 10 St Michael's Mount and the Poets Area.
3   See Oakfield Estate sales particulars p 62 ; Barry West, *The Street Names of Hitchin and Their Origins. Book 2: Eastern Hitchin* (HHS 1998) pp26,53
4   W Marshall, "Willes, Edward", *Oxford Dictionary of National Biography;* W Gibson, 'An eighteenth-century paradox: the career of the decipherer-bishop, Edward Willes', *British Journal for Eighteenth-Century Studies,* 12 (1989), pp69–76; David Kahn, *The Codebreakers. The Story of Secret Writing* (Scribner, New York, 1967, 1996) pp170–171, 174
5   *Victoria History of Bedfordshire* Vol 2 www.british-history.ac.uk/vch/beds/vol2/ pp308–313; HALS 58505; See Chapter 12 Highover and Farming in Walsworth.
6   BL Add Ms 45519 f5; Kenneth Ellis, *The Post Office in the Eighteenth Century: A Study in Administrative History* (University of Durham, 1958) pp127–131
7   Ellis, *The Post Office in the Eighteenth Century* pp127–131; Bishop Edward Willes' will TNA PROB11/993/84; *Victoria History of Middlesex* Volume 9: Hampstead www.british-history.ac.uk/vch/middx/vol9/pp66–71; www.westminster-abbey.org/our-history/people/willes-family
8   Kahn, *The Codebreakers* pp171, 187; BL Add Ms 24321 ff1–105, f106
9   W&SA 161/57/5; See Chapter 1.
10 Daphne Rance, *The Yeomen of Ippolyts. A country parish before 1800* (Cortney, Ashwell, 1996) pp121–122; Sir Francis Willes' will TNA PROB11/1734/3670
11 Rance, *The Yeomen of Ippolyts,* p122; Copy conveyance 28 June 1820 HALS Acc 6008
12 Daphne Rance, *St Ippolyts. A country parish in the nineteenth century* (Egon, 1987) pp44–45; Ippollitts enclosure award and map HALS QS/E/45; Philip J Wray, *A History of Preston in Hertfordshire* (Privately published 2015) p70; In c.1910 Home Farm was owned by Maud R Lovell HALS IR2/44/1
13 'Parishes: Biggleswade with Stratton and Holme', in *Victoria History of the County of Bedford: Volume 2,* ed. William Page (London, 1908), pp 209–215. *British History Online* www.british-history.ac.uk/vch/beds/vol2/pp209–215; HALS D/ P53/29/7
14 BL Add Ms 45519 ff103–105
15 W&SA 161/57/5, 161/70, 161/125; HALS DP/53/29/7; Maya Pieris, *Take 6 Carrots, 4 Heads of Celery, 8 Large Onions – The Receipts of a Hertfordshire Family* (HHS, 1994) p22

16 www.westminster-abbey.org/our-history/people/willes-family

17 Sir Francis Willes' will TNA PROB11/1734/3670

18 Hitchin tithe apportionment 1841 HALS DSA4/53/1; *London Gazette* 16 August 1839; 1841 census; *London Gazette* 30 December 1842

19 *Burke's Peerage and Baronetage* (1915) p216; "Some Famous Elopements." *The Strand Magazine*, 1907, 270. http://books.google.com/books?id=35MkAQAAIAAJ&q=lovell#v=snippet&q=lovell&f=false

F M L Thompson, *English Landed Society in the Nineteenth Century* (Routledge 1963, paperback reprint 1980) p286; GRO marriage certificate; 1851 census; *Edinburgh Gazette* 27 April 1847; Tytler, Sarah. "The Queen's Restoration Ball and the Guildhall Ball." In Life of Her Most Gracious Majesty the Queen – Volume 2. www.gutenberg.org/cache/epub/7086/pg7086.html;

20 Abstract of title to St Ibbs Bush 1876 HALS Acc 6008; *The New Domesday Book of Hertfordshire compiled from the Official Return of Owners of Land 1873* (Simson, Hertford, c.1873) pp99, 48, 63; Francis Frederic Lovell's will proved 4 Oct 1906; e.g. sale of a 7½ acre field in Hampstead for £4,000 in 1863 LMA E/MW/H/233 p501; See Thompson, *English Landed Society in the Nineteenth Century* pp110–113

21 W&SA 161/36; Gazetteer of New Forest Houses www.catherineglover.org.uk/NFHouses/HOUSE.html?HOUSE=87&MOD=this ; For a description of the park by Hampshire Gardens Trust see http://research.hgt.org.uk/item/hincheslea-house/ *London Gazette* 22 June 1860; 1871 census

22 *Edinburgh Gazette* 5 April 1867; *London Gazette* 24 November 1868, 11 December 1868, 29 December 1871, 16 July 1872, 13 June 1876

23 Conveyance of St Ibbs Bush 1876 HALS Acc 6008; Rance, *St Ippolyts. A country parish in the nineteenth century* pp116–117; Hitchin Tithe apportionment 1841 HALS DSA4/53/1; 1878 OS map 6 inches to 1 mile Herts XII West; *Hitchin Household Almanack 1872–96*

24 *Hampshire Advertiser* 29 December 1883; Lovell memorial in St Luke's Church, Sway, photographed by Richard Reeves; National Probate Index 1890; 1891 & 1901 census; Francis Frederic Lovell's will proved 4 Oct 1906

25 Nigel E Agar, *Behind the Plough. Agrarian Society in nineteenth-century Hertfordshire* (University of Hertfordshire, 2005) pp172–180; Rance, *St Ippolyts. A country parish in the nineteenth century* pp150–152; Wray, *A History of Preston in Hertfordshire* p69; In c.1910 Pond Farm (107 acres) was owned by Maud Lovell and rented to A Brown for £150 pa. See Hitchin 1913 Project www.hitchin1913.org.uk using Inland Revenue Valuation Office Field Books (TNA IR 58) and maps (HALS IR1)

26 Priscilla Douglas & Pauline Humphries, *Discovering Hitchin* (Egon, 1995) pp72, 79–82, 91; Hitchin rate book 1861 HALS Off Acc 1104 Box 5 UN81/4; See Hitchin 1913 www.hitchin1913.org.uk compared with the 1816 map of Hitchin and 1841 tithe apportionment.

27 Francis Frederic Lovell's will proved 4 Oct 1906; National Probate Index

28 See Chapter 14; Douglas & Humphries, *Discovering Hitchin*, p79; Hitchin 1913 www.hitchin1913.org.uk especially plots 4002–4016

29 1891, 1901 & 1911 censuses; Maud Rosalind Lovell's will proved 1941

30 Hitchin 1913 www.hitchin1913.org.uk; See Chapters 4 and 10; HUDC minutes 3 Mar & 17 Mar 1925 HALS ; Correspondence with Frank Newman & Son, Chartered Surveyors 1937 HALS Off Acc 1104 HUDC Box 3

31 Maud Rosalind Lovell's will proved 1941; Rosalind Ida Lovell's will proved 1946; *The Street Names of Hitchin and Their Origins. Book 3: Western Hitchin* (HHS 1999) p44; West, *The Street Names of Hitchin and Their Origins. Book 2: Eastern Hitchin* p53; See Chapter 7

32 Gazetteer of New Forest Houses www.catherineglover.org.uk/NFHouses/HOUSE.html?HOUSE=87&MOD=this

"Fine Dry Plots for Better Class Houses": the Brampton Park Estate

14

PAULINE HUMPHRIES

By 1908, Hitchin's population was nearing 12,000. Building expansion[1] northwards from the town centre had been proceeding steadily from the early 1870s. First to be built were Bunyan Road and Dukes Lane, with Ickleford Road boasting twenty three households by 1871. Lancaster Road and York Road were constructed in the late 1890s, on land previously owned by the Lovell family, and which stretched to the south side of Bearton Road. By the beginning of the 1900s development was beginning here. With the help of Matthew Foster, Agent to the Lovell Estate and a local builder, progress was relatively seamless and any friction between buyers, builders and the Hitchin Urban District Council soon resolved. The fact that Foster was a Councillor himself probably helped! By December 1907 the residents of Bearton Road South achieved their objective and the[2] Council agreed to the *"metalling and steam-rolling of the Roadway"*.

What next? Facing these new houses, which were to stretch up as far as the lane that we now call Old Hale Way, was an uninterrupted vista of trees, hedges and pasture land rolling northwards towards Ickleford. In January 1908 Maud Rosalind Lovell[3] sold *"ten acres of land in the Bearton Road, Ickleford Road area of the Parish of Hitchin"* for £4,000. The Agent for the buyer was to be Matthew Foster, head of the Company still busy on the south side of the road. What could possibly go wrong?

What should have been a smooth transition turned out to be problematical. Foster soon relinquished his position as the new buyer proved to be less co-operative than his previous employer. Theophilus Sneeds Eli Plowman was not a Hitchin man, and had little respect for the customary way of doing business. He was from Shefford, a shrewd businessman, and the owner of brick and tile pits at Stanpits, near Henlow. He soon proved to be an irritant to the Urban District Council.[4]

Well before building plots were advertised for sale, he had been in acrimonious discussion with them regarding the superiority of his own sewage scheme over theirs, even *"appearing before them"*. In the end he was forced to accept their route *"over Farmer Wallace's*

Advertisement promoting the new Brampton Park Estate. Note the sites for factories and a hotel. From the *Hertfordshire Express*, precise date unknown, but probably November /December 1909. (HHS Pat Gadd Thurstance Collection)

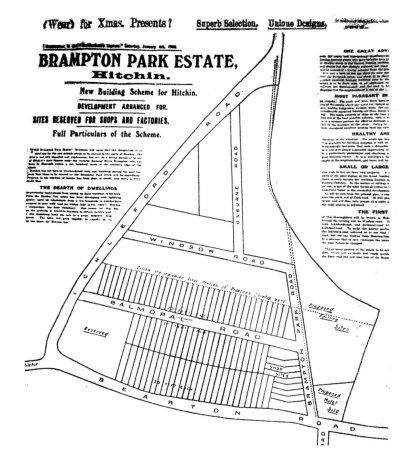

fields to the Sewage Farm", and had to agree to pay compensation for damage and disruption. As a parting shot, he demanded that *"all works be put out to tender"*. This set the tone for the fractious relationship which was to last until 1914.[5]

Building plots came onto the market in October 1909, (*"35/- per foot frontage, gas and water laid on"*). This equates to £1.75 in today's terms. All enquiries were to go to *"the Express offices in Hitchin"*.[6] No house was to cost less than £150, and all bricks were to be supplied by Mr Plowman for the first six years of the contract. Although a few plots were reserved by individuals the majority were purchased by local builders and tradesmen, who either sold on the completed houses or rented them out. Local firms such as Knight, Willmott, Monk, Pettengell and Clark, Brooker and Theobald identified their work by their named drain-covers and these are still visible on some of the properties.

Analysis of the 1901 Census for Hitchin[7] shows that 12% of the adult male working population were engaged in some aspect of the building trade. Although the basic lay-out of the new houses was probably fairly similar there was a wide variation of detail, some very imaginative, as can be appreciated by a stroll along the north side of Bearton Road. Earlier houses in Brampton Park Road display some pleasing polychromatic brickwork. These homes were far more than a product of a tradesmen's pattern book, incorporating distinctive porches, windows and decorative brickwork. Rail transport had revolutionised the building trade allowing easy access to slate, lead and glass, giving customers a wide choice of mass-produced fixtures and fittings, but local firms such as Gatward were still providing domestic ironware. Eli Plowman dug gravel from his pits on Bearton Road and lime for mortar was easily available from the Benslow area of town. In 1913 there was still a gravel and sandpit operating at Whitehill behind the (then) Whitehill Farm. Bricks were, of course, supplied by the builder himself.

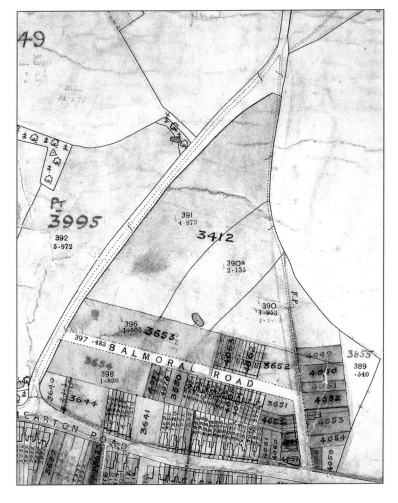

Extract from the 1910 Finance Act valuation maps, showing building progress by 1912. Plot 3412 is owned by Mr Plowman, but leased to Samuel Wallace for grazing. He also owned Plots 3641, 3644, and 3651–3654. The proposed hotel and factory sites have disappeared. (HALS IR1/75a)

Some local builders and businessmen had invested in multiple plots with a view to renting out the houses. "Buy-to-let" is not a new concept. Arthur Monk[8], with a yard in Bearton Road, was responsible for constructing a number of houses in Balmoral Road which he financed by taking out private mortgages. Tenants provided a steady income and many properties remained rented until the 1960s.

Typical tenants would have been the grandparents of Stephen Sears, who has a family connection with "Cotfield" in Brampton Park Road going back to 1914. They rented the house from the builder, Pettengell, for 10/6d a week (about 52p). Bearing in mind that the average wage for a clerk in a Hitchin office would have been the equivalent of about £1.50, this would have put the houses well beyond the means of the poorer sector of the population. *"Respectable and steadily-employed"* would have typified the new residents. In fact, when Stephen's grandfather died unexpectedly his widow and daughter were hard-pressed to stay in the house. His grandmother worked as a seamstress and took in a lodger. Her daughter earned 12/6d (about 63p) a week at the time as a junior shop assistant.

Eli Plowman and the Council were frequently at loggerheads during the building phase. He appears to have been disobliging[9]

Architectural features, north side of Bearton Road. There is much evidence of individual building style and detail. (Andrew Hyde Photographer www.AndrewHyde Photographer.co.uk)

(refusing to find work for the unemployed on his pathways) and was always pushing for more than his due. HUDC Minutes[10] are full of his requests for gas lamps, surfacing, and water-pipes. They are rebutted by demands that he fulfil his obligations before action be taken. Residents were incensed by the filthy state of the roads and pathways, which were his responsibility, and the cause of written complaints to both the Council and the local Press. His gravel pit in Bearton Road caused annoyance (although the HUDC was happy to fill it with town rubbish soon afterwards). When all private building ceased at the outbreak of war in 1914 the Estate roads were still in a parlous condition and the houses un-numbered (*"too many vacant plots"*).

Following 1918 life in Hitchin slowly returned to normal. By the early 1920s the fanciful original plans for the Brampton Park Estate had been abandoned. Now the emphasis was on housing for the more "aspirational" owner-occupier. There was space available. Plans to survey the remainder of Bearton Road towards Bedford Road had been shelved in 1913[11]; half of the northern side of Balmoral Road was vacant, as was a long stretch of Brampton Park Road.[12] The entire length of the lane soon to be known as Old Hale Way remained a stroller's paradise, fringed with fine trees at the southern end. Further up, near the Meads (then overgrown thickets) was the Sewage Farm, with its fields producing suspiciously large vegetables! Further on lay Ickleford.

In January 1924,[13] the Full Council proposed and passed that the Estate be adopted as *"highways repairable by the inhabitants at large"*. The long wait was over. At the same Meeting the Chairman, Mr G W Russell, enquired what lay-out was proposed for the remaining portion of land. In September he presented plans which were accepted by the Town Planner. Phase Two had begun.

Rare early postcard of Bearton Road looking west *c.*1914. The entrepreneurial Coleman family lately arrived from Bedford had been busily buying building plots on the estate, including the important plot on the corner of Brampton Park Road where they established a grocery. (Gerry Tidy)

The Burrows family and neighbours gather for a picnic beneath the oaks (joined for posterity by two nearby decorators!). A rare glimpse of the Estate in the early 1920s, before the second phase of building began. To the rear, the back gardens of Balmoral Road (north side); to the left, the rear of Brampton Park Road. The Sears' home (No 18) was then the last house in the road.
(Stephen Sears)

Two pieces of Government Legislation had made building development simpler. From 1923, Councils were allowed to loan money to prospective home owners, and could themselves borrow to finance this, and in the same year a Housing Act gave subsidies to private builders to enable them to build affordable homes for those able to buy them. Following this, and the adoption of the current estate roads,[14] Council Minutes are full of applications for planning permission, both from local builders and from private individuals. These were not for the earlier "build to let" houses, but for the new breed of owner-occupier.[15] Some bungalows began to appear in Brampton Park Road and Old Hale Way, with larger more traditional houses in Bearton and Balmoral Roads. G H Russell, son of Council Chairman G W Russell and an architect, designed houses that filled the vacant space in the latter. There were continuing applications for planning permission throughout the 1920s and 1930s, and for the HUDC loans which enabled people to buy the properties. Garages became popular from the late 1920s. In 1929 the Council bought Old Hale Meadow and designated it an Open Space.

Mrs Milly Grant standing proudly outside her new house, 50 Balmoral Road c. 1926.
(Marion Woodbridge)

Mr and Mrs Charles Grant were typical of the new buyers. Their daughter Marion Woodbridge, born at 50 Balmoral Road, recalls that her parents moved into their newly-built home when they married. Her father worked at Ransom's Distillery in Bancroft, cycling home for lunch. By the arrival of the Second World War the lay-out of the Estate was more-or-less complete. Air Raid Shelters were dug at the bottom of many gardens (although Marion Woodbridge's father, who was a Street Warden, announced that he would

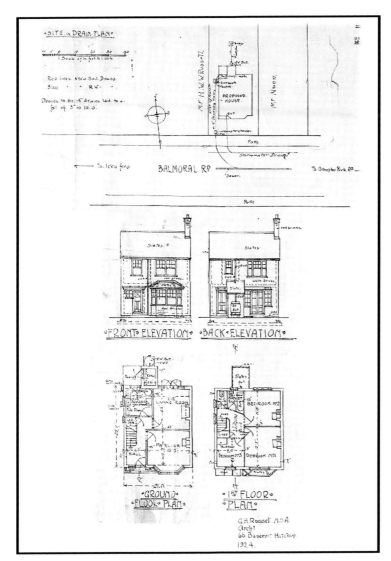

Excerpt from the Plan drawn up for Mr Smith, the prospective buyer of No 51 Balmoral Road, by local architect, G H Russell M.S.A., in 1924. (By kind permission of the current owners)

rather die in his bed than risk death from pneumonia by going down the garden). Stephen Sears' father in Brampton Park Road was in the GPO Home Guard and his mother was a member of the stalwart Fire Watching Team photographed for the local paper. Back gardens became vegetable plots, "blackout", stirrup-pumps and buckets became part of everyday life, and evacuees arrived. Some larger families were "shared" between smaller houses. Army lorries were parked under large trees in neighbouring fields for camouflage, and as "D-Day" approached, lined local side roads. Thankfully, nothing fell in this area, although Marion remembers huddling in bed with her mother, pillow over head, the night the "doodlebug" fell on Pirton. Her elder brother slept through it all. A

The Brampton Park Road Firewatching Team pose for the local newspaper c. 1940/1941, outside No.18. (Left to right): Mrs Cotton (?), Mrs Lawrence (No. 58), Mrs Marshall (No.57), Mrs Sears (No.18), Mrs Hills (No.56), Mrs Richmond (No.20), Mrs Jenkins (No.17), Mrs Bell (No.15?). (Stephen Sears)

neighbour, Mrs Collins owned a dog who uncannily barked before the Air Raid Warning Siren sounded.

Post-war, life returned to a rather austere "normal". Street-life was punctuated by regular visits from Notts-the-Bakers van, and Mr Flint, a Greengrocer from Westmill, whose horse and cart were also later to be motorised.

Patronising the "Co-op." milkman and coal-man meant enhanced "divi.", a welcome addition to the family budget. In the days before most local people owned a fridge (and here some houses still relied on gas as late as the 1950s), "top-up" daily shopping meant a trip into Bearton Road to Bavister's "General Stores", "an old-fashioned shop, broken biscuits, bacon, and paraffin" (Stephen Sears). Later this became a miniscule supermarket. On the opposite corner of Brampton Park Road stood "Birdsey's", supplier of newspapers, sweets (rationed until 1953) and cigarettes. Bicycles were the usual form of transport in the area, always wheeled "round the back".

In an era when "knowing your neighbour" was the norm, Marion Woodbridge remembers much friendly interaction between households, as well as acceptance and appreciation of idiosyncrasies. "Auntie D." who had *fallen on hard times* and ended-up in a rented "cottage" in Balmoral Road, spent many hours playing bezique, much to the neglect of her household duties. "Mr F." gained notoriety for being arrested *"drunk-in-charge of a bicycle"*.

In 1957, the Government passed a Housing Act placing an obligation on Local Authorities to up-grade sub-standard rented properties. From 1959 onwards the Council gave [16]Discretionary Improvement Grants to estate occupants whose *"sanitary conveniences, damp-proofing, and storage facilities"* fell below an acceptable standard. A number of applications were [17]granted for properties built during the early phase of the estate's development, for *"conversion of barn to bathroom"* and even *"provision of a fixed bath in a back bedroom"*. From this time onwards the proportion of rented properties decreased and the houses began to change hands.

Nothing stands still. Today the once empty estate roads are lined with cars and many of the new generation of occupants walk to the station each day for their daily commute. Tradesmen's vans and skips are a regular feature as owners seek to "upgrade" previous "upgrades". "Buy to let" has increased the number of rental properties once more. Women routinely work outside the home. Couples share domestic responsibilities. "Cleaning ladies" pay calls.

The original residents would have been amazed!

1   Hitchin Historical Society, *The Street Names of Hitchin and their Origins (Volume 3)* (Egon Publishers Ltd 1999)
2   Hitchin Urban District Council (HUDC) Minute Book (December 1907) HALS
3   HUDC Minute Book (Highways Committee) 1906 – 1910 (January 1908) HALS
4   Advertisement in the *Hertfordshire Express* (Autumn 1909) (HHS Pat Gadd Thurstance Collection)
5   HUDC Minute Book 1908 (March – May) HALS
6   House Deeds (36 Balmoral Road)
7   Research by Steve Fletcher (P.Douglas and P.Humphries, *Discovering Hitchin* – Appendix 1, Egon 1995)
8   HUDC Minute Book 1911–1914 (April 1914 for example) HALS
9   HUDC Minute Book 1908 (December) HALS
10 HUDC Minute Book 1906–1910 (January &December) Minute Book 1911–1914 (many instances) HALS
11 HUDC Minute Book 1911–1914 (December 1911) HALS
12 Robert Walmsley, *Around 1919: Boyhood memories of Hitchin* (AuthorGraphics Hitchin 1979)
13 HUDC Minute Book 1923–1926 (January 1924) HALS
14 HUDC Minute Book (1926–1927) HALS
15 HUDC Minute Book (1928–1929) HALS
16 HUDC Minute Book (1959–1960) HALS
17 HUDC Minute Book (1961–1962) HALS

"Fill her up!"
Petrol supplies in Hitchin

STEPHEN BRADFORD-BEST

Below left: An array of 2-gallon petrol cans from the earliest years of motoring, including six from Pratt's the company that first introduced this method of selling petrol and which became the government standard. (Iain Mansell)

Below right: A 1902 advertisement from Pratt's Motor Spirit for their sealed two-gallon cans of fuel. (*Grace's Guide to British Industrial History* www.gracesguide.co.uk)

Filling your car up with fuel in Hitchin is a regular necessity for many of us but when did we start and where did we first go for a supply? To clarify, the term 'petrol' had been coined to describe refined motor spirit in the 1870s and was patented by fuel distributor Carless, Capel & Leonard in 1892 but, although the word wasn't in common use until the late 1920s, I will refer to this fuel simply as petrol throughout this chapter.

It is generally accepted that the motor car was invented in Germany in 1885 independently by the pioneering Gottlieb Daimler and Karl Benz, but we were slow starters to exploit this invention in the UK. It was not until 1895 that the first motor car was imported to England, a French *Panhard et Levassor*, by the Hon. Evelyn Ellis. This was possibly because, with a 4mph speed limit until 1896, motor cars were poor competition for a horse and carriage being restricted not only by their maximum speed, but also by their limited range due to a scarcity of petrol supplies. The first car built in the UK was believed to have been a one-off home-built vehicle in 1894, but the first series-built cars, Harry Lawson's British Daimlers, didn't roll out of their Coventry factory until 1897. So there was little need for designated places supplying large volumes of petrol in the UK until the start of the 20th century when car production really got under way. In this early period petrol could

be purchased from ironmongers, hotels or even the chemist's shop. The airtight 2-gallon can, introduced by Pratt's, the UK brand of the Anglo-American Oil Co. in 1900, became the mandatory means of supplying petrol later that same year. Their competitors included the familiar Shell brand in red cans introduced in 1908. The cost of these cans of petrol, by then, was about 2s (or 5p per gallon, allowing for inflation, about £5.85 per gallon in 2018).

Sun Street in about 1920 with a splendid Argyll tourer – on the wrong side of the road! Has it just been supplied with petrol from Morgan's Garage? (John Read)

The Motor Car Act of 1903 required all vehicles to be registered by the local authority with a plate bearing the registration number displayed on the vehicle. The precise date that petrol-engined motor vehicles were first seen on the streets of Hitchin is not known but we do know that the first vehicle registered to a Hitchin resident was on 16 December 1903, although we don't know when he first acquired his motor car. That resident was Frederick Reynolds Carling, son of newspaper publisher William Carling, who lived in Bancroft. His vehicle was a British built 6hp Swift painted in dark blue, probably purchased from Flanders showroom in the Market Place, next to the Corn Exchange, as they were Swift agents. He replaced this voiturette with a larger 12hp Swift open tourer the following year and the original car passed to James Bowman of The Avenue, the miller of nearby Station Mills. The first motor car registered to a lady resident in the town, on 16 June 1904, was to Florence Hartland who lived at Rose Cottage in Walsworth Road, and whose vehicle was a 6½hp Napoleon also British built and painted dark blue. Other motor cars were subsequently registered to Hitchin residents, but probably less than twenty in the first decade of registration, together with several motorised bicycles, tricycles and one quadricycle, an Ariel registered to the Reverend George Bernard Gainsford of Birchfield, Verulam Road, the vicar of Holy Saviour Church. In addition to Hitchin owned cars, there would also have been visiting motor vehicles requiring a supply of petrol; amongst their sources may have been the ironmongers of Thomas Brooker & Sons in Walsworth Road and John Gatward & Son in the Market Place, or the Sun Hotel in Sun Street, or Perks & Llewellyn's chemist's shop in the High Street.

It is believed that one of the earliest garages in Hitchin was that of Ralph E Sanders & Son in Walsworth Road, built around 1905, which certainly had the first purpose-built car showroom in the town. Other garages in these early years included J Chalkley & Son in Brand Street and Slater Batty & Co in Bridge Street; it is very likely that they all supplied petrol, certainly the latter garage displayed a 'Pratts Motor Spirit' sign outside their premises pre-World War 1, as well as selling oil and other products required by motorists. Sanders dispensed petrol at their new garage in Bridge Street from a portable hand-cranked pump fitted to a large tank which was wheeled up to the customer's motor car. However, their main task would have been to repair cars, and their mechanics, who may have gained their engineering experience with agricultural machinery or horse-drawn vehicles, had to adapt their skills to the new means of transport and, indeed, to the growing variety of early motor cars built by different manufacturers in several European countries as well as the USA.

The first petrol pump in the UK is believed to have been installed outside a garage in Shrewsbury in 1915, but the first petrol filling station, selling National Benzole, was opened by the AA in

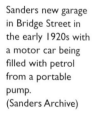

Sanders new garage in Bridge Street in the early 1920s with a motor car being filled with petrol from a portable pump.
(Sanders Archive)

Two petrol pumps with swinging arms outside the art deco style car showroom of Sanders in Walsworth Road built around 1920. (Sanders Archive)

Aldermaston in 1920, one of several around the country opened that year. It was not simply a commercial operation, but an attempt to get their members to buy British-made benzol fuel (a by-product of burning coal) as opposed to similar post revolution fuel from Russia, which was readily available but was perceived to be *"tantamount to supporting the Bolsheviks"*. Others soon followed their lead and existing garages, or new sites, were selected for the installation of one or more pumps surmounted by distinctive glass globes identifying the brand, like the familiar pecten shell (large scallop) chosen by Shell, as petrol from several different petrol companies was often supplied at the same site. Pratts offered to install and service a petrol pump, along with a 1,000-gallon tank, initially for £250 but later reduced to £165. Shell competed with a similar package. The makers of the pumps included Avery Hardoll and Britannic and, by 1923, 7,000 were in use around the country. It was necessary for the vendor to obtain a licence to sell petrol from the local authority.

The business premises and flats built in Hermitage Road in the late 1920s included a garage and workshop (now a bathroom showroom) run by CMI Garages Ltd. You can see the arms of the petrol pumps stretching across the pavement. (NHM)

Above: The surviving petrol pumps, but now no longer in use, outside Bert Wells' garage in West Hill around 1930 with a selection of customers' cars outside. (Pansy Mitchell)

Left: The Power petrol pump outside 'Jock' Thomson's garage in Queen Street about 1935 with his three sons, John, Neil and Gordon, on duty. (T N Thomson)

Where the first petrol pumps were installed in Hitchin is not known for sure, but Sanders certainly had two in front of their premises in Walsworth Road by the 1920s. These pumps had long arms holding the rubber pipes which swung out over the pavement to reach the cars. Appleby Bros., later becoming E T Cherry & Sons, in Nightingale Road had a similar arrangement as did CMI Garages Ltd, later known as Woolley's Garage, in Hermitage Road. Another garage, further up Nightingale Road from Cherry's, was Issott's, later George Ansell's, who sold cycles, motor cycles, petrol and paraffin until the late 1960s from the site now occupied by the Esso petrol station. Two pumps were installed outside the garages of E A Prime in Queen Street and Bert Wells in West Hill, the latter still there but not currently supplying fuel. The early pumps were hand-cranked but, by the later 1920s, pumps were fitted with electric motors to pump the petrol. In 1926 the price of petrol had increased to around 1s 4d per gallon (or 7p) and still cost a similar sum in 1936. A sign outside Thomson's garage in Queen Street promoted Power petrol at this price. The early pumps were sometimes installed on the premises of businesses for their exclusive supply, like Boxall's Taxis off Bucklersbury, or were installed in front of residential premises by entrepreneurial householders. Petrol companies started using snappy slogans to sell petrol like *"You can be sure of Shell!"*. Shell also commissioned attractive scenic posters by notable artists of the day like John Piper and Graham Sutherland. However, as the number of motor vehicles on the roads increased so did the need for designated places to supply their petrol. For the record, the tax on petrol, or correctly fuel duty, was first introduced in 1909 at 3d per gallon (or just over 1p).

During World War 2, and for a while after, 'pool' or unbranded low-octane petrol was rationed and only available in exchange for coupons. A red dye was added to commercial petrol and anyone caught using this fuel, having bought it on the black market, was severely punished. Rationing ended in 1950.

Although the number of petrol pumps had proliferated during the 1920s and 30s, it wasn't until after World War 2 that purpose-built service stations, mainly serving solely petrol and oil, were built in and around Hitchin. The pumps, mostly one brand due to the 'solus' agreements (vendors contracted to buy petrol from a single supplier), were often positioned on an 'island' so that waiting cars could be filled by the attendant on both sides of the pumps offering different grades of petrol. Do you remember Shell Economy, Esso Extra and BP Super-Plus? These petrol stations included the Willows and Oakfield Service Stations in Stevenage Road. In addition, H A Saunders Ltd offered a range of petrol at their new garage in Queen Street following their move from Brand Street. The various petrol companies renewed their sales battles with new slogans like *"Fill Up and Feel the Difference"* from Shell and *"Put a tiger in your tank!"* from Esso. In 1956, the price of petrol had increased to 5s 5d per gallon (or 27p).

By the 1960s the pumps were adapted for easy self-service by the motorist and the attendant was banished to a small kiosk or office close by where you paid for your petrol. The kiosk at Sanders new filling station in Walsworth Road opposite their showrooms, selling Regent petrol, was sited on the island. The supply of diesel fuel, commonly used by commercial vehicles, started to become popular for private cars around this time and service stations began to widen their services by offering drive-through car washes, oil changes and other repairs, and the kiosks gave way to small shops offering, at first, newspapers, sweets and cigarettes, but later a full range of groceries. Some garages, with car showrooms and originally just a couple of pumps, expanded their petrol sales, like Burr Brothers in

Below left: The new filling station opened in the 1960s by H A Saunders Ltd in Queen Street, this time selling BP petrol. (NHM)

Below right: The pay kiosk on the island of Sanders garage in Walsworth Road in the 1950s. (Sanders Archive)

Different grades of Shell petrol offered at Thomson's original garage and workshop in Queen Street shortly before it closed and was rebuilt in 1970. (Stephen Bradford-Best)

Thomson's new filling station, part of Woodcote House, opened in 1965. (T N Thomson)

Old Park Road and the newly built Portmill Service Station opened by J N Thomson & Sons in addition to their original premises further along Queen Street. There were still some old-style suppliers like Morgan's Garage, Reliant car agents, in Sun Street, then on a bus route through the town centre. Petrol companies also started offering gift promotions in exchange for tokens or vouchers received with the purchase of fuel, which included free mugs, and motoring prints and coins. Green Shield and similar stamps were also available. In 1966 the price of petrol remained at about 5s 5d per gallon.

By the 1970s out of town supermarkets began to be built which also offered cheaper petrol, as at Tesco in Baldock and Sainsbury's in Stevenage. It became increasingly difficult for the privately-owned service stations, and those suppliers of petrol from garage pumps at car dealerships, to compete on price and they gradually closed, or the pumps were removed from outside the showrooms and the tanks removed or filled with a mixture of sand and cement for safety. In 1976 the price of petrol had increased to 77p per gallon; doubling in price between 1972 and 1977 due to the Middle East oil crisis. It

Morgan's garage selling Shell petrol, as well as Reliant three-wheeled motor cars, in busy Sun Street during the 1960s. (NHM)

became possible to pay for petrol using a credit card at the pump when the petrol station was closed at night. Many of the in-town service stations are now run by the petrol companies themselves, as with Shell in Bedford Road, and the once secondary supply of groceries has grown to be a major part of a visit to the service station, M&S Simply Food at the BP Service Station in Stevenage Road being a good example. Other survivors are the Esso Service Station in Nightingale Road and the BP Westmill Filling Station in Bedford Road. In 2018 the price of petrol was £5.35 per gallon, including the fuel duty of £2.63 per gallon.

Whilst independent travel in motor cars continues, there will be a need for the supply of fuel but how this will evolve only time will tell. With the increase in the number of hybrid and electric vehicles, needing to be re-charged away from home by an electricity supply, perhaps petrol stations will be replaced by 'quick charge' electricity facilities sited at the sides of our roads or in our town and city centres.

Sources

Stephen Bradford-Best, *From Carriages to Cars* (HHS, 2014)

David Jeremiah, *Representation of British Motoring* (Manchester University Press, 2007)

Katherine Morrison and John Minnis, *Carscapes: the Motorcar, Architecture and Landscape in England* (Yale University Press, 2013)

Kenneth Richardson, *The British Motor Industry 1896–1939* (Macmillan, 1977)

Craig Horner ed. *Aspects of Motoring History. An annual Journal by the Society of Automotive Historians (in Britain)*

Hitchin Town Guides (HALS)

Web sources: wikipedia, Grace's Guide to British Industrial History
      www.gracesguide.co.uk

Origins of Hitchin's modern "Town Planning"

16

DAVID HOWLETT

Today government, local and national, often looks obsessed by "planning issues". Frequently, it seems, this obsession is at the expense of actually delivering any practical results. But British bureaucracy usually has origins in the best of intentions and town planning is no different.

Before 1900 there was little restriction on what happened to our landscapes. Government – such as for Royal Dockyards or Poor Law Unions – did what it needed. Big private companies behind big schemes – firstly mainly canals and then railways – did require Parliamentary sanction for their plans but this was not because these schemes transformed our towns and countryside (which they did) but because they impacted on individual property rights, a basic touchstone of politics, both national and local.

The Liberal government of 1906 is famous for pioneering social and welfare legislation and its ambitions also gave us the first Town Planning Act, in 1909. After 1918 came further significant planning regulation marking new roles for local authorities both to act on their own (such as in providing council housing) and to exercise more control over private interests. The novel scale, nature and stress of the Great War cannot be overstated: it required unprecedented interference by government in the whole fabric of national life and it was soon clear this involvement would not end with the peace.

In 1919 a Housing and Town Planning Act obliged local authorities to examine district needs more systematically, particularly in housing, and to devise plans for the future. Hitchin was then, logically, accepted as a natural unit of local government, but such units needed greater supervision. The *Hertfordshire Regional Planning Report 1927*, the first of its kind for any comparable County Council, noted local government

"*is ancient, historical and deeply rooted in our national life.... It dates...from times when inhabited areas were separate and even hostile, and had little or no relations with each other or with central government*".[1]

Proper planning would give better, coordinated, outcomes and Hertfordshire County Council worked with all its urban and rural district councils to this end.

Hitchin Urban District Council (HUDC) set about drawing up a future plan for the town. Mr Culpin, onetime secretary of the Garden City Association who had developed a London based architectural practice, was appointed "Town Planner" in 1919.[2] By 1924 preparation of the scheme was well underway with its first advertised airing and its acceptance by the Ministry of Health, the Whitehall department responsible. By 1925– 26, after a range of consultations with landowners, the County Council (on roads for example) and the Ministry, the plan (Map No.2) was formally adopted by the HUDC.[3]

The established town centre plus most of the suburbs built by about 1920 were largely excluded. The town centre was by now recognised as being of historic interest in its own right (as shown by the inspection visit of the Royal Commission on Historical Monuments in preparation for its county inventory of 1910)[4] and also as an important part of what made Hitchin an attractive place to live and work as a classic ancient market town. One town centre location that was included in future planning was around Hermitage Road: this area was designated for new shopping and business development so giving us the mainly 1920s–30s townscape we have today.

However, the main areas within the plan were those away from the historic town centre and 19th century suburbs. For the modern eye, what is striking are the plans for housing to the north, east and west of the town centre, especially how these are linked by new roads including southern and western by-passes. A proposed northern by-pass also stands out with spurs and a strategic crossing of the main railway line as it runs to Stotfold Road. Hertfordshire's embryonic consideration of Green Belt in the 1920s (importantly consolidated in 1947) did not stop Hitchin's housing plans lapping at the very borders of Letchworth, east of Stotfold Road.

The plan also includes areas for 'Light Industries' and 'Industrial Buildings' focused particularly on Miss Wilshere's land-holdings in the north-east which eventually became the Cadwell Lane and Wilbury Way industrial estates – despite her objections. Even so the HUDC was later criticised by the Chamber of Commerce for being overly concerned to preserve Hitchin as an attractive residential centre. These reservations were formalised in 1937 when discussions were underway on the preparation of an updated version of the Town Plan. The Chamber pointed out new employment zones were essential: too many inhabitants were forced to work outside the town (for example in the new industrial area of

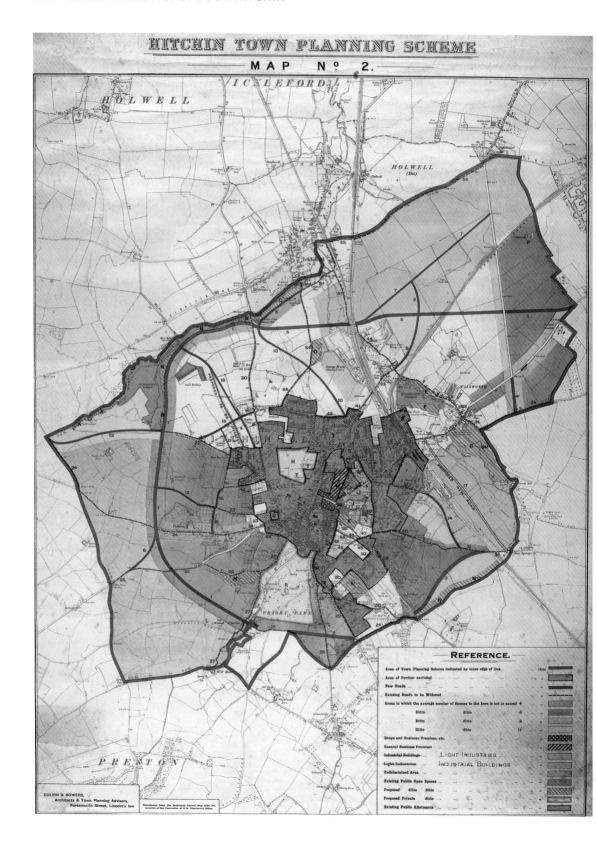

HITCHIN TOWN PLANNING SCHEME

MAP Nº 2.

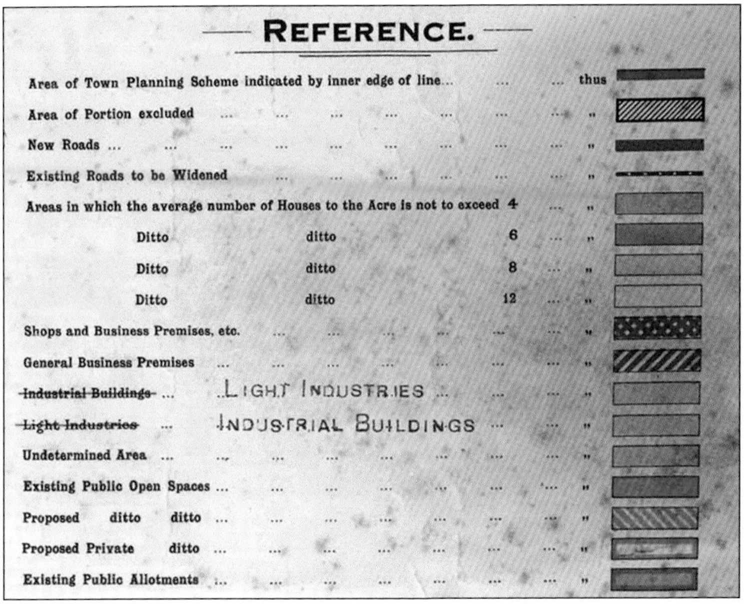

Opposite page:
Hitchin Town Planning
Scheme Map No. 2
1925–26 (HALS DE/
Ws/P24)

Left: Key to Hitchin
Town Planning
Scheme Map No. 2
1925–26 (HALS DE/
Ws/P24)

Letchworth) and this was seen as detrimental to the local economy. The Hitchin housing market might fail through over-supply unless the HUDC addressed the problem of providing new industrial sites which had good access by both road and rail.[5] These tensions also stimulated some early "Nimbyism"; the HUDC's dilemma was highlighted the same year. Hitchin firm George King proposed a new factory north of Wymondley Road not far from where it passes under the railway. This provoked objections from residents in and around The Avenue and the new 1930s ribbon-developed houses along Wymondley Road. The council decided against the proposed factory in an area now designated for residential use and suggested King's explored alternative local sites. After 1945, King's took advantage of the opportunities offered by the New Town at Stevenage.[6]

The area between Walsworth and Ninesprings east of the main railway line was designated in the plan as an 'Undetermined Area', although a new road (roughly along where St Michael's Road is today) was included. This designation reflected the indecision of the Great Northern, its successor the London and North Eastern Railway, and the council itself as to what this land might actually best be used for – council housing, private housing, railway uses, industrial, or ad hoc agriculture? This indecision lasted into the 1960s (see Chapter 10).

The 1925–26 plan was not all bricks, mortar and tarmac, however. Proposals were included to protect existing open areas such as Butts Close and part of Priory Park and for the designation of

Esther Seebohm's "very charming" footpath beside the River Purwell now running along the edge of Tennyson Avenue. (Bridget Howlett 2018)

new public open spaces such as in the Purwell Valley and around the suburban fringes of the town. Just as there was increasing awareness of Hitchin's historic environment there was new concern for its natural landscapes, although critics thought "not enough". For example, Miss Esther Seebohm of Little Benslow Hills soon noted:

> *"..with regard to the new Planning Scheme there seems very little space reserved for the future inhabitants of Hitchin for recreation and short walks…The one I see most of now – a very charming one and much frequented – is the strip of pasture land by the Purwell Stream over which there is already a right of way."*[7]

This enthusiasm for the natural was not matched by Mr Flint; he had just bought Purwell Mill and adjacent land from the Reverend Gainsford and intended to build houses there (!).

The 1925–26 Town Plan did not provide an exact template for Hitchin's development. But it did raise issues and provide initial parameters for new types of "Planning discussions" which still very much resonate in the town today – anyone for a southern by-pass?

1   W R Davidge, *Hertfordshire Regional Planning Report* (Hertfordshire Regional Planning Committee, 1927) p11
2   HUDC minutes 5 September 1919, 4 December 1923 HALS; Anthony Sutcliffe (ed), *British Town Planning: the formative years* (University of Leicester, 1981) pp38–39
3   Hitchin Town Planning Scheme: Map No.2 HALS DE/We/P24
4   Royal Commission on Historical Monuments (England), *An Inventory of the Historical Monuments in Hertfordshire* (HMSO 1911) pp117–125
5   HALS Off Acc 1104 HUDC Box 3 Town Planning
6   HUDC minutes 9 March 1937, 21 April 1937, 26 May 1937 HALS
7   Letter from Esther Seebohm 7 Dec 1937 HALS Off Acc 1104 HUDC Box 4 Objections to HUDC Planning Scheme

17

Westmill Estate

TERRY KNIGHT

Westmill Estate lies off Bedford Road in Hitchin and takes its name from Westmill Farm. However, on a street map of the town, published in 1947, it went by the name of Red Hill Estate and consisted of council houses in Redhill Road, North Place, South Place, Westmill Road, Westmill Road South, Mattocke Road and The Crescent and private houses in Nutleigh Grove. Since then it has grown considerably and now possesses far more social and private houses as well as a number of shops, a school, playing fields, a community centre and allotments. Bordering it is Oughtonhead Common and its nature reserve.

The early years

By the 1910s Hitchin Urban District Council wanted to demolish the Queen Street slums and in the early 1920s built the first 78 new homes at Sunnyside to rehouse the families. Their proposal for another estate at St Michael's Mount came to nothing so in 1925 an alternative scheme was devised for an estate of 500 houses at Westmill. Land was acquired from the Moss, Ransom and

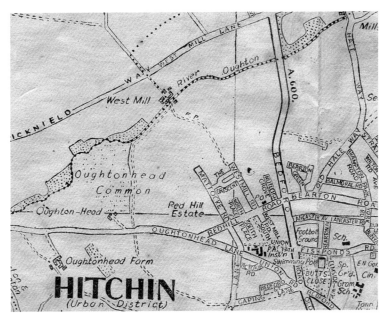

The Westmill or Red Hill Estate in 1947. Excerpt from *The "Neigbourhood" Map of Hitchin, Letchworth, Baldock and Stevenage*, Sun Map Company, Dunstable 1947. (Terry Knight)

Aerial photograph looking south of the Westmill Estate under construction 1928. The buildings in the centre are The Crescent, Westmill Road is on the left and Mattocke Road is on the right. (NHM)

Wilshere families amongst others. Building began in 1925 of the first phase of the estate adjoining Redhill Road.

June Leete, June Guthrie before she married, was born on Westmill Road South in 1931 when the estate was lit by gas lamps. The shops she remembers in Redhill Road included a grocer's and post office, a butcher's, a tobacconist and sweet shop and a fish and chip shop. On the other side of Nutleigh Grove was Walnut Tree Cafe and sweet shop, followed by a cycle shop and a gentlemen and ladies' hairdresser.

Derrick Conder by his tent in the big spinney at Oughtonhead. (Derrick Conder)

Derrick Conder formerly lived on Mattocke Road. In 1940 there were cornfields at the back and bottom of Mattocke Road together with The Crescent and Westmill Road backing on to allotments. The gap in the latter road, leading through the allotments, was a path called the Casty (derived from causeway) which went down to the River Oughton with Westmill Farm on the opposite bank. There was a pig farm where Hine Way/Westmill Road are now.

Janet Dilley moved to Redhill Road when she was three. Firework night was celebrated in The Crescent or at the bottom of Mattocke Road. A wooden hut, which stood on the corner of Redhill Road and Westmill Road, was used as a rent office until it was closed in 1977.

Mervyn Spokes lived with his maternal grandparents, Hubert and Rose French, and his parents on Redhill Road on the corner of Mattocke Road from 1947, when he was born, until 1951

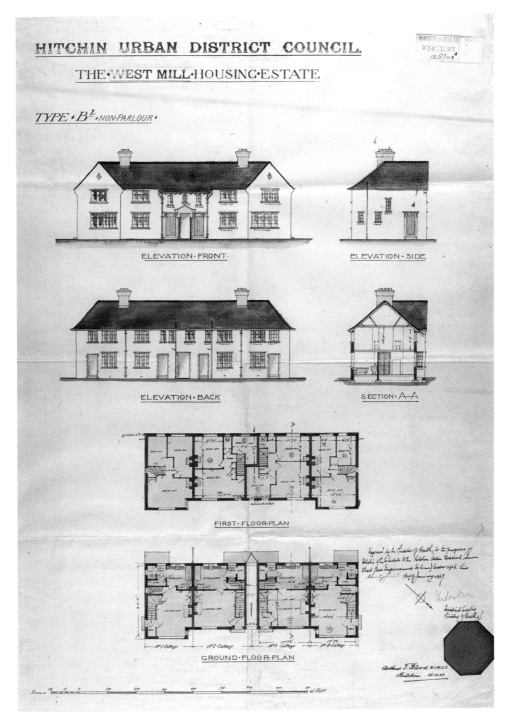

Architect's drawings for Non-Parlour Houses originally for Sunnyside Road 1923 were approved for the Westmill Estate in 1927. These houses designed by Arthur T. Blood, the HUDC Surveyor, were built in Mattocke Road. (HALS Off Acc 1104 Box 3)

Left: Joy Rosemary Spokes née French in the front garden of her home on Redhill Road in the summer of 1947.
(Mervyn Spokes)

Right: Washing hanging out in the snow. Back gardens of Mattocke Road in the hard winter of 1947 viewed from rear window of 28 Redhill Road. Part of The Crescent appears in the far right.
(Mervyn Spokes)

when he and his parents moved to Letchworth. He returned to his grandparents for holidays, Christmases and most weekends. He has many vivid memories of life on the estate which sadly cannot all be included here.

Mrs Brown kept the "Top Shop" at the top of Redhill Road, just into Lucas Lane, ideal for Tizer and ha'penny chews. He remembers fly papers hanging up and watching flies getting stuck to the papers. The Flints lived in North Place and ran a greengrocery business, using a horse and four wheel cart to carry their wares around. Just across from the entrance to Nutleigh Grove was Norman Clark's fish and chip shop. Another Mr Clarke on Redhill Road ran the barbers and Mervyn recalls his "two bob chop" (20p in decimal money), the haircut based on what was given to the military - short back and sides and a trim at the top.

Above: Commemorative plaque on houses in North Place.
(Alan Fleck 2018)

Right: Residents of North and South Place celebrate victory in World War II in North Place 1945.
(Terry Knight, source unknown)

Wally Minnis could be heard crying out *"Rag and bones"* as he travelled around Westmill on his horse and cart. Mervyn remembers *"I was to have my first two wheel bike from Wally and granddad took me down to Oughtonhead Common, no trees and bushes then, to teach me to ride it. What a day when I rode it back to Redhill Road!"*

Abraham Page, a very short man as wide as he was tall, rode a trade bike with a small front wheel and a carrier out front to hold a carpet bag to keep his tools in. He was a plumber for the council and lived on the corner of Redhill Road and Beaumont Close. Mervyn remembers that one day Abram, as he knew him, came home for lunch and whatever he had been doing, had left something hot in the bag and as a result it started to catch light and the fire brigade had to be called!

Mervyn Spokes on his tricycle bought from Wally Minnis the rag and bone man c.1949. (Mervyn Spokes)

Harry Todd and his family lived at the top of the lane leading down to Oughtonhead Common. Mervyn used to play with his sons and, on one of his visits, Harry was mowing hay in a field near his home and he let him drive the tractor for a brief while.

> *"I remember I was 12, the tractor was a slate grey coloured 1930s Case fitted with a Bamford semi mounted mower. This was my first drive of any kind of motor vehicle and, as a tractor enthusiast, memorable."*

> *"Mr Dando was the first person I ever saw with a Land Rover. He came to the Westmill area and set up a caravan site on Lucas Lane up towards Chalkdell. He seemed to have land on both sides of Lucas Lane and was an owner of a very ancient Fordson tractor on iron wheels which he kept in a corrugated shed on Oughtonhead Lane. Periodically he would bring it out to harrow the land opposite the caravan site."*

David Chivers, formerly from The Crescent and now living on Milestone Road, recalls Ken Logan, who had a shop in Hitchin, charging up wireless accumulators in his shed in North Place. At the top of The Crescent, where the road goes into Mattocke Road, lived Mr Crayton or Craydon who ran the local Sea Cadets on Bedford Road. He was a short stocky man who was always smartly dressed, even when riding his bicycle. David Chivers has further recollections of going to Clark's shop to buy fish and chips and scraps for dinner.

The estate expands

Doreen Barrett, who lives on Milestone Road, has been a resident on the estate for most of her life and seen many changes. The earlier estate she remembers was much smaller than it is today. People all knew each other and the community spirit was very good and the whole area was surrounded by countryside. In the late 1950s and 1960s plans were made to enlarge the estate. Land was taken to build from the dead ends of Mattocke Road and Westmill Road to a point very close to Oughtonhead Common. Burford Way became the limit and Westmill Road was extended to meet up with it. Modern council houses were built and extra shops and a community centre came into being in the area of John Barker Place which followed on from the dead end of Mattocke Road and met up with Westmill Road and Swinburne Avenue.

Cynthia Parker has lived on the Westmill Estate for 55 years – 35 years on Redhill Road and 20 years on Westmill Road. Her first son was born in 1959 and when she was expecting her second son in 1962 she and her husband went to see the council's housing manager and looked at a house on Redhill Road. They would have preferred to have stayed at Sunnyside where they were then living, but were told if they did not take it they would have to go to the bottom of the queue. Her parents moved to Westmill from Sunnyside in 1960. Cynthia remembers:

"A bus service of sorts, it used to come up Redhill Road and turn round at the top by the little shop. None of the Mums used the bus, we all had big prams and walked to the town and everywhere. We had a row of shops on Redhill Road, we had a grocery shop, a wool shop, a newsagent's, a butcher's, a fish shop. Across Nutleigh Grove we had Cummings, an amazing bicycle and toy shop (the children loved it) then a hairdresser, then some waste ground. We had a little shop at the Redhill Road end of the lane. You could get two rashers of bacon and two eggs and a small amount of butter. The shopkeeper used to weigh tea (loose) into small brown bags, same with sugar. It was a godsend because none of the families had much money in those days. All the shops closed at 1pm on Saturdays and that was that!

Cynthia Parker in her garden on Redhill Road.
(Cynthia Parker)

"Beyond the shop was a really big mobile home site, all of this was run by two brothers for many years. One of the brothers died and the other decided to sell the site to builders for private houses. Across the road from this was a piece of land allocated for Oughtonhead School but this wasn't built for a long,

long time. When my eldest son was ready for

long time. When my eldest son was ready for school it still wasn't finished so I used to walk him and his friend and my youngest son in a pram down to Strathmore School. We did this for seven weeks until the school was ready. Once the school started fundraising, lots of the parents (including us) went to discos, cheese and wine parties and school plays etc.

"The little shop was the last thing to be knocked down as it was a canteen for all the workmen on the building site. My Aunt Rose used to run the canteen. She made bacon rolls for the workmen and pies and sandwiches. I used to help her sometimes. I have never seen such big mugs of tea in all my life!"

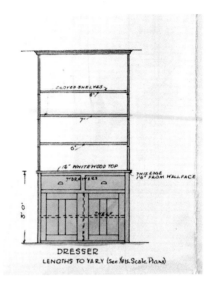

Design for a dresser for houses and flats on Westmill Estate by Arthur T Blood 1926. (HALS Off Acc 1104 Box 3)

The Angel's Reply, though on Bedford Road, was built on the site of Nutleigh Grove House. Despite many residents objecting to the plans it was opened in 1965 when the licence was transferred from the Angel Vaults in Sun Street which had closed in 1956. In its very early days the police were called on numerous occasions to the Angel's Reply and Cynthia Parker heard a story that one angry wife even took her husband's dinner there as he was always late getting home from the public house! More recently the Angel's Reply has been renamed The Angels and has become a very family friendly pub with play areas for children.

Cynthia says *"I loved living on Redhill Road and I now live on Westmill Road down the end near the Common (this was my Mum and Dad's house). I love this end as well. I would not want to live anywhere else. It is a lovely estate, the old part and the new part."*

The Angel's Reply 1988. (NHM)

Westmill Community Association

Westmill Community Association's origins can be traced back more than 50 years to 1964 when Len Worbey and Councillor Jim Reilly held a fete on Burford Way playing field to raise money to build changing rooms for their junior football team. In order to help Dora Price recruited some young Mums to hold another fete later that year. From this a volunteer group was formed by residents on the estate who managed to amass £500 in two years, a considerable sum of money.

In 1966 a barracks hut was purchased from RAF Henlow for £152 5s which was erected on Burford Way entirely with voluntary labour and opened in 1968. This early centre provided space for an over-60's group, bingo, whist drives, the youth club, a young Mums group and weekend lettings. During these years services were provided for the users including keeping the lights lit and the rain out!

A really strong faithful following resulted in the building of a new centre in 1974 with the support of North Hertfordshire District Council. Mick Furr became manager of the new centre. The provision of activities was widened to include facilities for the Bible Way Church of God and Universal Brotherhood, youth club discos and a luncheon club. The old centre was still used by Westmill Youth Football Club, Westmill Scouts and Cubs, Stevenage Pipe Band, Hitchin Pigeon Club and Offley Morris Men. In 1978 a welcome was extended to BBC television's Multi-Coloured Swap Shop with host Keith Chegwin. With support from the Youth Training Scheme it was possible to construct a front extension in 1982. This work made life more comfortable and enabled the committee to improve the bar facility. The centre received a Fundraising Genius Class One Certificate for Red Nose Day. The 50th anniversary of VJ Day in 1995 was marked with a dance which was attended by some members of the North Herts and South Beds Far East Prisoners of War Association.

Below left: Elizabeth Tomlin, Mick Furr, Rose Matthews and May Bullock ready for action behind the serving hatch in the first brick Community Centre. (Mick Furr)

Below right: Cynthia Parker at the kitchen sink in the Community Centre. (Cynthia Parker)

Left: Westmill
Community
Association
fundraising at
Walsworth Fete.
(Mick Furr)

Right: Mick Furr MBE
2008. (Mick Furr)

The mid-nineties were challenging times for the estate with some serious anti-social behaviour problems. This led to a concerted effort by police, the council, schools and youth services to provide more facilities for young people. The community association used vacant shops in John Barker Place to provide a Coffee Mill for youngsters and an Action in the Community Award enabled computer equipment to be provided for Coffee Mill users. A fruit and vegetable shop was opened for the convenience of residents on the estate. The community association made a bid to the National Lottery to build a basketball court and was granted £47,000.

During the first years of the new century the association was still being managed by Mick Furr and her indefatigable team who were in a continuous struggle to survive financially. The world itself was changing rapidly and support for all the activities at the centre was in decline. Despite these factors there were highlights. Mick Furr received an invitation to a Buckingham Palace Garden Party and in 2008 she was awarded the MBE for services to the community. It was an event she will remember for the rest of her life but she stressed at a celebration party she could not have done it without the support of all her stalwart helpers, past and present.

As part of North Herts Homes' proposal for the regeneration of John Barker Place plans were drawn up for a new community centre to be built there in 2005, but these and an alternative scheme came to nothing. In the meantime Mick Furr was coming up to 70 and she felt that a younger manager would be more suited for the future of the association, and a new manager was appointed. Before Mick Furr stepped down she requested that the association should ensure that the nursery at the old centre in Burford Way should be a charity in its own right so the new manager and committee did not have to worry about it. The new centre opened in 2016. The old community centre in John Barker Place was demolished the following year and a multi-use games area was built in its place. Football can still be played there today, so fulfilling Len Worbey's original dream.

Made in Hitchin: Backyard Industry and New Estates

18

DAVID HOWLETT AND STEPHEN BRADFORD-BEST

Hitchin, in its local history books and town guides, is usually described as a historic market town, implying that the buying and selling of goods and services are its key economic activities. They are, but things are not as straightforward as they seem – the traditional label also conceals a diverse manufacturing history that has been central to the town's story.

Market towns – more than markets

By the 1840s it was possible to describe a traditional market town as not being *"amongst the busy and bustling scenes of manufacturing industry"*.[1] Yet, before Britain's industrial revolution, such towns were actually key industrial centres. Their manufacturing had, for long, been focused on small scale workshops and yards within the market towns that were district centres. Such manufacture had its roots in activities in their surrounding countryside and was largely linked to their wider roles in agriculture, commerce, trades and services.

Hitchin was no exception. The town had been the main market centre of north Hertfordshire and south Bedfordshire for well over a millennium. It lay at the focus of an important and wealthy agricultural area; it was also within London's economic pull, even in the days of laborious road and water transport. Hitchin's early market was important in the buying and selling of grain, sheep, cattle, small animals and poultry and wool. Its industry served these trades. Livestock supported food processing, tanning, leatherworking and parchment making; wool supported some textiles and cloth processing and grain supported food and drink manufacture (especially milling, the making of malt and brewing) plus later niches such as straw plait making. In terms of the town's prosperity over some hundreds of years wool and malting were both of particular importance with the balance gradually shifting from the former to the latter.[2]

Hitchin's leather used for horses. (*The Official Programme of the Hitchin Celebrations of the Coronation of The King 1902*)

T. L. Raban, Saddler and Harness Maker,

✳ ✳ 17, HIGH STREET, HITCHIN.

Whips, Spurs, Brushes Sponges, Leathers, Embrocation, and every requisite for the Stable. All kinds of Gig and Cart Harness made on the lowest terms.

PORTMANTEAUX - - and Bags repaired.

HORSE CLIPPERS -

Agent for the "KING'S HEAD" HORSE CLOTHING, for Summer and Winter, Out-door and In-door, and Day and Night.

This Brand is second to none for quality, fit and wear.

There were also key ancillaries such as saddle and harness making, cart building, wheel-wrighting, carpentry, cabinet makers, iron-making and metal-working, brickmaking and building trades, clothing makers, and the production of baskets, sacks and ropes. Most of this was small scale but it all supported Hitchin's wider market functions in the local economy. Many of these 'making' activities were very long established and functioned well into more recent times. For example there was a large tannery off Bancroft, in the hands of the Russells by the late 19th century, which operated until the 1980s; lead processing was undertaken by Newton's the builders and plumbers dating from 1728 and they survived until a merger in the 1990s; the building trade also supported important lime making operations which continued into the 1960s; and the independent miller Bowman's – the last of a long line – only stopped grain processing at Ickleford Mill in 2016.

From the late 18th century the increased pace and complexity of the national economy stimulated more of what we would recognise as consumer demand. This reflected rising living standards; the trend was not uninterrupted but it was clear – gradually more people enjoyed more disposable income. Market towns responded by providing extra goods and services for their own catchments; many of the products desired were produced locally.[3] In Hitchin good examples that appeared in the 19th century are the making of domestic ironworks products by John Gatward, that of confectionery by Garratt and Cannon, Bentley's operating as a "Bedding and Furniture Manufacturer", the profusion of small scale local dressmakers and the growth of stationery, printing and bookbinders, particularly Paternoster and Hales.[4]

Garratt & Cannon, manufacturing confectioners, Bancroft, 1917. Note the funnels for packing gobstoppers. (Gillian Russell)

The arrival of the Great Northern Railway in 1850 was also important in changing Hitchin's role as a market town. One impact was to reinforce that role as a district centre, especially as the town was a junction, immediately for Cambridge and from 1857 for Bedford. A second impact was to connect the Hitchin economy to a much larger national market although this cut both ways. For example, local grain and malt production was initially boosted by opportunities for rail export but Hitchin's brickmaking soon came under increased competition from rail imported supplies and eventually grain suffered from imports too. A third impact was the gradual pull of the railway in locating more town industry nearer to the station and the goods yards.

Hitchin's special manufacturing niches emerge

Access to wider and more sophisticated markets also meant Hitchin developed new niches in manufacturing. Of particular importance were medical and pharmaceutical products. Even before the railway, in 1846, William Ransom, a Quaker businessman and chemist, established a herbal distillery off Bancroft. When Queen Victoria paused at the station in 1851 en route to Balmoral her loyal presentation included lavender water.[5] Ransom's Bancroft factory operated well into the 1990s with outputs from Lemsip to Body Shop lotions. Hitchin came particularly to specialise in lavender, becoming one of the three most important growing areas nationally, and with local manufacturing chemist Perks and Llewellyn (who traded until the early 1960s) achieving international renown with their lavender products.

Agricultural engineering became another niche specialism. However its full scale development eventually took place elsewhere underlining how smaller market towns were beginning to suffer limitations in the wider industrial economy of late Victorian Britain. By the mid 1850s Thomas Perkins had a showroom and offices next to the new Corn Exchange. His agricultural machinery works – from which stationary steam engines, hay and straw elevators, threshing machines and ploughs plus a range of smaller engineering goods emerged – was accessed off Paynes Park. Perkins successfully provided for an expanding range of customers but, after 1870, became involved in a larger scale Peterborough based business (in which today's Perkins Engines finds its origins), so the Hitchin operation was wound down.

Late Victorian Hitchin remained a success as a manufacturing centre and the town continued to attract new enterprises, especially to the vicinity of the railway. For example, Spencer Carter established an important boiler works (later Sharman's) off Cambridge Road in 1886; Innes (later George King), agricultural

Perkins agricultural engineers: foundry yard behind the Corn Exchange c.1870. (NHM LTS Vol 1 B p175)

machine makers, moved from Royston to Market Place in 1898 and then to Walsworth Road; Sanders (also originally from Royston) erected a large and purpose built coach and motor vehicle works on Walsworth Road between 1902–09; Bowman's opened state of the art Station Mills in 1901; and, in 1912, the Hertfordshire and Bedfordshire Bacon Factory Limited brought modern and upscaled food processing to a site in Nightingale Road. Many of these activities survived at least into the 1960s. All these enterprises shared an important characteristic of Hitchin's manufacturing hitherto – they were slotted individually into the townscape with little thought of being adjacent to other activities or residential areas. But Perkins' experience had shown that the future industrial economy would require more of "bigger business in bigger locations". Other key operations – such as brewing and malting – were also responding to regional concentration which reduced the number of local production centres. All this did not mean that there was no longer a role for the smaller market towns in manufacture, but it did show how that role might be delivered was changing.[6]

Hitchin's new Industrial Estates

By 1920, therefore, Hitchin faced major pressures on its manufacturing role. In 1903 Letchworth Garden City had been founded nearby and a planned approach to its industrial ambitions was implicit from the start – it had designated and specific areas for such development. The Great War massively expanded the role of government in the national economy and, after 1919, local authorities were required to adopt a more coordinated approach as to how their areas would function in future in the shape of Town Plans. The structure of industry itself was shifting with more emphasis on emerging light manufacturing operations rather than the traditional heavy outputs of coal, iron and steel and the tempo of its change was increasing. Hitchin, as an established market town which had evolved its role over a very long time, now faced both new opportunities but also new threats in its important manufacturing sector.

Hitchin Urban District Council's first coordinated Town Plan designated areas for various future uses including new industry and, importantly, supported these with new road and service links. Particular interest focused on the land around Cadwell Lane, north of the Hitchin to Cambridge railway. The Chamber of Commerce, concerned that Hitchin was becoming a picturesque residential centre with insufficient local employment, wanted the UDC to take the provision of new sites and infrastructure for industry much more seriously.[7] The first small scale and ad hoc development of new sites took place on Cadwell Lane, close to the railway, where the Ransoms had operated the Greystone Limeworks since 1857. A joinery works and timber yard for P H Barker and Son was established here by about 1930 (also using the railway) and, when the lime works were sold in 1933, Barker's bought more of the adjacent Ransom land. Other portions of the area were occupied by the Wallace brothers, then based on Grove Mill Farm and producing milk for the Bancroft Dairy. This farm also has a place in Hitchin's industrial estate history: D C Tibbles, which came to have a new factory unit on Wilbury Way after 1945, began its electrical transformer business in its outbuildings.

Grove Mill Farm at the junction of Wilbury Way and Cadwell Lane c.1965; original home of electrical equipment manufacturer D C Tibbles. (NHM Wilkinson Collection 11070-1003)

Light industry soon followed nearby on Burymead Road. Legal problems with continued common field rights over this land, for a long time also owned by the Ransoms, were resolved in 1934 and this opened the area for development. An early arrival – and symbol of the town's new light industry 'moderne' format – was the purpose built office and factory complex of the Hitchin Glove Company.

FACTORY AND OFFICES
HITCHIN, HERTS

THE
HITCHIN GLOVE COMPANY
LIMITED

Bury Mead Road. Hitchin

But it was land immediately north of the Cambridge branch and accessed by Wilbury Way that was potentially of most interest to the UDC for industrial development. This interest had been registered in the 1920s but its owner, Miss Wilshere, was not impressed. And, even though Miss Wilshere died in 1934, there was no movement on developing the site before another European war broke out in 1939. Then the Victaulic Company, a specialist hydraulics manufacturer, swiftly built a new factory on Wilbury Way to fulfil urgent wartime demands. After 1945 this plant was further expanded and soon provided a pivot around which other development was begun nearby.

Hitchin's new interwar light industry – glove making. (*Hitchin Official Guide* 1959 p37)

A prime mover in the further expansion of the Wilbury Way industrial area was an incomer, Frederick Bandet, a Czech, who wanted to move his leatherworking business from Baldock to a new purpose built factory. He purchased a site from William Wallace,

Wilbury Way's first factory – the Victaulic Company in the 1940s. (Viking Johnson)

Wilbury Way's post war development – Frederick Bandet's first brochure 1953. (W J Reader, *To Have and To Hold. An Account of Frederick Bandet's Life in Business,* Hunting Gate, 1983, p103)

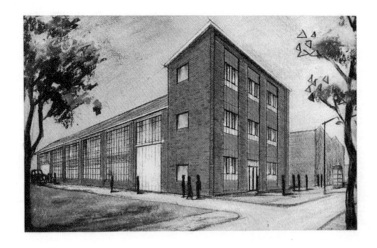

ERECTA (HITCHIN) LTD

Below left: Wilbury Way's post war development – the site expands c.1965. (NHM Wilkinson Collection 11070–0994)

Below right: Frederick Bandet's original factory eventually occupied by Vernon Instruments. (W J Reader, *To Have and To Hold. An Account of Frederick Bandet's Life in Business,* Hunting Gate, 1983, p83)

now the landowner, but faced problems in obtaining the required material licences and finding a builder amidst post-war rationing and austerity. The HUDC Surveyor advised against the enterprise saying the town had a shortage of labour but Bandet persisted, secured planning permission, decided to build the unit himself and completed it in 1949. But Bandet soon decided leatherworking was not for him, closed the operation and sold the factory, moving his energy into the development of industrial premises. In this way were laid the foundations of Erecta, later Hunting Gate, which took a key role in the construction and letting of the rest of the Wilbury Way industrial estate.[8]

HUDC was supportive, despite some locals worrying over a potential shift in the character of their historic market town, as the council again saw an alternative to losing local industrial initiative and employment to Letchworth. A new factor was that the blandishments of the New Town Commission posed a further challenge, as exemplified by the move of King's engineering works from Walsworth Road to a green field site at Stevenage. There was also the problem of County decision making. The Hertfordshire Development Plan of 1951 concluded there *"..is not a strong case for introducing any extensive industry into Hitchin…"* arguing new provision should be focused on Letchworth and Stevenage.[9]

CAM GEARS LTD

MANUFACTURERS OF STEERING GEARS FOR PRIVATE AND COMMERCIAL VEHICLES

Offer excellent opportunities to school-leavers

WILBURY WAY · HITCHIN · HERTS.

Telephone Hitchin 2341

Cam Gears (successor to George Kent) was based in Wilbury Way by 1962. (*Hitchin Official Guide* 1962 p37)

By 1953 Wilbury Way space had been let to English Electric and Bandet hoped to capitalise on this to attract other light electrical and engineering companies; the move of Tibbles is mentioned above. An early Erecta brochure lauded Hitchin's ideal situation close to, but not swamped by, London and its industrious population who wished to work *"..near their homes.."*.[10] Another success was that International Computers and Tabulators took their large factory unit in the early 1960s. The late 1950s and early 60s saw steady expansion in light industry so Wilbury Way was soon populated by a range of firms of varying sizes in addition to English Electric, Cam Gears, and the Victaulic. These personified the new generation of 'light industrial' estates. By 1960 the Hitchin Directory's list of *"Principal Hitchin Industries"* shows a wide variety of activity. It is clear how much of this was now concentrated on Wilbury Way and Burymead Road.[11]

The last portion of the Wilbury Way estate to be laid out – centred on Hunting Gate (so named because a nearby field access was said to be used by the Hunt) – was started in 1961. It is striking how, by this date, access to railway links was a faded priority. There was also additional small scale factory building on Wallace Way off Cadwell Lane around 1963 once the limeworks had closed. This witnessed another disagreement between the Urban District and the County Councils with the latter being keen the area remained limeworks, perhaps because it was still reluctant to see new industrial development away from its designated hubs.

By 1964, therefore, about a dozen industrial units were complete on Wilbury Way with the largest by then being taken

PRINCIPAL HITCHIN INDUSTRIES

(Hitchin Directory 1960)

Almco Supersheen Division of Gt. Britain Ltd, Bury Mead Road

Argosy Coachwork Ltd., Caravan Manufacturers, Wilbury Way

Bancroft Press Ltd., Printers and Stationers, 87 Bancroft

Barclay Corsets Ltd., Individually Designed Corset and Brassiere Manufacturers, Wilbury Way

Barker, P. H. and Son Ltd., Joinery Manufacturers and Timber Merchants, Hermitage Road

Bentley and Co. (Printers) Ltd., Printers and Carton Manufacturers, Wilbury Way

Bowman, J. and Sons Ltd., Millers, Station Flour Mills

Brown, W., Engineers' Pattern Maker, Bury Mead Road

Carling, W. and Co. Ltd., Printers and Newspaper Proprietors, "Express" Works

Elcontrol Ltd., Industrial Electronic Engineers, Wilbury Way

English Electric Co. Ltd., The, Wilbury Way

Garratt and Cannon Ltd., Sweet Manufacturers and Wholesale Confectioners and Tobacconists, Bancroft

Genito Urinary Manufacturing Co. Ltd., The, Surgical Instrument Manufacturers, Tithe Barn, Tilehouse Street

Harkness, R. & Co. Ltd., Rose Growers, Cambridge Road

Hertfordshire Truck Co. Ltd., Engineers and Truck Manufacturers, Wilbury Way

Herts. and Beds. Co-operative Bacon Factory Ltd., Nightingale Road

Herts. Bronze Powder Works Ltd., Bronze Powder Manufacturers, Bury Mead Road

Hitchin Glove Co. Ltd., The, Glove Manufacturers, Bury Mead Road

Hitchin Rubber Works Ltd., Tyre Retreads, Cambridge Road

Kelso Knitwear Ltd., Bury Mead Road

Kent, Geo. Ltd., Engineers, Wilbury Way

Plasmoulds Ltd., Pattern Makers and Founders, Wilbury Way

Ransom, W. & Son Ltd., Manufacturing Chemists, Bancroft

Russell, G. W. and Sons Ltd., Tanners, Fellmongers, Parchment Makers, Bancroft

Sharman Engineering Co. Ltd., The, Boilermakers and Engineers, Cambridge Road

Slingsby, H. G. Ltd., Truck and Ladder Manufacturers, Wilbury Way

Squires Dairies Ltd., Wilbury Way

Tibbles, D. C. and Co. Ltd., Manufacturers of Electrical Equipment, British Sampson Works, Wilbury Way

Townsend and Crowther Ltd., Instrument Makers, Cambridge Road

Victaulic Co. Ltd., The, Pipe Joint Manufacturers, Wilbury Way

Wilmond Enginering Co. Ltd., Mechanical and General Engineers, Bury Mead Road

Wilbury Way today still showing Frederick Bandet's distinctive style. (Alan Fleck 2017)

by International Computers. There was some inevitable churn in tenants – such as the departure of English Electric – but overall the estate was a success. Still today, through the survival of several distinct Bandet-designed buildings, the supervising hand of the area remains evident. In 1971 Bandet bought the freehold of the Wilbury Way estate from the Wallace family. The area remains principally one of light industry although now dominated more by smaller 'cottage' type businesses than larger concerns such as Cam Gears, which closed in 1984. Following national trends 'making' is now less dominant and service uses have increased such as accountants and nursery care. But the area still has its 'makers' and remains a vibrant source of local employment; variety has been further augmented by two important Sikh temples.

The 1950s also saw new enterprises developed along Burymead Road. By 1960 Almco Supersheen (industrial polishing and finishing products), Brown's (patternmakers), Herts. Bronze Powder Works, Kelso Knitwear and Wilmond Engineering were there. The Erecta company was involved here too as is still shown by the distinctive Bandet-style buildings at the junction with Grove Road.[12] This area also remains a mix of small businesses although, again, manufacture has often been replaced by service and retail activities such as the new Brookers building supplies operation on Bilton Road.

Back to the Future in Yards?

Despite the importance of the industrial estates over the past eighty years the town proper still hosted a range, usually relatively small scale and specialised, of industrial activities. Examples include the catchily named Genito-Urinary Manufacturing Company off Tilehouse Street (specialist medical equipment) which operated into the 1960s, Townsend and Crowther instrument makers on Cambridge Road, Sharpe's who produced silk Trade Union banners on Walsworth Road and W B Moss continued to make its own distinctive pork pies. A clutch of small businesses (including precision parts for jet fighters) was found in workshops at Jeeves Yard into the 1990s. It is true that many town centre sites (such as Russell's Tannery and Ransom's off Bancroft and Sharman's off Cambridge Road) have been switched to supermarket retail or residential uses in the past thirty years. But, in that time, 'production' activities have significantly changed and today value is often added through the use of internet and digitally based techniques as much as machines; the separation of 'work' and 'home' has again become much more blurred. Perhaps, in this context, there might be new shifts back to using town centre yards as locations of production. It will not be the same as before: for instance, there will be no more "sweet and sour pongs" generated by the smells of combined Ransom and Russell processes or the distinctive sticky sweetness from Garratt and Cannons and the Lucas Brewery. But it will be employment and wealth generation to keep Hitchin functioning for future generations as "an ancient market town".

1   Quoted, Jonathan Brown, *The English Market Town* (Crowood Press, 1986) p65
2   See for example, Anthony M Foster, *The Book of Hitchin* (Barracuda Books, 1981); Keith J and Tony Fitzpatrick-Matthews, *The Archaeology of Hitchin from Prehistory to the Present* (NHM & HHS, 2008)
3   See Anthony M Foster and Lionel M Munby, *Market Town. Hitchin in the Nineteenth Century* (HHS, 1987) pp1–14
4   See for example *Hitchin Household Almanack*, 1872–96 (Paternoster & Hales)
5   Richard Holton, "The Great Northern Railway at Hitchin", *Hertfordshire Past and Present No 14* 1974 pp15–16
6   See Alan Fleck and Helen Poole, *Old Hitchin: Portrait of an English Market Town* (1999); Richard Field, *Hitchin: A Pictorial History* (Phillimore, 1991); *Hitchin Household Almanack* annually 1872–96
7   See Chapter 16
8   W J Reader, *To Have and to Hold. An Account of Frederick Bandet's Life in Business* (Hunting Gate, 1983)
9   E H Doubleday, *Hertfordshire: Survey Report and Analysis of County Development Plan* (HCC, 1951) p42
10 Reader, *To Have and to Hold*, p104
11 Reader, *To Have and to Hold*, p125; *Hitchin Directory* 1960 p29
12 See for example *Hitchin Directory* 1960 and *Hitchin Official Guide* 1962

A look at some 1960s buildings in Hitchin

19

CHRIS HONEY

Hitchin expanded rapidly during the 60s. There were some large developments like the completion of the Oakfield Estate, the eastern side of both the Purwell and the Rosehill Estates, the western side of the Westmill Estate, parts of the Willows Estate off the Charlton road, the Cedarwood Estate (better known as the Foster Drive area off Blackhorse Lane) and finally developments either side of Whitehill Road including the school. Some of these were built by local firms like M & F. O. Foster and S. J. Thompson, but the larger developments were established by national companies like George Wimpey and Fairview Homes. Factory units and warehouses were added to the industrial estate and Eastern Gas extended its plant at Cadwell Lane.[1]

Changes in and around the town centre were smaller, more individual and frequently more controversial either because they looked out of character with their neighbours or due to them replacing buildings of greater aesthetic merit. Conservation or restoration was given little regard during the 60s, instead bold new edifices were preferred with 'form fitting function'. In isolation these were sometimes impressive, but when inserted between older buildings looked discordant. Also when period styling was applied this often reduced the design quality of the building. There is insufficient space in this publication to include all of these developments so those of more interest are recorded here. We will start our discovery with one of the most notorious.

Safeways Building, 18–19 Bancroft. Now occupied by Wilko, probably Hitchin's most hated building because of that which it replaced (Waters House, a fine Georgian building) and its prominent position on the axis of Hermitage Road, you can't miss it! The house was included on the List of Buildings of Architectural and Historic Interest. The original application, in January 1964, proposed conversion and extension of the dwelling into shops and offices. Outline approval was given provided the existing elevation was retained with sympathetically designed shop fronts inserted. Well the rumour is that the front facade fell down during construction! So, later, permission was granted for a 'modern' insertion. A good example of how not to marry new with old.[2]

Above: Waters House 1962. Alfred Waters was an ironmonger, furniture dealer and remover. (NHM)

Right: Safeway. This bold block pays no regard to its neighbours. When Safeway built a new store (now Waitrose) on Bedford Road in the late 1980s, this building became Wilkinson's. (NHM 386–11)

The Croft, 11 Bancroft, further south on the same side. You would be forgiven for assuming this was not a 60s development because it is a reproduction of the former facade with shops inserted in the ground floor. In fact Hitchin Property Trust and their architect Hugh D Bidwell maintained that it was not practical to use the existing building and applied for a demolition order and replacement with shops and offices over plus a four storey block of flats behind. In 1960 Hitchin Urban District Council declared that the existing front elevation should be preserved and The Ministry of Housing and Local Development dismissed the proposed new development as unsympathetic in December 1961. Eventually HUDC Town Planning and Development Committee decided that the applicant could demolish the existing building due to its poor construction and absence of proper foundations, but reconstruct a replica in 1964.[3]

Above: The Croft. The facade is 19th century but the building dates back a further 400 years when it was thought to have been a wealthy wool merchant's hall house. (NHM 140–12)

Left: A present day view of The Croft pastiche reproduction. (Chris Honey 2018)

Near the corner of Hermitage Road [post 1924]. The lower portion was a medieval hall house. Its facade though 17th century contained an interior at least 200 years older.
(NHM 409-12)

Today's view of the same site.
(Chris Honey 2017)

On the opposite side stood **Hall House** (117 to 119 Bancroft) and **Jackson's House** (120 Bancroft). The former was a late 14th/ early 15th century building which was demolished in 1963. HCC planning officer, G F Oliver, in a letter dated 3 April 1964 to A King, HUDC surveyor, commented:

> "This is a very long stretch which is made up of buildings of different ages, heights, materials and qualities but has considerable character. They are just the sort of buildings which are typical of an old town like Hitchin. Then come two public houses not listed, the first 17th century and the second mid 19th century."[4]

The application to develop five shops and later a sixth on the site of George Jackson's house (a medieval timber framed building with a similar aged wall painting in one room) was granted in May 1965 but not before it fell down despite a previous preservation order! The architect R W Patterson of Ian Fraser & Associates, who represented The Shop Construction Group of Companies, attempted to replicate the gables of the previous buildings, but it has to be said without their charm. The Council took advantage of this change by widening Portmill Lane.

Later in 1968 the Co-op were granted permission to develop a food hall and home centre on 114–116 Bancroft (demolished in 1958) with a return frontage to Hermitage Road. The building did not last for long before succumbing to 'concrete cancer' in its frame.[5]

Land adjoining 121/123 Bancroft and Church House, this is on the southern side of Portmill Lane. Two 17th century public houses, the Crown and the White Lion, plus other old buildings were replaced by Taylor Woodrow Industrial with a supermarket, a public house and four shops.

The proposed severe look by W S Hattrell & Partners, in association with W E Eddleston FRIBA, was later partially softened by a break in the roof line and a change to clay roof tiles plus smaller upper storey windows, before being granted permission in October 1965. A lot of wrangling took place with regard to vehicle access to the rear from Portmill Lane car park but was eventually solved by giving some land at the front of the development to the Council for pavement widening. The land for Church House was donated by the Edith Wilshere Charity; it consists of a meeting hall, offices, kitchen and toilets with two flats above. A sculpted mural by Anthony Holloway adorns the wall beside the main entrance. The

Below left: The Crown built in 1654 was for a while a parcels depot for the Great Northern Railway. The White Lion Inn was probably from the same period.
(NHM 260–04)

Below right: Today's view looking south.
(Chris Honey 2017)

building at 121 Bancroft was modified and extended rearwards in June 1964 to become a self service store on the ground floor with offices above by architects White and Travis. Now an M&S Food store, you may remember it as part of Tescos.[6]

Further south on the opposite side beyond the junction with Brand Street stands 9/10 High Street, still referred to as the **Woolworths Building**. Woolworths had severely truncated the Cock Inn when building its shop in the 1930s, then in 1961 it purchased Perks and Llewellyn on the other side and demolished it. This was despite HUDC wanting at least the upper floor of the Grade II listed building retained. In this they were supported by the Georgian Society and The Hitchin Society, but to no avail as the architect convinced others that this would not be viable. The resulting proposal had a bland modern appearance, so the Architects Advisory Panel was consulted. It felt that a neo Georgian front a little like the facade of the Woolworths Oxford store, designed by the revered Sir William Holford, should be adopted. Well that is how it turned out when a new front designed by Kelleth Ablett was approved in October 1962. There was a lot more wrangling over the roof top car park and access ramp to the rear which delayed building until 1964. The store finally opened in August 1965.[7]

Now pass through Market Place to **3 Sun Street.** This is where the Angel Vaults Inn stood until July 1956 when it received a "Dangerous Structure Notice" after a 14th century beam and plasterwork fell down in the main part of the building. It could have been strengthened but was immediately demolished leaving the site vacant until 1963 when Central and Provincial Properties proposed two shops and a supermarket in its place. HUDC gained some land in front for road widening and granted permission for the three storey and adjoining two storey replacement in April 1965. The result lacks any quality or charm and does no justice to the site next to the Sun Hotel.

The response to this loss was an application by McMullen & Sons to erect the Angel's Reply beside the junction of Redhill and Bedford roads. Built by B. G. Cox & Co of Letchworth it is mainly one storey with part two storey accommodation for staff. It was

Above: A mid 1930s view of the Woolworths 3d & 6d store, later to become Timothy Whites then Boots, and the reduced Cock Inn. (Gerry Tidy)

Left: Present day view of the 'Woolworths' building (Chris Honey 2018)

granted permission in March 1963. See photograph on page 157. This property has been extensively altered and added to in recent years.[8]

A little walk now through Market Place, the Arcade and across Paynes Park to **Hitchin Library Extension**. Designed by Martin

Above: The Angel Vaults Inn. Though the date 1450 appeared on the facade, the roof construction could have been 14th century. (NHM)

Right: Present day view of 3 Sun Street. (Chris Honey 2017)

Hitchin Library Extension. A good example of an unquestionably modern building complementing its 19th century neighbour Charnwood House which housed the Public Library from 1939 and Museum from 1941 until 2012. (Chris Honey 2017)

Priestman together with the County Architect Geoffrey Fardell and built by local firm M & F O Foster, it is unquestionably the finest 60s development in Hitchin. This bold and successful modern building featured under floor electric heating, large windows and architect designed beech shelving. It still satisfactorily serves the Hitchin population more than 50 years later. Consent for the proposal was forthcoming from both HCC in March 1963 and HUDC in May the same year and it gained a Civic Trust Award in 1965. In 2003 a Hitchin History mural by Henry and Joyce Collins (1973), which was previously attached to the former Sainsbury building in Brand Street, was appropriately sited here alongside the main entrance.[9]

Cross back over Paynes Park and proceed along Cooper's Alley to the corner of Tilehouse Street and Wratten Road East. Formerly occupied by the Wratten malting house **Midland House** is another example of a 60s brutal intervention. Designed by local architect Norman Hyde and built by Hitchin firm M & F O Foster it dominates this area and because of the elevated site can be seen from afar. Both HCC and HUDC recommended refusal of this application but after an appeal was launched permission was granted in May 1963 when the applicant agreed to move it back from the road edge. Originally intended to be the regional headquarters for natural gas conversion it became bank offices.[10]

You may remember **Crown & Sceptre House** in Bridge Street, beside the bridge over the Hiz. This was built by Hitchin based Erecta Contractors on the site where the Lucas brewery stood until 1963. Designed by Alexander Finder & Associates for the Shellwood Group of Companies who leased it out to the Inland

The Wratten malting house owned by the Lucas family, Quaker brewers.
(NHM 348–10)

Revenue, the Ministry of Labour & National Insurance and the Ministry of Pensions. It was a brick faced building with a flat concrete roof brutally inserted into this charming street. The only physical advantage gained was some road widening at this point. It was demolished in 2007 and replaced with a block of flats.[11]

Now we view **Austin House** on the corner of Bridge Street and Queen Street. Built as a motor showroom and petrol service station with offices above and an extensive car parking space for H A Saunders, this development occupies a large site. Designed by architect Alan Stubbs and erected by Kirk & Kirk, it took two

Below left: Midland House.
(Chris Honey 2017)

Below right: Crown House, Bridge Street 2004. (Alan Fleck)

Above: The old
jettied buildings of
the Triangle at the
junction of Bridge
Street and Queen
Street. To the right
are cottages removed
for Cannon House.
(Gerry Tidy)

Left: Present Day.
Austin House on the
left, the petrol pumps
pictured on page
143 were removed
many years ago,
and Cannon House
opposite.
(Alan Fleck 2017)

years for permission to be granted in October 1961. This was partly because the Ministry of Housing and Local Government objected to demolishing two medieval cottages on the site. Prime's Garage in Queen Street and the High View Commercial Hotel in Bridge Street were also removed. There were discussions about providing a public car park, possibly below ground, but eventually a land swap was agreed so that HUDC could have the road widened on this corner. A typical 60s style, this building is now occupied by ASDA and until recently by Carpetright with vacant office space above.[12]

A view of the newly completed St Mary's Square and canalised river Hiz with the King's Head beyond in the early 1930s. (Simon Walker)

Woodcote House in 1971. The Rolls Royce is appropriate as Norman Royce, the architect, was a relation of the automobile creator. Also see picture on page 144. (Chris Honey)

On the opposite side of Queen Street lies **Cannon House**, a late 50s early 60s block of 24 flats designed by Anthony King on the site of old cottages. It is an unremarkable 'Council style' edifice. This can't be said of **Woodcote House/Balliol Chambers** situated on the corner of Queen Street and Hollow Lane. The land it occupies was cleared of slum dwellings during the 1920s and used to store demounted stalls from Hitchin Market and for car parking. Some buildings were left at the northern end including the King's Head public house which was demolished in 1961 to encompass the widening and straightening of Queen Street. In 1963 Parway Joint Estates commissioned a well known and respected architectural practice, Norman Royce and Partners, to design a petrol filling

Kennedy Court. This is the largest of five blocks, the others being Abbiss House, Chapman House, Russell House and Hazelwood Court. (Chris Honey 2017)

station, car showroom, public house, flats and offices for this site. After a lot of negotiating, their proposal was granted permission by HUDC in March 1964. You may not like Woodcote House, it does not fit in with the general aesthetic of Hitchin, but at least it stands on an isolated site, not in close proximity to older properties. It has its troubles like 'concrete cancer', roof leaks and underground water ingress, so it requires constant maintenance and repair, but it still exudes that bold optimistic look of the early 60s which has become quite fashionable again.[13]

A short diversion into Whinbush Road and Hazelwood Close before turning back towards the town centre reveals five blocks of Council flats. Four of these are in the same style the largest being Kennedy Court designed by Anthony King HUDC Surveyor and built by David Chaston Ltd in 1964. It is a four storey brick building containing 24 one bedroom flats. The cantilevered access walkways and balconies display metal balustrades reminiscent of the Festival of Britain style.[14]

Pass into Hermitage Road and on the left side at Nos 71–81 is a three storey development of seven shops with flats over and car parking behind. This was designed by the Felix Walter Group of architects and built by Greenhaven (Hitchin) Ltd on the site of the Hermitage Cinema. The proposal was supported by County and District officers Martin Priestman and Anthony King and granted permission in December 1965. One unfortunate change was the replacement of the proposed aluminium panels on the front facade to a brick facing which required crude metal angle supports overtly bolted to the structure for support. This building is presently due to be refaced with off white panels and will acquire two extra storeys.[15]

Above: Hermitage Road. The Hermitage Cinema was built in 1931/2 by John Ray Ltd. Barkers Warehouse had modified its front to a Tudor style in the 1920s. (Gerry Tidy)

Right: Today's view of the poorly maintained facade including a buddleia on the second floor. (Chris Honey 2017)

Next door once stood **Hitchin Post Office, Hermitage Road.** This was built on the site of Barker's timber yard by local firm M & F O Foster to a design by John Stevens, a Ministry of Works architect. The design of the building addressed the problem of how to accommodate the expansion of business and future developments, for example by including easily moved internal partitions, and paved the way for subsequent post office buildings.

Hitchin Post Office pictured not long after completion. A post box, clock and public telephones are situated below the 'Post Office and Savings Bank' sign. (HHS Collection)

Other innovations included self-service machines for postal orders, stamps and letter cards mounted outside but under cover. The Daily Telegraph reported that "...*The building's simple design, with external walls of the three storey frontage in hand made russet bricks, suits the scale of the street...*". It opened in February 1962 having taken a year to build at a considerably reduced cost to that estimated. This was demolished in 2014 many years after the Post Office had moved to Martins in Market Place and then to Brookers. The site including the sorting office in Portmill Lane was developed into shops, luxury flats and an hotel.[16]

So now we can see Wilko's again at the Bancroft/Hermitage Road junction where we began our 60s journey.

Finally further out of town to the east of Hitchin Station beside the Cambridge Road lies **North Hertfordshire College**. The 60s saw a large expansion in further education provision, Hitchin being no exception. In January 1962 the County Architect Geoffrey Fardell put forward a proposal to extend the facilities for what was then known as the Hitchin College of Further Education. The application was for a large development of reinforced concrete frame buildings with latticed elevations of fenestration and grey vitreous enamel panels alternating with red brick faced facades. Permission was granted to start construction in October 1962. The majority of these were upgraded and refaced or added to in 2014.[17]

Hitchin College of
Further Education
before 2014.
(IMG_3791 North
Hertfordshire
College)

1 NHDC planning archives planning applications; OS Maps of Hitchin, TL12NE 1960, TL1730NW 1964, TL1930NE 1965, TL2029NE 1965, TL2030NW 1965, TL1828 and TL1928 both 1966; Alan Fleck, *Hitchin in Old Photographs* (Alan Sutton, 1994); Richard Field, *Hitchin: a Pictorial History* (Phillimore, 1991)

2 NHDC Planning Application N/128–64; Brent Smith, *Hitchin – The Best and Worst. A Personal View* (Privately published 2009)

3 HUDC minutes 1960–1964 HALS; NHDC Planning Application N/433–60

4 NHDC Planning Application N/1006–63

5 NHDC Planning Applications N/404–65 and N/122–67; Brent Smith, *Hitchin – The Best and Worst*; 'Then and Now', *North Herts Gazette* 1 March 1986

6 NHDC Planning Applications N/179–65, N/277–65, N/968–65 and N/229–61

7 NHDC Planning Applications N/1071–61 and N/891–63

8 NHDC Planning Application N/877–63 and N/147–63; Brent Smith, *Hitchin – The Best and Worst*

9 NHDC Planning Application N/232-63 and N/147-63; Brent Smith, *Hitchin – The Best and Worst*; Hertfordshire County Library, internal information note

10 NHDC Planning Application N/190–63

11 NHDC Planning Application N/934–62

12 NHDC Planning Application N/954–59

13 NHDC Planning Applications N/307/57 Cannon House, N/124–64, N/1389–64 Woodcote House

14 NHDC Planning Application N/309–64

15 NHDC Planning Application N/852–65

16 Simon Walker, *Hitchin Journal* Vol. 24 No 1 2014 pages 23–25; www.visitpostalmuseum.org www.britishpostofficearchitects.weebly.com/hitchin.html

17 NHDC Planning Application N/793–62

Bibliography

Agar, Nigel E, *Behind the Plough. Agrarian society in nineteenth-century Hertfordshire* (University of Hertfordshire, 2005)

Agar, Nigel, "'Homes fit for Heroes' – the Hertfordshire experience", *Herts Past & Present 3rd series no 22* Autumn 2013

Birch, Jacky, Douglas, Scilla, et al, *Educating Our Own. The Masters of Hitchin Boys' British School 1810–1929* (British Schools Museum, 2008)

Bradford-Best, Stephen, *From Carriages to Cars* (HHS, 2014)

Brown, Jonathan, *The English Market Town. A Social and Economic History 1750–1914* (Crowood Press, 1986)

Bryant, G E, & Baker, G P, ed. *A Quaker Journal Being the Diary and Reminiscences of William Lucas of Hitchin (1804–1861) A Member of the Society of Friends* (Hutchinson, 1933)

Crosby, Tony, Douglas, Priscilla, Fletcher, Steve, et al., *Jeeves Yard. A dynasty of Hitchin builders and brickmakers* (HHS, 2003)

Davidge, W R, *Hertfordshire Regional Planning Report* (Hertfordshire Regional Planning Committee, 1927)

Day, Edie, *From Day to Day an autobiography by Edie Day* (Privately published n.d.)

Doubleday, E H, *Hertfordshire: Survey Report and Analysis of County Development Plan* (HCC, 1951)

Douglas, Priscilla, and Humphries, Pauline, *Discovering Hitchin* (Egon, 1995)

Ellis, Kenneth, *The Post Office in the Eighteenth Century: A Study in Administrative History* (University of Durham, 1958)

Everett, Andrew, *Visionary Pragmatist: Sir Vincent Raven* (Tempus, 2006)

Farris, Noel, *The Wymondleys* (Hertfordshire Publications, 1989)

Field, Richard, *Hitchin: a Pictorial History* (Phillimore, 1991)

Fitzpatrick-Matthews, Keith J and Tony, *The Archaeology of Hitchin from Prehistory to the Present* (NHM & HHS, 2008)

Fleck, Alan, *Hitchin in Camera. The Town and District* (Quotes Limited of Buckingham, 1986)

Fleck, Alan, *A Hitchin Century in Camera* (Quotes Limited of Buckingham, 1988)

Fleck, Alan, *Hitchin in Old Photographs* (Alan Sutton, 1994)

Fleck, Alan, & Poole, Helen, *Old Hitchin: Portrait of an English Market Town* (Phillimore, 1999)

Foster, Anthony M, *The Book of Hitchin* (Barracuda Books, 1981)

Foster, Anthony M and Munby, Lionel M, *Market Town. Hitchin in the Nineteenth Century* (HHS, 1987)

Gadd, Pat, *Fifty Years of Change in Hitchin circa 1930-1980* (AuthorGraphics, Hitchin, 1980)

Gadd, Pat, "Hitchin Inns" (Unpublished typescript, 1987)

Gibson, W, "An eighteenth-century paradox: the career of the decipherer-bishop, Edward Willes", *British Journal for Eighteenth-Century Studies*, 12 (1989), 69–76

Gover, J E B, Mawer, A, and Stenton, F M, *The Place-Names of Hertfordshire* (English Place Name Society, 1938)

Harwood, Kate, "Park Piece Detached Gardens (now Gaping Lane)" Hertfordshire Gardens Trust, 2017 http://hertsgardenstrust.org.uk/wp-content/uploads/2017/09/Gaping%20Lane%20Detached%20Gardens.pdf

Hine, Reginald L, *The History of Hitchin Vol I* (Allen & Unwin, 1927) *Vol. II* (Allen & Unwin, 1929)

Hitchin Historical Society, *The Street Names of Hitchin and Their Origins. Book 3: Western Hitchin* (HHS, 1999)

Hitchin Historical Society, *Hitchin Arcade Then and Now* (HHS, 2007)

Hitchin Household Almanack 1872–1896 (Paternoster & Hales)

Holton, Richard, "The Great Northern Railway at Hitchin", *Hertfordshire Past and Present No 14* 1974 pp8–30

Horner, Craig, ed. *Aspects of Motoring History. An annual Journal by the Society of Automotive Historians (in Britain)*

Howard, Phil, *Take the Train From Hitchin. A journey into our local railway heritage* (HHS, 2006)

Howlett, Bridget (ed), *Survey of the Royal Manor of Hitchin, 1676* (Hertfordshire Record Society, 2000)

Howlett, Bridget, *Hitchin Priory Park. The history of a landscape park and gardens* (HHS, 2004)

Howlett, Bridget, *Maydencroft. A Manor, hunting park, farm and brickworks Near Hitchin* (HHS, 2012)

Jeremiah, David, *Representation of British Motoring* (Manchester University Press, 2007)

Kahn, David, *The Codebreakers. The Story of Secret Writing* (Scribner, New York, 1967, 1996)

Lakeman, Albert ed., *Concrete Cottages, Small Garages and Farm Buildings* (Concrete Publications, 1918) https://archive.org/stream/concretecottages00lakerich/concretecottages00lakerich_djvu.txt

Latchmore, E Aillie, *A Venture of Faith. The Story of Hitchin Clubland* (Privately published *c.*1970)

Latchmore, E Aillie, *People, Places and Past Times of Hitchin* (Privately published 1974)

Lucas, John, *Phebe's Hitchin Book* (HHS, 2009)

Moore, Cyril, *Hertfordshire Windmills and Windmillers* (Windsup, 1999)

Morgan, Richard, "The Rev Thomas Whitehurst Rector of Colmworth", *History in Bedfordshire Vol 6 No 2* Spring 2013

Morrison, Katherine, and Minnis, John, *Carscapes: the Motorcar, Architecture and Landscape in England* (Yale University Press, 2013)

Oxford Dictionary of National Biography (Oxford, 2004) accessed online via Hertfordshire Libraries

Page, William (ed), *The Victoria History of the County of Hertford Vol 3* (1912) www.british-history.ac.uk/search/series/vch--herts

Pieris, Maya, *Take 6 Carrots, 4 Heads of Celery, 8 Large Onions – The Receipts of a Hertfordshire Family* (HHS, 1994)

Polden, Patrick, *A History of the County Court 1846–1971* (Cambridge University Press, 1999)

Rance, Daphne, *St Ippolyts. A country parish in the nineteenth century* (Egon, 1987)

Rance, Daphne, *The Yeomen of Ippolyts. A country parish before 1800* (Cortney, 1996)

Ranger, William, *Report to the General Board of Health – Hitchin* (HMSO, 1849)

Ransom, William, "An account of British and Roman remains found in the neighbourhood of Hitchin", *Transactions of the Hertfordshire Natural History Society Vol IV* 1886

Reader, W J, *To Have and To Hold. An Account of Frederick Bandet's Life in Business* (Hunting Gate, 1983)

Richardson, Kenneth, *The British Motor Industry 1896–1939* (Macmillan, 1977)

Rowe, Anne, *Medieval Parks of Hertfordshire* (University of Hertfordshire, 2009)

Rowe, Anne, and Williamson, Tom, *Hertfordshire a landscape history* (University of Hertfordshire, 2013)

Royal Commission on Historical Monuments (England), *An Inventory of the Historical Monuments in Hertfordshire* (HMSO, 1911)

Seebohm, Frederic, *The English Village Community* (Longman, 1883)

Slater, Terry, and Goose, Nigel (ed), *A County of Small Towns. The development of Hertfordshire's urban landscape to 1800* (University of Hertfordshire, 2008)

Smith, Brent, *Hitchin – The Best and Worst. A Personal View* (Privately published 2009)

Sutcliffe, Anthony (ed), *British Town Planning: the formative years* (University of Leicester, 1981)

Talbot, Derek, *A Diary of Events as Recorded at Hitchin South Signal Box Between 1st January 1906 and 22nd September 1968* (2nd edition Great Northern Railway Society, 2017)

Taplin, Valerie, and Stewart, Audrey, *Two Minutes to the Station. The Tale of Hitchin's Victorian Triangle* (HHS, 2010)

The New Domesday Book of Hertfordshire compiled from the Official Return of Owners of Land 1873 (Simson, Hertford, *c*.1873)

Thompson, F M L, *English Landed Society in the Nineteenth Century* (Routledge 1963, paperback reprint 1980)

Thornes, Rosemary, and Slater, Terry, "Detached gardens and the urban fringe of eighteenth-and-nineteenth-century English provincial towns", *Journal of Historical Geography* 53 July 2016 pp28–44

Urwick, William, *Nonconformity in Herts. Being lectures upon the Nonconforming Worthies of St. Albans, and Memorials of Puritanism and Nonconformity in all the Parishes of the County of Hertford* (Hazell, Watson and Viney, 1884)

Walker, Janet, and Watson, Margaret, *A Stroll round the Village of Old Walsworth* (Privately published 1997)

Walker, Simon, "The Post Office, Hermitage Road", *Hitchin Journal* Vol. 24 No 1 2014 pp 23–25

Walmsley, Robert, *Around 1919, Boyhood Memories of Hitchin* (AuthorGraphics Ltd, Hitchin 1979)

West, Barry, *The Street Names of Hitchin and Their Origins Book 2: Eastern Hitchin* (Egon, 1998)

Western, H G, *A History of Ickleford* (Privately published 1975)

Whitaker, Allan, *Brewers in Hertfordshire. A historical gazetteer* (University of Hertfordshire, 2006)

Willis, Margaret, *The Gardens of the British Working Class* (Yale University Press, 2014)

Wray, Philip J, *A History of Preston in Hertfordshire* (Privately published 2015)

Young, John N, *Great Northern Suburban* (David & Charles, 1977)

Novelty postcard
c.1921. (Terry Knight)

GOOD LUCK FROM **HITCHIN**

Index

Abbiss, Bill, 75
Ablett, Kelleth, 176
Albon, James, 92
Allen family, 34
allotments, 14–16, 19, 89, 94–96, 151–152
Allwoods Farm, 108–109
Anchor PH, 106
Angel's Reply PH, 157, 177–178
Angel Vaults, 104, 157, 176–178
Arcade, 76, 178
Arlesey, 20, 61, 110
Avenue, The, 33, 69, 139, 149
Avery, George, 46, 48

Bacon Factory, 83, 163, 168
Balmoral Road, 124, 132–137
Bancroft, 14, 42, 45, 47, 75–78, 81–82, 85–86, 134, 139, 161–162, 164, 168, 170–176
Bandet, Frederick, 165–169
banks, 17, 26, 32, 47, 85, 185
Baptists, 25, 27, 37
Barker's, joiners, 18, 35–36, 164, 168, 184
Barrett, Doreen, 156
Baulk Path, 10
Bearton Avenue, 125
Bearton Farm, 117, 119, 123
Bearton Green, 3–6
Bearton Road, 3–6, 20, 117, 123–125, 129–136
Beaver, George, 55, 60
Bedford Road, 11–12, 20, 59, 71, 73, 123, 126, 145, 155, 157, 172, 177
Bedford Street, 15–20
Beggarly Shot, 1, 87
Benslow Bridge, 74, 89–97
Benslow Lane, 35, 73–79, 124
Bethel Lane, 25, 34–35, 37
Bidwell, Hugh D, 172
Blackhorse Lane, 77, 171
Blood, Arthur T, inside front & back covers, 153, 157

Bolton, Benjamin, 28
Bowman's, millers, 139, 161, 163, 168
Bowyer, John, 8
Bowyer, William, 9
Brampton Park Estate, 124–125, 129–137
Brand Street, 32, 46, 48, 80–81, 85, 140, 143, 179
Braund, William, 17
brewing, xiii, 26, 32, 51–52, 58–61, 160, 163, 179–180
brickmaking, 9, 17, 20, 25–30, 35–38, 110, 123, 126, 129, 161–162
Bridge Street, 51, 59, 140, 179–181
British Schools, 27–28, 30, 42, 100
Broadmead, 66, 68
Brooker's, 130, 140, 169, 185
Bucklersbury, xiv, 50, 76, 142
Bullock, Mary, 158
Bunyan Road, 124, 129
Burford Field, 2–5
Burford Way, 156, 158–159
Burns Close, 98
Burrows family, 134
Bury Field, 1–5, 8–9, 125
Burymead Road, 165, 167–169
Butcher's Lane, 25–26, 29
Butts Close, 3–6, 11, 73, 149
Byde, Thomas Plumer, 7, 117
Byron Close, 98

Cadwell Lane, 4–6, 147, 164, 167, 171
Cam Gears, 167–169
Cambridge Road, 7, 24, 89–107, 120, 162, 168–170, 185–186
Campbell, W Lawson, 82
Cannon's Nurseries, 75
Capswell Brook, 3, 6, 11, 16, 75
Carling, William, 85, 139, 168
Catholics, 81

Cemetery, 38–39
Cemetery Road, 35, 38
Chalk Dell, 12–13, 155
Chalk Dell Path, 14–15
Chamber of Commerce, 147, 164
Chaucer Way, 94, 97
Chennells family, 114
Chivers, David, 155
Church House, 175–176
Churchyard, ix–x, 48, 76
cinemas, 42, 183–184
Clowes, Winchester, 9, 38
Coleman, James, 27, 32
Coleman family, 133
Coleridge Close, 87, 97, 126
Collins, Henry & Joyce, 179
community centres, 98, 100–101, 156, 158–159
concrete cottages, 19–22
Conder, Derrick, 152
Congregationalists, 36
Conquest Close, 30
Conygrees, 4–6
Co-operative Society, 40, 136, 168, 175
Corn Exchange, 44, 162–163
County Court, 80–86
Cox, William, 32
Crescent, The, 151–155
Cricketers PH, 12
Croft, The, 45, 172–173
Culpin, Ewart, 147

dairies, xiv, 164, 168
Dashwood Thomas, 63–64, 85
Dawson William, 47
Day, Edie, 40
Debenham, Samuel, 46–48
Delmé-Radcliffe family, 8, 25, 36, 85, 119, 121, 125
Dilley, Janet, 152
Dimsey, Thomas, 27–28
Duke of Wellington PH, 26, 30
Dukes Lane, 129

Eddleston, W E, 175
Edwards, Albert W, 112–114
enclosure, 1, 6–10, 24, 87, 110–111, 118–119
English Electric, 167–169
Erecta, 166–167, 169, 179
Exton, William, 8, 100
Eynsford Court, 37

Fardell, Geoffrey, 179, 186
Farrow's Stores, 36–37
Fells' Nurseries, 25, 71
Field, Thomas, 9, 25–29, 31
Fire Brigade, 19–21, 40, 105
Firs, The, 12, 59, 71
Fish Pond Fields, 3–6
Fishponds Road, 125
Flint, greengrocer, 136, 154
Flint, Reginald, 94, 150
Forester family, 109–110
Foster, M & F O, 171, 179, 184
Foster, Mary, 25
Foster, Matthew, 61, 115, 129
Foster, Maurice, 36–37
Foundry Road, 18, 20–21
Fountain PH, 31, 69
French family, 152, 154
Friends Burial Ground, 49, 118, 122
Furr, Mick, 158–159

Gainsford, G B, 102, 140, 150
Gaping Hills, 11–22, 54–56, 58
Gaping Lane, 11–22
garages, i, xiv, 83, 107, 138–145, 181–183
Garratt & Cannnon, 161, 168
Gatward, J, 17–18, 131, 140, 161
Gibson Close, 98
Grant family, 134–135
gravel pits, 19–20, 35, 131, 133
Grays Lane, 6, 9, 13–14, 58
green belt, 11, 147
Grove Mill, 100, 104–105, 107
Grove Mill Farm, 164
Grove Road, 75, 114, 169
Grovelands Estate, 114
Gypsy Lane, 87–88

Hailey, Thomas, 112
Halsey Drive, 127
Hardy Close, 97
Harkness & Co, 64, 72, 75, 168

Hawkins, John, 84
Hawkins & Co, 81, 84–85
Heathfield Road, 10
Henlow, 129, 158
Henniker, Sir John, 112
Hermitage Road, 35–36, 42, 79, 141–142, 147, 168, 171, 174–175, 183–186
Herts County Council, 15, 40, 84, 96–97, 146–147, 167, 174, 179, 186
High Dane, 114
High Street, 17–18, 46, 49–50, 75, 85, 140, 176–177
Highbury Road, 14, 67
Highover, 4–7, 108–114, 116
Highover Estate, 103, 109
Highover Way, 102, 114
Hillview Estate, 91, 98
Hine, Florence, 92
Hine, Reginald, 5, 82
Hitchin Boys' School, 6, 89, 92
Hitchin Girls' School, vii
Hitchin Glove Co, 165, 168
Hitchin Hill, 14, 24–34, 37, 181
Hitchin Hill Path, 25–26, 28–33
Hitchin Local Board, 19–21, 105
Hitchin Market, 76–77, 85, 112, 160–164, 182
Hitchin New Town, 9, 24–33
Hitchin UDC, 22, 92–96, 102, 115, 125–126, 129, 133–137, 147–156, 164–167, 172–183
Hiz, River, 3, 41, 100, 179, 182
Hollow Lane, 40, 182
Holloway, Anthony, 175–176
Holy Saviour Church, 112, 140
Hubbard, Henry, 39
Hunting Gate, 166–167
Hyde, Norman, 179

Ickleford, 3, 73, 111, 119, 129, 133, 161
Ickleford Road, 124, 129
Innes & Co, 92, 162–163
International Computers, 167–9
Ippollitts, 60–64, 116–123, 127
Ippollitts Brook, 63–65, 67, 70, 88–89, 97

Jackson, George, 19, 79, 174–175
Jackson, Joseph, 19–22
James, Bill, 75

James, John, 34, 59
Jeeves, George, 17–20, 28, 61–63
John Barker Place, 156, 158–159
Joshua, John, 41–42

Keats Way, 97
Kendale Road, 41–42
Kent, George, 167–169
Kershaw's Hill, 40
King, Anthony, 174, 182–183
King, George, 149, 162–163, 167
Kingshott School, 60–65
Kingswood Avenue, 96
Knight, James, 125, 130

Lancaster Avenue, 124–125
Lancaster Road, 124, 129
Latchmore, Aillie, 39
Latchmore, Thomas B, 43–50
Latchmore, Thomas W, 49–50
Latchmore Close, 37
Leete, June, 152
Letchworth, 6, 86, 91, 108, 147–149, 154, 163, 167, 177
Library, 178–179
lime making, 20, 35, 90, 131, 161, 164, 167
Lindsay Avenue, ii, 68
Lindsell family, 85
Lister family, 56–57
Logsdon, Edwin, 19–22
London Road, 24–32, 118
Lovell, Francis, 62, 115, 119–127
Lovell, Maud, 92–93, 115, 121–122, 125–127, 129
Lovell Close, 115, 127
Lucas, Francis, 85
Lucas, Geoffry, 30
Lucas, Samuel, 12, 52, 55–56, 58, 61, 108
Lucas, Wm VI, 17, 44, 51–61
Lucas, William Tindall, 85, 122
Lucas family, 9, 34, 44, 51–64, 67, 71, 124, 180
Lucas Lane, 6, 11–13, 22, 75, 154–155

McKay, George & Nellie, 33
McMurtrie, Donald S A, 82
Magistrates' Court, 32, 63, 74, 77, 82–86
Malein/Maling, Wm, 89, 110
malting, 160–163, 179–180

Manor Crescent, 67–68
Manton Road, 67–69
Maples, The, 31
Market Place, viii, 18, 44–45, 48, 139–140, 163, 185
Mary Exton School, 97, 100
Matthews, Rose, 158
Mattocke Road, 151–156
Mattok, Nicholas, 109
Meadowbank, 10
Methodists, 30, 32
Milestone Road, 155–156
Minnis, Herbert, 36
Minnis, Wally, 155
Monk, Arthur G, 130, 132
Montserrat, 26–27, 31–33
Moremead Field, 1, 4–5, 8
Morgan's Garage, 83, 139, 144–5
Moss family, 39, 151, 170
Moulden, Eliza, 22
Moulden, Henry G, 49–50, 85
Moules, Leonard, 59
Museum, ix, 45–46, 48–49, 179

Nash family, 89
Newton's builders, 40, 161
Newton's Way, 40
Nichols, George A, 48–49
Nightingale Road, 37, 71, 73, 76, 83, 142, 145, 163, 168
Ninesprings, 24, 87–95, 100, 149
Ninesprings Way, 67–70
North Hertfordshire College, vii, 96, 105, 185–186
North Herts District Council, 16, 158–159
North Place, 151, 154–155
nurseries, 25, 64–65, 71–79
Nutleigh Grove, 151–157

Oakfield Avenue, ii, 65–68
Oakfield Estate, 31, 63–70, 75, 127, 143, 171
Oakfield House, 59–65, 67, 85
Offley, 55, 158
Offley Road, 9, 55
Old Hale Way, 3–6, 124, 129, 133–134
Old Park Road, 3–6, 11–17, 83, 144
Orchard House, 40–41, 67
Orchard Road, 102–103

Oughton, River, 8, 57, 152
Oughtonhead Common, 3–6, 56–57, 151–152, 155–156
Oughtonhead Farm, 52–60, 125
Oughtonhead Lane, 155
Oughtonhead School, 156–157
Oughtonhead Way, 11–18, 20

Park Lane, 6, 13
Park Piece, 12–22
Park Way, 24, 31
Parker, Cynthia, 156–158
Parkinson, Sir Lindsay, 65–69
Passingham Ave, 35, 41, 115
Pateman, John, 93
Patterson, R W, 175
Paynes Park, 40, 49, 162, 178–9
Pedder, Richard, 112
Perkins, Thomas, 162–163
Perks & Llewellyn, 140, 162, 176
Pettengell, John, 112
Pettengell & Clark, 40, 130, 132
photographers, 36, 43–50
Pierson, Joseph M, 26, 32
Pierson, Thomas G, 28
Pinehill Hospital, 73, 124
Pirton, 64, 119, 136
Pirton Road, 9, 11, 122
Plowman, Eli, 129–132
Poets Estate, 69, 86–98, 126–127
police, 29, 40, 74, 80–86, 159
Portmill Lane, 81, 84–85, 175, 186
Preston, 32, 85, 119, 123
Price, Dora, 158
Priestman, Martin, 178–179, 183
Prime's Garage, 142, 181
Priory Park, 25, 48, 149
Pulter family, 109–110
Pulters Way, 36–37, 41
Punfold Park, 6, 12–13
Purwell, River, 3, 6, 88, 92, 100, 104, 118, 126, 150
Purwell Estate, 103, 171, 126
Purwell Field, 2–8, 87, 126–127
Purwell Lane, 96, 102
Purwell Meadows, 3, 90, 150
Purwell Mill, 87–89, 94–95, 100, 104, 150
Pym, Wollaston, 12, 17

Quakers, 8, 34, 39, 46–49, 51–63, 118, 122, 162, 180

Queen Street, i, xiv, 30, 36, 39–42, 76–77, 92, 142–144, 180–183

Raban, T L, saddler, 160
Radcliffe Arms, xiv, 74
Radcliffe Road, 37, 76
railwaymen, 29, 36–37, 91, 93
railways, 29, 65–69, 73–74, 77, 88–100, 120, 146–149, 162–167, 175
Ransom, Alfred, 35, 61, 124
Ransom, John, 100, 119, 123
Ransom, Joseph, 57, 117
Ransom, Joshua, 8, 105, 123
Ransom, Theodore, 35, 92, 164–5
Ransom, W & Son, 134, 162, 170
Ransom, William, 46–47, 73
Ransom's Recreation Ground, 1
Ray, John, 184
Read, John, 35–36, 41
Redhill Road, 151–157, 177
Reilly, Jim, 158
Riddy Path, 62, 67
Roberts, G P, 9
Rosehill Estate, 114, 171
Rosenberg, 9
Royce, Norman, 182–183
Royston, 82, 86, 163
Rugley, John, xiii
Russell, G H, 134–135
Russell, G W, 133–134, 161
Russell's Slip, 8

Sailor Boy PH, 100, 103, 106
St Faith's Church, 102
St Ibbs Bush, 118–122, 127
St Ibbs Farm, 119, 123
St John's Church, 37–38, 40
St John's Road, 25, 34–41, 124, 126
St Mary's Church, 30, 38, 50
St Mary's Square, 42, 76, 182
St Michael's Mount, 87–98, 126
St Michael's Road, 87–88, 91, 96–98, 149
sand pits, 25, 35, 131
Sanders, R E, 140–143, 163
Saunders, H A, 143, 180–181
Sears, Stephen, 132, 134–136
Seebohm, Esther, 150

Seebohm, Frederic, 1–3, 47, 51–52, 82
Selby, Frank, 92
sewage, 105, 129–130, 133
Sharman's, 162, 168, 170
Sharp, Frank C, 50
Sharpe, Abel, 28
Shefford, 107, 129
Ship PH, 102, 106–107
Shot[t]ling Mill, 5, 104
Sir John Barleycorn, 11, 15, 17
Skimpot, 87–91, 95–96, 98
Skynners' Almshouses, 75, 117
Smith, Nellie, 100–101
Society for Bettering the Condition of the Poor, 14–15
South Place, 151, 154
Spital Field, 2–5
Spokes, Mervyn, 152, 154–155
Standhill Field, 1, 4–5, 25
Standhill Road, 35, 37–38, 40
Station Mills, 139, 163, 168
Station Road, xiv, 48
Stevenage, 22, 59, 71, 86, 96, 144, 149, 158, 167
Stevenage Road, 24–31, 60–61, 65, 143, 145
Stotfold Road, 4–7, 95, 110, 147
Strathmore Avenue, 3, 10
Strathmore School, 157
straw plaiting, 29, 160
Stubbs, Alan, 180–181
Sun Hotel/Inn, 17, 19, 140
Sun Street, 29, 50–52, 58–60, 83, 104, 139, 144–145, 176–178
Sunnyside Estate, inside front cover, 38–42, 92, 151, 153, 156
Sunnyside Sawmills, 35
Swadling, Fred, 102
Swan Inn, 18
Swinburne Avenue, 156
Switzer, Bamlet N, 29–30
Sykes, Sir Francis, 112

tanning, 110, 160–161, 168, 170
Taylor, Samuel, 17
Taylor Woodrow, 175
Tennyson Avenue, 97, 150
Theobald, A, 130

Thompson, John, 46
Thompson, Lawson, 48, 85
Thompson, S J, 171
Thomson, J N, i, xiv, 142, 144
Three Moorhens, 25–26, 29, 42
Tibbles, D C, 164, 167–168
Tilehouse Street, 32, 46, 58, 61, 85, 168–169, 179–180
Times, Charles, 81
Times, William Onslow, 81–82, 84–85, 92, 125
Tomlin, Elizabeth, 158
town planning, 94–96, 133–134, 146–150, 163–167, 171–186
Tristram, Mary, xiii
Tudor Court, 9
Tuke, James Hack, 17, 20, 45

Union Road, 14–15
Upchurch, Bill, 75
Upchurch family, 90

Victaulic Company, 165, 167–8
Victoria Road, 71

Wallace family, 9, 126, 129–131, 164–165, 169
Wallace Way, 167
Walsworth, 1, 4–7, 69, 75, 89, 100–114, 116, 147–149, 164–169
Walsworth Common, 10, 100, 102, 108–109, 159
Walsworth House, 90, 92, 96, 105–106, 112
Walsworth Road, xiv, 1, 20, 48, 76, 112, 139–143, 163, 167–170
Walsworth School, 100–101
Wardale, John Reynolds, 17
Waters, Alfred, 171–172
Wedgewood Way, 98
Wellingham Avenue, 126
Wells, Bert, 142
Welshman's Croft, 3–5, 8–9
Westmill Estate, inside front & back covers, 73, 93, 136, 151–159, 171
Westmill Farm, 34, 151–152
Westmill Rd, 151–152, 156–157

Wheeler family, 71–79
Whinbush Rd, 71, 73, 75, 183
Whitehill Road, iii, 34–35, 38, 41, 65, 77, 131, 171
Whitehurst, Thomas, 7, 110–112, 116
Wilbury Way, 147, 164–169
Willes, Edward, 115–116
Willes, Sir Francis, 116–120
William IV PH, 26, 31
Wm Ransom School, 1, 73, 75
Williams, Joseph, 22
Willian Road, 6, 102, 109
Willmott, J, 92, 130
Willows Estate, 143, 171
Wilshere, Charles Willes, 15, 105, 119, 121, 125
Wilshere, John, 112, 119
Wilshere, Miss, 15, 92, 105, 147, 152, 165, 175
Wilshere, Thomas, 119–120
Wilshere, William, 111–112, 119
Wilshere, Wm MP, 12–15, 100
Wilson, Terry, 95
Wimpey, George, 41, 87, 96–98
Windmill Cottages, 89, 95–96
windmills, 55–56, 89, 120
Woodbridge, Marion, 134–137
Woodcote House, 144, 182–183
Woolgrove Road, 6, 100–104, 107–109, 114
Worbey, Alec, 35, 77, 94
Worbey, Brian, 36–37, 40–41
Worbey, Len, 158–159
Worbey family, 35, 40–41, 67, 70, 77, 94, 96, 126
Workhouse, 12–14, 71, 75
World War I, 35, 49, 72, 92, 101–102, 125, 133, 146, 163–164
World War II, 38, 42, 77, 102, 134–136, 143, 154, 165
Wratten Road, 14, 58, 179–180
Wright, George, 32
Wymondley, 3, 109–110, 113
Wymondley Road, 67–69, 89–90, 96–97, 127, 149

York Road, 124, 129